Scandals in past and contemporary politics

MANCHESTER
1824

Manchester University Press

Scandals in past and contemporary politics

edited by
John Garrard & **James L. Newell**

Manchester University Press
Manchester and New York

distributed exclusively in the USA by Palgrave

Published by Manchester University Press
Oxford Road, Manchester M13 9NR, UK
and Room 400, 175 Fifth Avenue, New York, NY 10010, USA
www.manchesteruniversitypress.co.uk

Distributed exclusively in the USA by
Palgrave, 175 Fifth Avenue, New York,
NY 10010, USA

Distributed exclusively in Canada by
UBC Press, University of British Columbia, 2029 West Mall,
Vancouver, BC, Canada V6T 1Z2

British Library Cataloguing-in-Publication Data
A catalogue record for this book is available from the British Library

Library of Congress Cataloging-in-Publication Data applied for

ISBN   0 7190 6551 8   *hardback*
EAN   978 0 7190 6551 4

First published 2006

14 13 12 11 10 09 08 07 06   10 9 8 7 6 5 4 3 2 1

Typeset in Photina
by Graphicraft Limited, Hong Kong
Printed in Great Britain
by CPI, Bath

Contents

List of boxes and tables

Boxes

Tables

List of contributors

Hélène Bilger-Street is Lecturer in French in the Department of European Studies and Modern Languages of the University of Bath. She is a graduate of the Universities of Paris and Liverpool. She has interests in parliamentary scrutiny in France and Britain, and is currently writing a book on political scandal in France 1986–2002. Her publications include 'Du Royaume Uni au Royaume des Nations et Régions', *Annuaire Européen d'Administration Publique*, vol. 23, 2000 (with F. F. Ridley), and 'The Municipal Elections of 2001', *Modern and Contemporary France*, 9(4), November 2001 (with Sue Milner). She also teaches a course on political scandal.

Miguel Caínzos is Associate Professor of Sociology at the University of Santiago de Compostela, Spain. He is the author of various articles on sociological theory, social stratification and political sociology. He has also contributed to several edition volumes, including *Agency and Structure: Reorienting Social Theory* (Gordon and Breach, 1994) and *Corruption in Contemporary Politics* (Palgrave Macmillan, 2003). His current research focuses on different aspects of Spanish class structure, relationships between social inequalities and patterns of political behaviour in contemporary democracies, and the influence of citizens' evaluation of public policies and party leaders on their voting decisions.

Marion Demoissier is Senior Lecturer in French and European Studies at the University of Bath. She is the author of *Recollections of France: Memories, Identities and Heritage in Contemporary France* (Berghahn, 2000) and of numerous articles and book chapters on various aspects of French culture and anthropology. She is currently working on wine consumption and culture in France, and is preparing a book on the political structuring of cultural identities in Europe.

Anne-Maree Farrell is currently Lecturer at the Law School, Lancaster University. Her research interests include law, science and public policy making, with a particular focus on risk regulation and the role of scientific expertise. She is currently completing her PhD, which involves a comparative study of public policy making arising out of HIV contamination of the blood supply in France, the United Kingdom and Ireland.

Jenny Fleming is Fellow at the Regulatory Institutions Network (RegNet) in the Research School of Social Sciences at the Australian National University, Canberra. She is a former Research Fellow with the Key Centre for Ethics, Law, Justice and Governance at Griffith University, Brisbane, from where she holds a doctorate. She is the co-editor with I. Holland of *Motivating Ministers to Morality* (Ashgate, 2001), and of *Government Reformed: Values and New Political Institutions* (Ashgate, 2003).

She publishes widely on police management, police unionism and criminal justice administration. Her research interests include police–government relations and the politics of criminal justice.

John Garrard is Senior Lecturer in Politics and Contemporary History in the School of English, Sociology, Politics and Contemporary History, and member of the European Studies Research Institute, at the University of Salford. Although primarily a historian, his research interests lie on the borderlines between history and political science. His publications include *The English and Immigration: A Comparative Study of the Jewish Influx 1880–1910* (Oxford University Press, 1970); *Leadership and Power in Victorian Industrial Towns 1830–1880* (Manchester University Press, 1983); *The Great Salford Gas Scandal of 1887* (British Gas Northwestern, 1988); and *Democratisation in Britain: Elites, Civil Society and Reform since 1800* (Palgrave, 2002). He is currently editing a book on the mayoralty for Ashgate.

Fernando Jiménez is Associate Professor of political science at the University of Santiago de Compostela (currently at the University of Murcia) and Fellow of the Instituto Juan March (Madrid). Since his book *Detrás del escándalo político* [Behind political scandal] (Tusquets, 1995), his research has focused mainly on the politics of scandal. His most recent papers – mostly co-authored with Miguel Caínzos – pay special attention to the electoral consequences of these affairs.

Kleomenis S. Koutsoukis is Professor of Political Science at Panteion University, Athens, Chair of the Department of Political Science and Director of the Centre for Political Research. In this capacity, he organised, in November 2003, an international conference on 'Corruption and Scandals in Public Administration and Politics'. He is the author of *Political Pathology* (Papazissis, 1998). While most of his publications are in Greek, he has also produced a number of works in English, most notably, *Political Conflict in Southern Europe: Regulation, Regression and Morphogenesis*, with E. Ziegenhagen (Praeger, 1992).

Jeroen Maesschalck is Senior Researcher at the Public Management Institute of the Katholieke Universiteit Leuven (Belgium), where he undertakes and supervises research on public sector ethics and public personnel management. He is also Research Fellow in Integrity of Governance at the Free University Amsterdam and co-chair of the Study Group on Ethics and Integrity of Governance of the European Group of Public Administration (EGPA). His publications include articles on public sector ethics and scandals in the journals, *Public Administration*, *International Public Management Journal*, and *Public Integrity*.

Chris Moncrieff has worked continuously for the Press Association in Parliament since 1962, and was Political Editor from 1982 to 1994 when officially, but not *de facto*, he retired. He travelled the world with Margaret Thatcher and John Major, and was awarded the CBE in 1989. He is author of *Living on a Deadline: A History of the Press Association* (Virgin, 2001).

Gary Murphy is Senior Lecturer in Government in the School of Law and Government at Dublin City University. He has published widely on the Irish State in a number of journals and texts, and is currently engaged in research on the relationship between political elites and the citizenry in terms of democratic accountability. He is the author of *Economic Realignment and the Politics of EEC Entry in Ireland* (Maunsel Press, 2003) and is currently co-editor of *Irish Political Studies*, the leading journal in Irish political science, published by Taylor & Francis.

James L. Newell is Professor of Politics at the University of Salford. His recent publications include: *Parties and Democracy in Italy* (Ashgate, 2000); *The Italian General Election* *of 2001: Berlusconi's Victory* (ed.) (Manchester University Press, 2002); *Corruption in Contemporary Politics* (ed. with Martin Bull) (Palgrave Macmillan, 2003); *Criminal Finances and Organising Crime in Europe* (ed. with Petrus C. Van Duyne and Klaus Von Lampe) (Wolf Legal Publishers, 2003); *Threats and Phantoms of Organised Crime, Corruption and Terrorism: Critical and European Perspectives* (ed. with Petrus C. Van Duyne, Klaus Von Lampe and Matjaž Jagar) (Wolf Legal Publishers, 2004). He is co-convenor of the UK Political Studies Association's Italian Politics Specialist Group and co-editor of the journal, *European Political Science.*

Véronique Pujas is Research Fellow at the Centre National de la Recherche Scientifique, Grenoble. She has published extensively on white-collar crime and corruption in West European democracies. She teaches comparative politics and corruption issues at the Institut d'Etudes Politiques in Grenoble.

Robin Theobald is Professor of Organisation Studies, in the Westminster Business School at the University of Westminster. He has also taught at the City University (London) and the University of Jos, Nigeria. He is the author of *Corruption, Development and Underdevelopment* (Macmillan, 1990) and, with Vicky Randall, of *Political Change and Underdevelopment* (Macmillan, 1997). He has also written numerous articles in the area of corruption, patronage and bureaucracy.

Eric M. Uslaner is Professor of Government and Politics at the University of Maryland (College Park). He is the author of seven books, the editor of four others, and has published over 100 articles in journals and edited volumes. His current research focuses on trust, civic engagement and corruption in the United States, Romania and cross-nationally. His most recent books are *The Moral Foundations of Trust* (Cambridge University Press, 2002); *The Movers and the Shirkers: Downsians and Ideologues in the Senate* (University of Michigan Press, 1999); and *Social Capital and the Transition to Democracy* (ed. with Gabriel Badescu) (Routledge, 2003).

Robert Williams is Professor of Politics at the University of Durham. He has been Visiting Professor/Fellow at a number of universities including Harvard University, the Australian National University, Lewis and Clark College, Flinders University and the University of Western Ontario. He has also been appointed Guest Professor at Renmin University, Beijing. His publications include *Political Scandals in the USA* (Edinburgh University Press, 1998), *Politics and Corruption* (4 vols) (Edward Elgar, 2000) and *Party Finance and Political Corruption* (Macmillan, 2000). His current research centres on political ethics, corruption and scandal.

Julia Wishnevsky is former Researcher with Radio Free Europe/Radio Liberty, Inc., and author of *The Evolution of the Russian Communist Party* (The Jamestown Foundation, 1999). She has also written numerous articles on Russia and the Soviet Union.

List of abbreviations

ANES	American National Election Study
BSE	Bovine Spongiform Encephalopathy ('Mad cow disease')
BTSB	Blood Transfusion Service Board (Ireland)
CECS	Centre for the Study of Social Change (*Centro de Estudios del Cambio Social*)
CIA	Central Intelligence Agency
CJC	Criminal Justice Commission (Australia)
DC	Christian Democratic Party (Italy)
EIB	European Investment Bank
EIC	East India Company
EU	European Union
FBI	Federal Bureau of Investigation
FSB	Federal Security Service (Russia)
ILP	Independent Labour Party
IMF	International Monetary Fund
JMSE	Joseph Murphy Structural Engineering (Ireland)
KGB	Committee for State Security (Soviet Union)
LDP	Liberal Democratic Party (Japan)
LDPR	Russian Liberal Democratic Party
MoU	Memorandum of Understanding
ND	New Democracy (*Nea Demokratia*)
OECD	Organisation for Economic Co-operation and Development
PA	Press Association
PASOK	Panhellenic Socialist Movement (*Panellinio Sosialistiko Kinima*)
PC	Parliamentary Commissioner
PCI	Italian Communist Party
PCJC	Parliamentary Criminal Justice Committee
PP	People's Party (Spain)
PRI	Institutional Revolutionary Party (Mexico)
PSI	Italian Socialist Party
PSOE	Spanish Socialist Worker's Party
QPU	Queensland Police Union
RPR	*Rassemblement Pour la République* (France)

RTÉ	*Radio Telefís Éireann* (Ireland)
SDF	Social Democratic Federation
TD	Deputy to the *Dáil* (Ireland)
US	United States
USA	United States of America
USSR	Union of Soviet Socialist Republics

Introduction

James L. Newell

On 17 February 1992, Mario Chiesa was going about his business as usual. That afternoon he had an appointment with Luca Magni, the thirty-two-year-old proprietor of a small cleaning firm who had agreed to pay 14 million lire in exchange for a 140 million lire cleaning contract at the old people's home Chiesa managed. At about half-past-five after a long telephone conversation, Chiesa was able to show the waiting Magni into his office and to take the envelope containing the 7 million lire, which Magni said was all that he could manage for the time being. The remaining seven he would bring the following week. As Magni turned to leave, he was almost bowled over by a plain-clothes policeman coming in the opposite direction.

The police had suspected for some time that the head of the Milanese old people's home, the Baggina, had a case to answer. A few months earlier he had sought to reduce the amount of alimony he was required to pay to his ex-wife, Laura Sala – whereupon the latter went to the authorities with details of her ex-husband's florid financial affairs. Fifteen billion lire in various bank accounts in Italy and abroad seemed suspicious, and in the autumn of 1991 Public Prosecutor, Antonio di Pietro, asked the Milan Flying Squad to eavesdrop on Chiesa's telephone conversations. But Chiesa was too cautious – or very well informed. Thus it was not until Luca Magni went to the *Carabinieri* complaining about the bribe he had been asked to pay that di Pietro was able to lure Chiesa into his trap. Preparing a small briefcase containing marked banknotes and a number of listening devices, di Pietro was able to convince Magni to present himself at Chiesa's office with the briefcase and four *Carabinieri* who would lie in wait outside. When the *Carabinieri* burst in, Chiesa asked to be allowed to use the bathroom, where he was shortly caught flushing the 37 million lire proceeds of another bribe down the toilet. Thus began the deepest and most long-lasting corruption scandal in Italy's post-war history.

A member of the Italian Socialist Party (PSI), Chiesa had made little effort to hide the ambition that he might one day become Mayor of Milan. A member of the faction headed by Paolo Pilittieri, brother-in-law of party leader and one-time Prime Minister, Bettino Craxi, Chiesa had begun his political career as the secretary of a party branch in a remote suburb of Milan. From there he had moved up in the party. Taking advantage of the established system of governing party control, for patronage purposes, of large parts of the state apparatus, he had first been an administrator at the Sacco hospital in Milan, then a provincial councillor, and, from 1986, head of the Baggina. By 1990, he had his own modest electoral following of about 7,000 votes, which he expected to place at the disposition of whomsoever, further up the party hierarchy, could help him to advance further. Normally the clientelist system was such that, when members got into trouble with the judicial authorities, the party would quickly erect a large protective wall around them.[1] But Chiesa had been caught 'with his hands in the marmalade'[2] and a general election was due on 5 April. Frequently the object of media satire for its shaky grasp of probity, the party abandoned him to his fate. He was, in Craxi's words, '*un mariuolo*' ('a little rascal') who had thrown 'a shadow over the entire image of a party which, in fifty years in Milan – not five but fifty – [had] never had an administrator convicted for grave crimes against the public administration'. Faced with this evidence that his political career was in ruins, Chiesa decided to empty the sack.

What came to light was a massive network of 'mutually beneficial linkages' (Waters, 1994: 170) between the political parties and powerful economic groups in the city: a situation in which those who were obliged to pay bribe money did not wait for it to be asked of them but rather knew that in that particular environment the payment of back-handers was normal and so conformed to the system. It was a system so pervasive and routine that those involved, while aware that what they were doing was *illegal*, had clearly lost the sense that it was in any way *reprehensible* – as was vividly revealed by the suicide note written by the Socialist deputy, Sergio Moroni, who killed himself on 2 September 1992 having been accused of receiving numerous bribes for public works contracts:

> I began my political activity in the PSI when I was very young, only 17 years of age. I still remember passionately many political and ideological battles, *but I made a mistake in accepting the 'system', believing that accepting contributions and help for the party was justified in a context in which this was the normal practice.* (Colaprico, 1996: 31–2, author's translation and emphasis)

'Normal practice', though it may have been, it was illegal all the same and because of this it required there to be, among those involved, a trust that would necessarily have been very difficult to establish – but very easy to break in the event of the slightest suspicion that the wall of silence surrounding the network had been breached. Public prosecutors interviewing Chiesa and those he implicated were clearly aware of this, turning it to their advantage in using preventative custody laws to create for suspects a kind of 'prisoner's dilemma' – leading to a veritable rush on the part of politicians, administrators and entrepreneurs, to confess the part they had played in networks of corrupt exchange. Suspects, held *incommunicado*, would be offered the choice of remaining in prison or else released if they confessed. Accomplices, knowing that they too would be picked up in the event of a confession but not knowing exactly how much had been revealed, thus had an incentive to tell 'their side of the story' as soon as possible, before the confessions of those in prison had gone 'too far' (Newell, forthcoming).

Thus it was that the scandal spread. On 3 May the Milanese public prosecutor's office issued requests for the lifting of the parliamentary immunity of the ex-Mayors of Milan, Carlo Tognoli and Paolo Pilittieri, and by the middle of the month the notorious *avvisi di garanzia* advising them that they were under judicial investigation had been received by the Christian Democrats' (DC's) administrative secretary, Severino Citaristi, and by the leader of the Republican group in the Chamber of Deputies, Antonio Del Pennino. Meanwhile, in Milan, the investigations quickly spread from the Baggina to the municipal transport company, to the *Ente Comunale di Assistenza*, to the Sacco and Fatebenefratelli hospitals, to the airport authority, to the *Piccolo Teatro*, and revealed bribes ranging from those in connection with the 2000 billion lire contract for the realisation of the airport project, Malpensa 2000, to the 100,000 lire back-handers paid by the undertakers working for the Baggina (Della Porta, 1993: 220).

By mid-July, arrest warrants had been issued in Florence and the Veneto and, with the issue of an *avviso* to ex-Foreign Secretary, Gianni De Michelis, and the arrest of the builder, Salvatore Ligresti, the investigations had begun to involve politicians and businessmen of the very highest rank. The 15 December 1992 was to become an unforgettable date in the history of the scandal. It saw an officer of the *Carabinieri* deliver to the luxury suite of the hotel Raphael in Rome an *avviso di garanzia* addressed to the Socialist leader, Bettino Craxi, himself.

In March 1993 it was the turn of the ranking politicians of the DC and the other governing parties. Towards the end of the month an *avviso di garanzia* was served on no less a figure than the Health Minister, the Liberals' Francesco De Lorenzo. Keeping him company were: former Interior Minister Antonio Gava; Enzo Scotti, who had resigned as Foreign Secretary the previous July; Paolo Cirino Pomicino, one-time Minister of the Budget; Giulio Di Donato, one-time vice-secretary of the PSI. Finally, on 27 March, with the accusation of Mafia involvement, it was the turn of the 'boss of bosses', the former DC Prime Minister, Giulio Andreotti, himself. By the end of 1993 no fewer than 251 members of Parliament were under judicial investigation, including four former prime ministers, five ex-party leaders, and seven members of the Cabinet. Ten suspects had killed themselves (Bull and Newell, 1995: 74; Nelken, 1996: 109; Newell, 2000: 56).

The downfall and humiliation of so many powerful figures delighted public opinion. Italians had always had an especially low opinion of politicians and the parties they represented and, if they kept on voting for them in high numbers year after year, it was less because of any positive commitment than because of the negative feeling that they had little choice. That is, they supported them either for reasons of clientelism – which, by turning citizens' *rights* into *favours*, itself bred cynicism and resentment – or because they were frightened by the prospect of the Communists taking power, or both.[3] They knew that the world of politics was dark and labyrinthine, and that its practitioners were powerful people with the ability to 'fix things' in such a way that they were immune from the impositions of a hostile state that ordinary citizens had to endure. Consequently, the sight of once untouchable figures at last getting their come-uppance was intoxicating – and rendered all the more powerful by the awareness of ordinary citizens that, if they had once felt compelled to vote for the established parties, that was no longer true. For the politicians' power to blackmail voters by raising the spectre of Communism had collapsed along with the Berlin Wall.[4] As a result, that delicious combination of outrage and joy was allowed to express itself with all its righteously indignant force. With voters turning their backs on them in droves and their memberships melting away, the parties that had governed the country continuously since the war soon realised that they were undergoing a process of electoral and organisational meltdown.

It was a heady atmosphere. Not since the country's World Cup victory in 1982 had there been such an outpouring of public excitement. As the revelations touched higher and higher levels of the political system, as the established parties' vote totals plummeted to lower and lower depths, the widespread view that what was happening was Italy's version of Eastern Europe's 'velvet revolutions', was captured in the events of a single day. On 29 April 1992, Parliament refused to grant the magistrates' request to lift Bettino Craxi's parliamentary immunity in connection with four of the six charges he then faced. As Craxi himself continued to insist that he was a scapegoat and the victim of a plot, since all parties had taken illicit contributions to finance their activities, a flood of street protests and letters, telephone calls and faxes to national newspapers demonstrated popular derision and disgust at Parliament's decision. As Craxi left his Rome residence to attend a television interview he was greeted by a hostile crowd throwing small coins and chanting '*Buffone!, Buffone!*'[5] – an incident which stood as a metaphor for the fate of an entire political class (Newell, 2000: 56).

As scandals go, there are few to rival this one. It might even qualify, in some meaningful sense, as the twentieth century's 'greatest scandal'. For it did indeed result in the break-up of Italy's main governing parties – leading eventually to the transformation of the entire party system and the onset of a process of regime transition. It therefore demonstrated, more strikingly perhaps than any other could, the sheer profundity of the political consequences that scandals often have.

This would by itself constitute a sufficient reason for considering the academic study of scandals as something important – but there are additional reasons. One of these has to do with what scandals tell us about public values and how they are changing. As Garrard puts it in his contribution to this volume, scandals are 'indicator events'. This is so because whatever else it does, conduct deemed scandalous by definition offends public values. But public values are constantly shifting – so that scandals are likely to arise when those engaging in behaviour that was once tolerated suddenly find themselves on the wrong side of a shifting moral borderline.

But if we accept the reasons given in the previous two paragraphs as being valid, then perhaps the most important reason for studying scandals is that they have come to be an increasingly prominent feature of public life in modern societies over the past thirty or forty years. On the one hand, this has had to do with the development of the mass media of communications, which have rendered the lives of the individuals who walk on the public stage 'much more visible than they ever were in the past' (Thompson, 2000: 6). On the other hand, it has had to do with the growing significance of scandals, in an age when parties' policy differences are much harder to detect than in the past, as weapons in the competition to mobilise voters. As Ginsberg and Shefter (2002: 14) have put it, recent scandals 'reflect a major change in the conduct of . . . politics . . . and the growing importance of "politics by other means" '.

Finally, scandals are phenomena we tend, though not invariably, to associate with liberal democracies. For liberal democratic arrangements by definition rest on norms of 'due process' and a necessary condition for the outbreak of scandals is that standards of correct behaviour, of which due-process norms are a sub-set, be infringed. If this is borne in mind, then the foregoing paragraphs suggest that we have at least three reasons for thinking that the study of scandals can tell us much about the nature of liberal democratic regimes and how they function.

But what exactly *is* a 'scandal'? A moment's reflection reveals that, conceptually speaking, scandal is by no means easy to pin down. Partly this has to do with the heavy evaluative load the term carries when we use it in everyday parlance. Thus, there are plenty of events and episodes each one of us regards as 'scandalous'. Depending on our points of view, we might choose to call British and American invasion of Iraq 'scandalous', as we might the level of crime on our streets or the decision to cut the link between pensions and earnings. But the problem is: how can we define scandal as an objective social phenomenon independent of our own individual perceptions and evaluations of right and wrong?

There would seem to be at least three criteria that need to be fulfilled in order for the term 'scandal' to have relevance. That is, it refers to situations in which:

1 significant, but deliberately concealed, breaches of standards of correct behaviour are suddenly brought to light;
2 such breaches are communicated to an audience wider than those immediately involved;
3 the audience is consequently 'scandalised'.

Of course one is immediately aware that each of these criteria raises as many problems as it solves. What is a 'significant' breach? Who makes up the audience to which such breaches are communicated? What proportion of the members of such an audience have to be scandalised before we are willing to apply the term? These are by no means trivial questions. One might ask in what sense the Monica Lewinsky affair was actually a 'scandal', bearing in mind that well over half the American population apparently regarded the behaviour of the man at the centre of it as a matter of strictly *private* rather than of any *public* relevance (Uslaner, this volume). For reasons such as these, as editors we have left contributors free to work with those understandings of the term that they think are best, given their areas of study, rather than tying them down to any one definition. For, one of the purposes of this book is precisely to contribute to debate on this issue, rather than to offer research based on some a priori definition that may then turn out to be flawed. In that sense, the purpose of this book is very much one of 'theory-building' rather than of 'theory-testing'.

Exploratory in intent, then, the book's other essential purposes are to throw light on three interrelated sets of questions: (1) Under what conditions do scandals take place? (2) How do they unfold and how are they perpetuated? (3) What effects, if any, do they have upon public values, the perceptions of politicians, legal frameworks, and the legitimacy of political institutions and systems?

In considering the first of these issues, Garrard's analysis in Part I of the volume suggests that the answer to the question posed earlier – namely, how 'significant' must breaches of standards be in order to form the basis of a scandal? – is something that has vertical and horizontal dimensions. That is, he argues that, for breaches to trigger a scandal, they must either be committed by senior public figures or else, if committed by lesser mortals, be widespread. To this one might add the further suggestion that the two dimensions will – presumably – govern the 'scale' of a scandal (measured in terms of the size of it's 'audience') – bribery on the part of a local councillor scandalising the municipality's residents but failing to arouse most other people; bribery on the part of a Cabinet minister, arousing the entire population. But unless wrong-doing is discovered at the moment it takes place, or shortly thereafter, there can be no scandal. As Williams notes: President Kennedy's reckless sexual liaisons cannot be scandalous because it is not possible retrospectively to 'discover' a scandal. Perhaps the reason for this, in turn, is that transgressions that are 'water under the bridge' cannot pose any threat to the established order or to the public interest in the present. That transgressions be perceived as in some way damaging, at least potentially, to the interests of some of the public does indeed seem to be a further necessary condition for the outbreak of a scandal. Thus, it is highly probable that the phenomenon highlighted by Pujas – the increasingly high profile taken by business and accounting scandals in recent years – is not unrelated, in an era of pension funds and increasingly widespread share ownership, to the tendency for the interests of ordinary citizens to be far more closely tied to the performance of business and of stock markets than ever they were in the past.

That for breaches to be scandalous they must touch the interests of large numbers of people immediately draws attention to an issue examined by many of the contributors to this volume: the role of the media in the genesis and unfolding of scandals. For scandals cannot occur unless breaches are publicised, while media organisations, as commercial entities, will only publicise breaches in which the public is likely to be interested. Have the media become too eager to denigrate politicians and other public figures, perhaps to the detriment of informed discussion of policy? Garrard thinks that this may be the case, but former journalist, Chris Moncrieff, in his contribution in Part II, on how scandals unfold, disagrees. Offering an 'insider's account' of the role of Fleet Street in the reporting – and indeed manufacture – of some of the most memorable of British scandals, he argues, from a normative point of view, that politicians are 'fair game if they step out of line. They are constantly preaching at us, so if they err, then they get what they deserve.' Be this as it may, as the chapters by Fleming, Murphy and Uslaner suggest, empirically the successful exposure of behaviour deemed scandalous is no guarantee of an improvement in standards and, indeed, excessive zeal on the part of investigators – journalists and others – may even have consequences that fly in the face of those they intend.

The four historical case studies in Part III suggest – and this would be confirmed by the *Tangentopoli* (Bribe City) scandal described above – that scandals are typically associated with periods of rapid social and political change. Thus, as Koutsoukis shows, the two most devastating scandals in Greek history arose out of conduct threatening collective social goals at moments of profound transformation of Greek society, while, echoing an earlier point made by Garrard, Theobald (p. 148) argues that the trial of Warren Hastings in 1788 was to be explained in part by growing urbanisation, which 'created a public eager for news, gossip, entertainment, scandal – in short, for spectacle'. In their study of scandals involving presidents of the French fifth republic, Bilger-Street and Demossier follow Pujas' suggestion in seeing corruption allegations surrounding President Chirac as indicative of important shifts in the relationship between the judiciary and the press. In her analysis of what was possibly the greatest health scandal in twentieth-century Ireland, the Hepatitis C/Anti-D blood contamination episode, Farrell shows the significant part in the scandal's emergence that was played by growing secularisation and the country's successful integration into the global economy. All four studies point to the apparent importance in explaining the occurrence of scandals of competing sets of values on the part of the individuals and groups involved in them.

Finally, the chapters in Part IV reverse perspectives to explore the potential consequences of scandals, and are revealing of the conditions under which they have consequences of greater or lesser magnitude. One factor that seems to be important is the degree to which they draw attention to significant political problems. If they do, then they are likely to be highly damaging to the reputations of those involved. On the other hand, if they arise out of conduct that speaks more to the personal qualities of the transgressors than anything else, they may actually lead to an *enhancement* of reputations. A good example of this is Vladimir Zhirinovsky, founder and leader of the far-right Russian Liberal Democratic Party. As Wishnevsky points out, in a cultural context in which Russians do not expect the personal conduct of public figures to be above that of ordinary citizens, Zhirinovsky has successfully indulged in all kinds of outrageous acts designed to keep him at the forefront of media attention and to appeal to those who have suffered from the market-oriented reforms of the post-Communist era. The challenge to the assumption that scandals must necessarily have devastating consequences for those involved is then continued by Jiménez and Caínzos in their analysis of the conditions that need to be fulfilled if they are to affect electoral behaviour. Reviewing a large number of empirical studies of the electoral effects of scandals, they argue that 'voters differ in terms of the way they process the negative information associated with scandals' (p. 12) and that under certain circumstances they may be willing to trade tolerance of politicians involved in them for the defence of policy positions they consider to be important. In any given instance, the way voters react will depend heavily upon the conclusions they reach about those involved *as compared* with the *alternatives* on offer. Finally, the chapter by Maesschalck, focussed on the Belgian case, asks about the conditions under which scandals give rise to policy change, drawing on 'grid-group theory' to explore the precise part played by the Dutroux scandal in bringing about, after two centuries of debate, 'the most important changes to the structure of the Belgian police ever implemented' (p. 218).

All the chapters presented in this volume are revised versions of papers originally presented at a conference on 'Political Scandals Past and Present' organised by the editors at the University of Salford, 21–23 June 2001. Towards the organisation of the conference, and thus, indirectly, towards the production of this volume, the British Academy and the European Studies Research Institute, University of Salford, offered generous sponsorship, which, as editors, we wish to acknowledge with thanks. We are also enormously grateful to Wendy Dodgson and Louise Graham, who undertook all the administrative work associated with the conference.

One of the purposes of the conference was to continue analysis of themes considered in a volume, *Corruption in Contemporary Politics*, edited by James Newell together with Martin Bull (2003). Though, conceptually, the two must be clearly distinguished, corruption is, of course, a phenomenon with which scandal is often closely related – and, perhaps, the kind of transgression that most frequently gives rise to it. In that sense, the present volume may be seen as a companion to the earlier work. It takes the analysis a crucial stage beyond *Corruption* to the point where corruption, or some other abuse of power, becomes scandalous. This stage is important because it is only through the generation of scandal that the behaviour in question becomes *widely perceived* as abusive and is thereby enabled to have society-wide effects. And because scandals provide opportunities for legal or other amendments, the increasingly frequent outbreak of corruption episodes in the advanced democracies since the 1980s suggests that the study of scandal, past and present, is an essential means of understanding the way in which early twenty-first century democracies govern themselves.

Notes

1 Thus it had been with Antonio Natali, President of the Milanese underground system. When accused in 1987 of accepting bribes in connection with construction work, he had managed to get himself elected to the upper house of Parliament, the Senate – a majority of whose members had then obligingly voted against the judicial authorities' request that his parliamentary immunity be lifted.
2 The expression was di Pietro's.
3 From 1945, the Italian Communist Party (PCI) consistently challenged the Christian Democrats for the status of the country's largest party but was constantly confined to the Opposition owing to its unacceptability as a coalition partner to the remaining parties.
4 As a result of the Wall's collapse, in 1991, the PCI transformed itself into a *non*-Communist party with a new name: the Democratic Party of the Left.
5 A word that conveys far more contempt than its English equivalent, 'buffoon'.

References

Bull, M. J. and J. L. Newell (1995), 'Italy Changes Course? The 1994 Elections and the Victory of the Right', *Parliamentary Affairs*, 46: 2, 72–99.

Bull, M. J. and J. L. Newell (eds) (2003), *Corruption in Contemporary Politics*, Houndmills, Palgrave-Macmillan.

Colaprico, P. (1996), *Capire Tangentopoli*, Milano, il Saggiatore.

Della Porta, D. (1993), 'La capitale immorale: le tangenti di Milano', in S. Hellman and G. Pasquino (eds), *Politica in Italia: I fatti dell'anno e le interpretazioni*, Bologna, il Mulino.

Ginsberg, B. and M. Shefter (2002), *Politics by Other Means: Politicians, Persecutors, and the Press from Watergate to Whitewater*, 3rd edition, New York and London, W. W. Norton.

Nelken, D. (1996), 'The Judges and Political Corruption in Italy', *Journal of Law and Society*, 23: 1, 95–112.

Newell, J. L. (2000), *Parties and Democracy in Italy*, Aldershot, Ashgate.

Newell, J. L. (forthcoming), 'Corruption Mitigating Policies: The Case of Italy', *Modern Italy*.

Thompson, J. B. (2000), *Political Scandal: Power and Visibility in the Media Age*, Cambridge, Polity.

Waters, S. (1994), ' "Tantentopoli" and the Emergence of a New Political Order in Italy', *West European Politics*, 17: 1, 169–82.

Part I

Theoretical and comparative perspectives

1

Scandals: an overview

John Garrard

This chapter contains some thoughts about what scandals are, the conditions under which they tend to arise, what influence they can have, and why they should interest observers of the past and present. The observations rest partly upon my own research, partly upon what other studies have suggested. The initial evidence comes from before 1914. However, I have also used more recent examples from Britain and America in the fairly unoriginal belief that, although scandals vary greatly according to culture and time, they also have certain recurring features rendering them eloquent about the societies wherein they occur, and allowing useful comparison (and contrast) across time and culture.

Some scandals

We start with three examples, selected purely because I know about them, and because they illustrate certain enduring features of a substantial class of scandals. We begin in Salford where, in February 1887, prompted by the Gas Committee, Samuel Hunter, the Corporation's gas manager for the previous eleven years, sued Ellis Lever for criminal libel (Garrard, 1988). Hunter was not just a corporation official, but also a major social figure in Manchester and Salford. Lever, one of the North's largest coal contractors, had persistently alleged that 'bribery, corruption and fraud [had] prevailed in the borough . . . for many years', and claimed that Hunter had been accepting bribes on contracts for coal, cannel (a type of coke) and gas equipment to the exclusion of honest contractors. The case aroused extensive publicity not just in Salford and Manchester, but also in newspapers across the North. It also received significant attention amongst the London dailies, even more in the several periodicals for professional gas engineers, amongst whom Hunter was a minor but significant rising star.

After a three-day trial, Ellis Lever was acquitted. He was immediately hailed in the press and by many amongst the middle-class public as a hero, striking a great and cleansing blow for public and commercial ethics in a dirty and corrupt world where backhanders were increasingly common. His subsequent journeyings received considerable publicity, doubly so when he embarked on a public campaign not just to cleanse Salford (where he alleged much uncovered ordure remained), but also numerous other allegedly venal northern towns. For a while, Salford particularly, and the gas industry generally, became horrifying by-words for corruption. In the gas-engineering press, editorials, articles and numerous, often breast-beating, letters from gas managers all suggested that bribes (or 'commissions' as many preferred to call them) had long been normal accompaniments to contract negotiation within the municipal and private gas industry across the country. Many said the 'system' had partly arisen as implicit compensation, recognised by all sides, for the allegedly inadequate salaries and rightfully high social expectations of gas managers. Many pointed to the close relations between managers and contractors of all sorts that were typical of the industry and almost endemic in a profession that, whilst proud of its learning, expertise and skill, was strongly entrepreneurial, and slipped almost seamlessly into business activity. In the wider daily press, letters and editorials alleged that such practices were widespread in commercial life as a whole. For the *Yorkshire Post* (16 February 1887, p. 4), 'the thing is stupendous even in an age of rottenness of business . . . methods'. The *Gas and Water Review* (11 February 1887, p. 138) pronounced the whole 'world . . . a gigantic augean stable'. One correspondent to the *Manchester Examiner* ('Draco', 7 February 1887, p. 2) demanded an end to 'those immoral transactions, acts of bribery . . . daily going on in our midst . . . bringing into disrepute . . . commercial credit . . . and sapping the integrity of the nation'.

Salford's gas committee immediately resigned. After some hesitation, the Corporation sued their manager. They did this not on grounds of bribery (offering and accepting bribes were not then criminal offences for municipal officials) but because of alleged perjury at Ellis Lever's trial, and the forgery of the gas committee chairman's signature on a letter in 1880, supposedly allowing a coal firm to continue paying the manager his commissions. So great was the publicity, it was felt impossible to find an unbiased Lancashire jury. Consequently, the trial was transferred to London where, in March 1888, Hunter pleaded guilty. After further delay, he was sentenced, rather savagely given the charges but clearly as an example to others, to five years penal servitude.

After several months of tortuous negotiations with the Council before and after sentencing, Hunter agreed to start naming the many firms who had bribed him. Salford then instituted legal proceedings against them, mostly preliminary to out-of-court settlements, whereby they paid substantial sums in compensation for the over-charges written into contracts to finance the manager's commissions. The last contractor named was Ellis Lever, Hunter's chief accuser, champion of the cleansing righteous, whom Salford thereupon joyously sued to the bitter legal end. In effective return, the municipal elite signed a petition originated by Hunter's solicitors pleading, unsuccessfully, for some mitigation of sentence. Councillors always denied this was a *quid pro quo*, though it undoubtedly was. However, many also probably agreed with the gas committee's ex-chairman (Alderman Mackinson, *Salford Reporter*, 24 August 1889, p. 7) that 'there are thousands . . . who do the same . . . as Hunter . . . His particular offence is that he has been found out.' They also probably concurred with a local doctor ('Medico', *Salford Reporter*, 17 January 1891, p. 4) that, 'it seems almost impossible that such a man . . . could be subjected to a felon's prison for receiving a few royalties . . . a man who would grace any social position . . . dying in a felon's jail [to] the distress . . . of a respectable family and friends'.

In fact, much more than just 'a few royalties' were involved: the minimum estimate of his benefits was £11,000 at contemporary values, and the real figure was probably far higher. However, Hunter too felt he had done nothing wrong. Outwardly, he was not amoral. He was a Wesleyan lay preacher who actively contributed to local charities, and was a sympathetic employer of gas workers. Ellis Lever's accusations had allegedly begun partly after Hunter had refused to co-operate in his efforts to blacken the name of a rival coal contractor. Hunter left jail on a ticket-of-leave in March 1892, telling a newspaper that, though he *had* taken commissions, these constituted 'no serious breach of morality'. He posed as a much-wronged man whose downward career had begun when he was Rochdale's gas manager, saying that he had consulted his minister about the many good things on offer from contractors. This Man of God had told him that there was 'no harm in taking a friendly gift'. Hunter claimed to have spent 'many years trying to be a religious man' (*Sunday Chronicle* quoted by the *Rochdale Observer*, 30 September 1892, p. 4).

The gas scandal was one of several rather similar events around this time. Caught up in reverberations emanating from Salford, several other industrial towns also experienced commission-based gas scandals. These, and the much more spectacular goings-on revealed by the Royal Commission inquiring into the affairs of London's Metropolitan Board of Works, produced the 1889 Public Bodies Corrupt Practices Act.

The year 1888 was a vintage year for scandals, even in Salford. Shortly after the town's gas manager was convicted, its town clerk disappeared. He reappeared briefly in Folkestone and Paris, eventually holing up in San Francisco, along with £800 of Corporation money and £15,000 he, as a solicitor, held in trust for a Peterborough family. He provided an unwitting trailer for a much more spectacular scandal that reached its climax in a London court in 1900. Here, amidst massive publicity, Benjamin Lake, the Law Society's ex-President, was given twelve years penal servitude for defrauding clients of £173,772. He had carelessly gone bankrupt after using trust money in land and building speculation. This scandal caused the same sort of crisis amongst solicitors as a profession that Samuel Hunter had created for gas engineers. This was heightened because the ensuing professional breast-beating revealed that the tendency of solicitors to 'mix' their clients' money with their own was very widespread, even amongst those whom the *Solicitors' Journal* (2 February 1901, p. 231) called 'very respectable solicitors'.

More spectacular and more widely reported than either of the foregoing, notwithstanding determined attempts from within the political elite to suppress inquiry, was the much-later scandal arising after the collapse of John Poulson's architectural business in north-east England in 1972. The subsequent bankruptcy examination showed that Poulson had over many years used extravagant and widespread bribery, hospitality and gifts to persuade municipal councillors and officials to grant him redevelopment contracts. Subsequent criminal proceedings drew in many regional politicians and officials in the north-east and in Scotland, and some civil servants, and produced extended prison sentences not just for Poulson but also for twenty others, including T. Dan Smith, charismatic leader of Newcastle City Council and the inspiration behind the city's redevelopment. Over the next five years, enquiry followed enquiry, with massive media publicity, culminating in a Royal Commission and a Commons Select Committee. The scope of Poulson's network of generosity and reciprocal obligation became apparent. MPs in all parties, even front-bench figures like Reginald Maudling, also became unwillingly, but hardly innocently, involved. Some of this amounted to simple, if remarkably generous, hospitality by Poulson; some involved gifts ranging from horse-racing tickets to suits of clothing, cars or house extensions. Some constituted unashamed and extensive bribery. The lines separating the marginally legitimate from the downright illegal were almost imperceptible. The BBC's correspondent, David Wheeler, noted: 'What makes corruption so difficult to stamp out is that those who practice it often don't really believe they are doing wrong. They're simply trying to get things done . . . to motivate people in the right direction' ('Public Affairs', 1990, no. 4).

Smith himself was certainly one of these. In a BBC interview ('Public Affairs', 1990, no. 2), some years after emerging from prison, he observed:

> the implication of so many . . . authors . . . was that I was a crooked councillor . . . Nothing could be further from the truth . . . I think (Poulson) behaved in a way . . . common to most businesses, of offering holidays, entertainment. If that is corrupt . . . the boxes at Ascot and Wimbledon are full of the recipients of the same kind of inducements. I'm not condoning it, but it's a matter of how you interpret business ethics . . . what Poulson did was typically common of business practices then and now.

Alderman Cunningham ('Public Affairs', 1990, no. 2), late chairman of Durham's Police Authority, recipient of much Poulson generosity including a paid-for holiday in Portugal and another of those imprisoned, claimed, 'if I am corrupt then the entire country is corrupt'. Even Poulson felt somewhat victimised.

Main characteristics

These examples illustrate what the introduction to this chapter has already noted about scandals. They are public phenomena, wherein hitherto private behaviour, sometimes resting upon private systems of mores and values, often long-persistent and tolerated, is publicly revealed, widely deemed morally outrageous, and thereby comes to scandalise large numbers of people. Scandals rest on public values, help define them, and do not have fixed contents. These vary according to time and location. 'Commissions' had probably been central features of the gas and other sectors of British industry for many decades, and consented to by most of those involved. They were only just beginning to seem fully scandalous in the century's final decades, partly because of scandals like Salford's. More familiar in this respect for British historians is the changing content of electoral scandal (electoral malpractices capable of scandalising people) over the 200 years since around 1800 – from a situation, for example, where the giving and receiving of bribes was frequently 'customary' to one where it has become deeply heinous. Again, scandals have probably been important agencies of change. Similarly, the clientelism and brokerage, so long normal political staples in Ireland, would arouse outrage in Britain and Scandinavia, and, as the result of scandals, may finally be starting to do so in Ireland (Ridley and Doig, 1995). In general, in Europe and North America at least, apart from the crucial area of sex where it is probably rising, the threshold for being genuinely scandalised has declined, and with increasing speed, over the years.

Scandals mostly, and almost necessarily, involve *public people*: politicians, public officials, and/or people in positions of *public trust* – positions that involve them being trusted by substantial numbers of others and being assumed to deploy high standards of personal conduct. They may be politicians, company officials, officers of civil organisations, high-profile lawyers like Benjamin Lake, clergymen, or public servants like social workers, policemen, teachers, or indeed gas engineers. As Robert Williams (1998: 6) has noted, what matters is 'not . . . the conduct itself but its relation to a public role, and the attendant expectations of that role'. Often these public persons are also *publicly visible* and celebrated in some way – royals; politicians; social, economic or political leaders in inward-looking nineteenth-century towns, where mass visibility was possible; sports persons or film stars. Others (more humble citizens or employees, or professional criminals) may well also be involved, but their presence cannot generally generate scandals unless they are involved in large numbers. Single directors of banks can easily produce scandals; ordinary bank clerks rarely manage it. Gas managers can induce scandals; gas fitters cannot, unless their particular 'fiddles' occur on a systemic scale, and only sometimes then. More often perhaps, where ordinary citizens are involved, they tend to emerge as innocent *victims* of *situations deemed scandalous*, and produced by neglect or abuse by public persons or authorities. Most large nineteenth-century towns went through regular cycles of public-health scandals: the sudden revelation or rediscovery of horrendous death rates, or the discovery that they had not declined since the last scandal, or that council regulations, however stringent, were not being enforced, sometimes due to alleged neglect or chicanery by relevant public officials.

Public people are mostly essential to the emergence of scandals for various reasons. Only they have access to extended means of behaving scandalously, and they are trusted to behave otherwise. Only public persons have the authority to keep such behaviour private for long periods of time, as did all three of those in the scandals above. This often produces second-order scandals possibly more serious than the original sin, since they involve greater amounts of irregularity or illegality. Examples include Samuel Hunter's perjury at Ellis Lever's trial; Bill Clinton's denial of sexual impropriety in the White House; Richard Nixon's attempts to cover up involvement in Watergate (Thompson, 2000: 17). Expectations of such people rest upon public values, and scandals necessarily outrage those values. Their presence is what most often engages media attention. Finally, their appearance, particularly where they are celebrated, gives scandals their public appeal, rendering the behaviour in question not just outrageous, but positively enjoyable for those watching – who thereby allow themselves to be scandalised. One of scandals' great appeals is the sense of high, mighty and dignified individuals being 'cut down to size', being rendered absurd, undignified. This is why scandals, whether financial, political or sexual, have long provided radicals with vivid, even pornographic (McCalman, 1988), ways of ridiculing and thereby de-legitimising elites and the systems they preside over. The opportunities became increasingly evident from the later eighteenth century onwards, with emerging mass politicisation and the emerging mass media. Thus the gas scandal presented local socialists with irresistible opportunities for ridicule and moral opprobrium, since Salford's council of businessmen was made to look seedy, absurd and deliciously typical of their kind.

On the other hand, the threshold and content of scandal can also vary according to the sort of public person involved. In our age, some can get away with far more than others. Politicians, clergymen and others in positions of public trust are most constrained and vulnerable. Footballers' or film stars' sexual exploits, whilst often 'interesting', only occasionally seem scandalous even to the tabloids. However, politicians caught with half-masted trousers, particularly alongside persons other than their wives, better still in their places of political business, still have as much scandalous potential as they did in the nineteenth century. This is so even if the numbers of people actually scandalised, rather than merely amused, is declining. Major businessmen can get away with more financial sharp practice than politicians before triggering scandals. Indeed, the mismatch between expectations in the public and business worlds may well be a potent generator of conduct that turns out to be scandalous, particularly for businessmen-turned-politicians, or where politics, as it increasingly does due to government's ever-expanding role, involves contact and negotiation with business. This was certainly an ingredient in the Poulson scandal. The numerous politics–business scandals of the late nineteenth and early twentieth centuries – the gas scandal being one and the Marconi scandal another – may mark the point where expectations of the two began clearly diverging.

Partly as a result of the foregoing, and partly because they so often lead to formal enquiry, scandals (perhaps like other dramatic occurrences such as disasters) are indicator events. They are points of social declaration and declamation, saying much about the society and/or political system wherein they occur. Read carefully, and with due attention for unwitting as well as witting testimony, as well as – crucially – for the agendas of the media reporting them, they can highlight important characteristics. Salford's gas scandal was eloquent about the increasing influence of expert municipal servants compared with that of the businessmen-turned-councillors who formed so large a proportion of councils in large industrial towns, and who were beset by 'the increasing pressure of business', both their own and the council's. It proclaimed much about the hazy borderlines between professional and entrepreneurial activity: for Samuel Hunter, like many of his kind, this involved not just enterprising attitudes towards supplementing his salary on the side, but also owning several businesses founded upon his gas-engineering expertise. Allowing for scandals' ability to produce moral panics, it may also have advertised much that was customary in business life. Misty borderlines were also evident in Salford's subsequent 'Town Clerk Scandal', and the later Lake scandal: solicitors intermixed the terms 'practice' and 'business' to describe their central activity, and still do, and used their access to family-trust money and expertise in areas like land transfer to invest and speculate. So equally did and do architects like Poulson. Above all, scandals say much about 'sharp practice' in any society, and about what of that activity can scandalise people. In other words, they are eloquent about the changing and constant content of public values. As the gas scandal showed, they can become crucial points where people express and define their anxieties about perceived trends in the world around them. Meanwhile, the Poulson scandal was continuously eloquent about links between politics and business in a world where national and local governments were major initiators of urban redevelopment. Similarly, the more recent Enron scandal was described by one commentator as 'a magnifying glass allowing us to see clearly . . . how government and business operate today' (Andrew Leonard, quoted in the *Guardian*, 16 January 2002, p. 3).

Underpinning this is the fact that scandals also tend to be perceived as systemic in some way. This explains why they can have cleansing, but also (for the system concerned or those presiding over it) dangerous and de-legitimising, consequences. One implication of some of the discussion immediately above is that, sometimes they actually *are* systemic, or at least symptomatic. Evidence emerging from the formal enquiries following initial scandalous revelations often suggests this. Scandals appear to proceed from the ways a given system (whether governmental, professional or organisational) fundamentally works, or from the way it is changing: the increasing pressure from contractors upon late nineteenth-century gas managers or mid-twentieth-century council leaders; the vast increase in private-sector lobbyists around modern legislatures; the opportunities and temptations that privatisation creates for MPs.

Scandals come in various kinds. They can be classified according to the field where the abuse primarily occurs: political (abuses of power), financial or sexual. They can also be classified according to the number of participants, and the character of the behaviour deemed scandalous.

Thus, firstly, they may involve *single* scandalous actions by some publicly celebrated person: for example, the troubles during 1999–2001 of Jonathan Aitken and Geoffrey Archer. More often, even where individuals are the primary participants, the behaviour in question is, or is taken as, symptomatic of much wider patterns, involving far more people of the same kind – perhaps entire 'regimes'. Samuel Hunter came to be seen as a gas manager who had been found out, his behaviour indicative of how others within the gas industry routinely conducted themselves. The Lake scandal became symptomatic of practices amongst solicitors that were 'normal'. This explains why scandals arise, still more why they grow; it also explains their ability to produce moral panics – situations wherein a whole group, even a whole society, apparently places itself in the dock. The more this is so, as argued later, the more influence scandals can have on public values.

Second and consequently, scandals often come in groups, particularly where they involve the same kind of behaviour. This may be less because such practices have suddenly become more common than because behaviour, which in the past was widely practiced and tolerated, comes up against a public tolerance that is changing (partly because of initial revelations), and/or media competitively eager to reveal. This helps explain the rash of scandals over 'commission-taking' by public officials in late nineteenth-century towns; also those over MPs taking cash for asking questions before the 1997 election. These points also partly explain the capacity of scandals, as we shall see, to taint, even erode, the legitimacy of an entire political class.

Third, the behaviour in question may be clearly heinous and criminal, dramatically assaulting public values: for example, child abuse by social workers or teachers or the embezzlement of public funds. More often, it is located in a grey zone, on the hazy borderlines between what is publicly permissible and impermissible. This is an area of activity that Anthony Barker (1992: 21) has called 'not unlawful' rather than either illegal or legal. As evident from our initial examples, the individuals and/or groups involved may even see their behaviour as morally defensible, or neutral, or at least capable of being rendered respectable. Thus they use words like 'commissions' or 'perquisites' to describe what others saw as bribes for the award of municipal contracts by gas engineers and probably by many others across the country in the late nineteenth century. The *Journal of Gas Lighting* (24 January 1888, p. 137), in one of many similar editorials on Salford's tribulations, chipped away at this borderline in 1888, likening:

> the commercial morality of gas-works officials in bulk . . . to the condition of their own manufactured product with respect to chemical purity. Downright knavery and sulfurated hydrogen are alike forbidden; but after this line has been drawn

there are varying degrees of moral obliquity in men and chemical impurity in gas
which seem to be endured . . . as a matter of course.

Bribing firms, meanwhile, with the even looser moral frameworks probably
customary in the business world, 'may [have regarded] the granting of such
bribes as a legitimate factor in pushing business' (*Gas World*, 12 March
1887, p. 261). Similar attitudes were evident amongst the many respectable
nineteenth-century solicitors who 'mixed' their own finances with money
held in trust for child or female beneficiaries of wills, and speculated cheerfully
with both. The same was true of many small-town electors and party agents
throughout the eighteenth and much of the nineteenth centuries who saw bribes
in return for appropriate voting as customary and unexceptionable supplements
to scarce income. The fact that English cathedral towns were amongst the worst
offenders suggests that religiosity did not necessarily preclude such expectations. In our own age, many Conservative MPs probably saw the taking of payments from businessmen for asking questions as normal extensions of their
roles as constituency representatives and/or interest-group consultants, and
perfectly appropriate supplements to income. Meanwhile, Williams (1998: 98)
has noted that, until the scandals of the late 1970s, it was generally understood that lobbyists plied American congressmen with trips abroad and campaign contributions as normal ways of achieving goodwill and access, while
congressmen saw them as legitimate perks, too small to be regarded as real
bribes. Overall, this marginality has implications, as we shall see, for the
conditions under which scandals arise, and their possible impact.

Finally, though scandals vary greatly, most have been argued (Thompson,
2000: 17) to have a natural evolution or internal logic, with at least two, more
normally three, stages, all stemming from the very public character of those
involved and the media that reveals them. There is first the initial conduct,
often continuing over an extended period, and its revelation in the press, on
television or elsewhere. Second, there are often-determined attempts to deny
wrongdoing and cover things up. This phase may well involve conduct of a
morally darker and/or legally dubious, and thus more scandalous, sort than
the original behaviour: at least extended lying, often perjury in court or public enquiries, perhaps the suborning of witnesses. Third, where the attempt
fails, or sometimes conversely as part of an attempt to sweep matters under
the carpet, there is often a formal enquiry stage.

Conditions under which scandals arise

Scandals, being public events, and often involving morally marginal behaviour, tend to arise in particular sorts of circumstance and context. This means
that, whilst corruption is and has been widespread, scandals have tended in
the past (though much more uncertainly in the present) to be less common
and require more critical situations. In the present, as I will argue later,
scandals may be starting to have a life independent of misconduct.

Unlike corruption, if scandals, particularly political ones, are to occur – if masses of people are to be scandalised – the regime has to be either liberal or at least inefficiently authoritarian. Efficient authoritarian regimes (whether governmental or private) may be highly corrupt, but rarely have to tolerate scandals, unless they decide to use them to discredit political opponents. Liberal-democratic regimes, or ones moving that way, may be most likely to experience scandals. This is not because they are more corrupt, rather because their populations are more politicised, their media more independent and because such regimes are likely to rest upon increasing presuppositions of accountability and equality between rulers and ruled – assumptions that citizens are as good as the elites presiding over them. Indeed scandals may reinforce this characteristic, increasing the ordinariness, even the contempt-ibility, of politicians. Such assumptions are combined with implicit and not always compatible expectations that politicians, being repositories of trust, and part of 'responsible government', can be judged by higher standards of probity across much of their conduct. Democratising regimes may also be susceptible to scandal because political change is causing expectations of public conduct to shift (highly important for reasons explored later) or because a politicised public can increasingly enforce accountability on previously unaccountable public officials. Besides, in democratic or democratising regimes, despising politicians is easy and probably enjoyable, and liberal polities by definition can levy few penalties against so doing. If, as later suggested, the media have their own agendas when unearthing and transmitting scandals, it would be wrong to think of the citizenry of liberal democracies, particularly in our own time, as blank sheets. Overall, such environments are highly favourable to scandal-generation.

Connectedly, scandals require some means of spreading information about the revealed behaviour. They require a visible public arena, and the presence of a relatively open and vibrant media of communication, whether newspapers, television or the internet. Except for government-generated scandals about opponents, the media also probably need to be competitive and eager for circulation and profit. They have at least two roles in scandal generation. First (though not the only agencies involved) they *unearth* corrupt or questionable conduct and condemn it. This is particularly so where there is a watch-dog or muck-raking tradition, as there was amongst nineteenth-century American newspapers, or amongst parts of the British local weekly press, especially where this was encouraged by fierce competition between partisan rivals. This spirit of determined investigation has become increasingly evident in liberal democracies in recent times. It has occurred under the influence of vibrant partisanship, albeit decreasingly informed by policy disagreement, fierce com-petition for circulation and thereby advertising revenue, and, particularly so far as quality newspapers and television programmes are concerned, ever-more elevated, even over-inflated, conceptions of Fourth Estate duty. For some obser-vers, including this one, the watchdog has become a 'rottweiler' (Williams, 1998: 128), with all that animal's destructive potentialities. Secondly, having unearthed it, the media *spread news* of questionable behaviour, thereby rendering it truly *scandalous*. In self-absorbed nineteenth-century towns, local weeklies massively spread information within the locality about dubious behaviour as about other things. By picking it up from one another, they also often conveyed news of scandals from place to place, generalising initially local phenomena, sometimes contributing to a sense of moral crisis. The London dailies were instrumental in broadcasting information about scandalous conduct by national politicians: *The Times*' reports of divorce proceedings were instrumental in destroying the reputations of Charles Dilke and Charles Parnell in the 1880s. In nineteenth-century professions, professional journals became the means of publicly communicating news and opinion about dubious conduct, providing agencies through which occupational experience could be compared, and values redefined. Newspapers, television and more recently the Internet have been central to keeping the various political, financial and sexual scandals of recent decades before the public. In all cases, the media portray themselves, perhaps accurately, as the guardians and definers of public standards.

As this begins suggesting, the media are not just neutral investigators and transmitters. They had, and have, their own agendas. Scandals undermine enemies (sometimes even rival editors), sell newspapers and thereby indirectly attract advertising revenue, and enhance the reputations of television commentators. This lends particular force to the notion that modern scandals (since the eighteenth century) are 'mediated' (Thompson, 2000: 31), shaped to varying degrees by the priorities of those reporting them. This has rightly led some commentators to wonder whether the priorities of capitalist (even public-service) media competition have produced behaviour dysfunctional for the liberal democracies that modern industrial capitalism tends to produce – perhaps a special case of the inner contradictions that A. J. Lee (1976) argued were implicit in the relationship between capitalist media and the functions required of them by healthy liberal democracies. Whilst the latter require the spread of serious information and debate, the competitive priorities of the former, particularly mass-circulation tabloids, point increasingly to sensationalism, titillation, entertainment and trivialisation. There is also an increasing addiction to *bad* news – of dysfunction, things going wrong, promises being broken. The overall result is arguably that political elites increasingly become objects of a public cynicism, at best only partly connected with the real probity or otherwise of what they do. With its daily 'shocking' revelations of the normal processes of government, the recent Hutton enquiry (though not the eventual report) into the events surrounding the suicide of David Kelly is, for this writer, a case in point. Particularly in regard to sexual matters, tabloids especially now appear able to produce 'pseudo-scandals', vacuous in content, and independent of any real scandalisation of their readers. The victims, politicians, thus become objects not of shock but of cynicism and derision. They thereby lose their ability to focus public attention on policy initiatives, for reasons quite independent of the merits or otherwise of those policies and their initiators (Doig, 1990: 15; Thompson, 2000: ch. 8; Williams, 1998).

Given the media's crucial role in scandal-generation, it follows that scandals most often occur in significantly urbanised societies, and in urban rather than rural places. Only in such locations are there sufficient means of gaining widespread public attention – via the media. Only in urban places do public values have the shifting quality that can render previously accept-able behaviour scandalous. The point must be made cautiously, however. Nineteenth-century towns were certainly highly encouraging locations for scan-dal generation since, inward-looking and community conscious as they were, they possessed absorbing public arenas, presided over by local newspapers eager to fill them with information. Late twentieth-century urban places, however, are more ambivalent in this respect, at least in Britain. The means of gen-erating and spreading news are massive. However, due to local newspapers' effective disappearance (free sheets hardly qualify as news-carriers), local, as distinct from national, government is becoming invisible. So perhaps are its abuses, aside from those capable of connecting with national anxieties.

As we have begun implying in the comments about the moral marginality of much scandalous behaviour, scandals often arise where private value-systems and private means of 'getting by' ('perquisites' and the like) come up against public, especially official, values and means. Connectedly, they also occur where publicly pronounced values are revealed to be at variance with what significant numbers of people actually do. This may explain why scandals are probably more likely to occur in politics (where public value-systems have great-est sway, where expectations of probity are high, and where relevant public people are most prone to moral proclamation) than in other sectors of life. It also explains why scandals are particularly likely at the meeting-points between political and business life, where the codes and expectations of conduct asso-ciated with them may be at variance. Since around the mid-nineteenth cen-tury, these points have multiplied considerably with growing regulation of business activity, increasing taxation, government's increasing use of private contractors in its public operations, the regulation of privatised utilities, the increasing need of each side for 'information, advice and consent' from the other (Finer, 1966: 4). The examples outlined at the start of this chapter also suggest scandals are likely at the meeting-points between business and pro-fessional life, or more accurately in the wide, hazy area between them, where competing value-systems or ways of getting by are again in tension.

It follows that, merely because many are scandalised, there is no automatic implication of moral consensus about the conduct in question. Indeed, scan-dals may arise where two value-systems or at least value-priorities come into conflict. To some degree, this has been involved in recent politico-sexual scandals in Britain, even more the USA, though the priorities of the tabloid press are at least equally important. Conflicting moral priorities have more certainly been at play in the scandal from the late 1990s involving human organ retention by major hospitals. On the one hand, relatives of the deceased and many of the public have been outraged by perceived invasions of patient autonomy; on the other, medical staff have been at least partly persuaded by desires to do future patients good by facilitating research.

Scandals often arise when, and indicate that, public standards and values are shifting. People engaged in hitherto-tolerated or condoned private behaviour suddenly find themselves on the wrong side of a moving public moral borderline, one probably shifting under the impact of similar scandals: during the nineteenth century, 'commissions' became increasingly perceived as bribes; 'customary' payments for desired electoral behaviour were more widely perceived as actively *venal* rather than just *venial*. For these sorts of reasons, the Victorians were probably more potent generators of scandal (financial, electoral and sexual), at least in relation to government and politics, than their immediate predecessors. The influence of evangelicalism, nonconformity and morally self-confident, middle-class, urban elites, bent on spreading their values to more of the social and political fabric above and below, made this particularly likely, even if it did not necessarily ensure moral consensus. So too did the downward and upward spread of respectability, and the decreasing tolerance of sexual 'excess' amongst the respectable classes: arguably important factors fuelling the Dilke and Parnell divorce scandals of the late nineteenth century (Weeks, 1981: 86). Similar sorts of change, though no longer religiously inspired, probably help explain the outbreak of scandals in recent decades involving business and politics in Europe and the USA. As Williams (1998: 89) has noted of the many scandals involving Congressmen and gifts available from lobbyists:

> legislators need to understand what constitutes proper conduct and where the boundaries of unacceptable conduct lie. These have proved difficult to define both because they have rarely been made explicit and because they have evolved over time, often in response to scandals. Thus scandals sometimes arise because legislators are behaving in accordance with a code or practice that has become outmoded.

The examples quoted here suggest that changing public values underpin scandals rather more frequently than just 'sometimes'. So too do recent parliamentary cash-for-questions scandals. Lord Nolan perhaps implied this in a letter to the then Prime Minister, John Major: 'changes . . . in the roles and working environments of politicians and other public servants have led to confusion over what is and what is not acceptable behaviour' (quoted by Ridley and Doig, 1995: 14). What were once normal aspects of the relationship between MPs and lobby groups, for whom they acted as consultants, rather rapidly became publicly unacceptable. Remunerated enquirers have suddenly found themselves on the wrong side of a borderline shifting in the direction of greater probity, or perhaps where what counts as probity has changed. Certainly, what Anthony Birch (1971: 102) described as respectable and routine in both Britain and the US was producing scandals by the 1990s, and is now largely prohibited:

In both countries, group interests have spokesmen in the national legislature and feed these spokesmen with specialised information for use in debate and committee work. A few groups draft legislation for their spokesmen to present, while many persuade their spokesmen to move amendments to Bills sponsored by the executive. In Britain, it is thought perfectly proper for MPs acting in this way to be paid fees or salaries by the groups.

The impact of scandals

As these examples suggest, because they are public events, because they are 'mediated', because they scandalise and because of what they often show and confirm about public values, scandals can have substantial influence. Not only can they indicate shifting public attitudes and values; they can also shift them further in the same direction – normally towards greater probity. This may be expressed in new legislation or regulation, or greater eagerness to enforce existing regulation. This is particularly so when scandals move beyond the initial revelatory stage into official enquiry and report. Salford's gas scandal, and the ensuing enquiry, produced a new gas committee bent on much closer supervision of all aspects of production and contracting, and a new gas manager willing to comply. It sparked several similar scandals elsewhere. Alongside the more dramatic revelations from a Royal Commission enquiring into how the London Metropolitan Board of Works misconducted its business, these helped produce the 1889 Public Bodies Corrupt Practices Act, amongst other things, rendering criminal the bribery of municipal (though significantly not private utility) officials. The scandalised public outcry following W. T. Stead's 'Maiden Tribute' articles in the *Pall Mall Gazette* produced the 1885 Criminal Law Amendment Act, raising the age of sexual consent. Several decades earlier, revelations from the regular parliamentary enquiries into electoral corruption eventually produced the 1852 Election Commissioners, and 1854 Corrupt Practices Acts. The first decreed the creation of Royal Commissions to investigate future election petitions. Their formal hearings in the relevant constituencies, their subsequent reports to Parliament and the reportage of both in the local and daily press, created potentially powerful engines for scandal-generation. The sense of being held up to more general public opprobrium probably helped erode small-town perceptions of the giving and accepting of bribes as agreeable and customary accompaniments to elections. This probably substantially helped create an atmosphere wherein the far more stringent 1883 Corrupt and Illegal Practices Act was possible and enforceable. In the later twentieth century, the rash of House and Senate scandals caused hitherto-tolerant Congressmen, beset by the perceived hostility of their constituents, to create ethics committees in the 1960s, and then increasingly stringent codes of conduct in subsequent decades. All this both expressed and accelerated tightening public perceptions of what was permissible in relationships between legislator and lobby group. In the 1990s, Britain's cash-for-questions and other scandals produced the standing Nolan Committee of enquiry into 'concerns about standards of conduct of all holders of public office', and ultimately a new Code of Conduct for MPs, amongst other things banning advocacy for private interest groups.

As this suggests, scandals often have cleansing and beneficial effects upon the institutions or regimes wherein they occur. Certainly, they tend to narrow the boundaries of permissible conduct for those in positions of public trust – either directly through legislative enactment or codes, and/or perceptions by public figures of tightening boundaries of public tolerance. Where significant parts of the public have become scandalised by some perceived neglect or abuse by public authorities, scandals can induce those authorities to reform. In our own age, scandals involving child abuse represent clear examples. In the nineteenth century, more than one local authority was persuaded to tighten its public health regulations by revelations of high death rates. The effect was particularly evident where, as in Salford for much of the late nineteenth century, the town periodically found itself around the unenviable top of governmental death-rate tables. This was particularly so where mortality was linkable to un-enforced bylaws. Local newspapers were likely to play important roles here, as did the *Salford Weekly News* during January–March 1877 when it spilled tens of thousands of words of dramatic outrage about Salford's 'Social and Sanitary State', reinforcing its long-held belief that 'the entire borough is little better than a valley of death' (17 February 1871, p. 2). What were involved here were not just revelations of human suffering and the perceived neglect of public duty. As in many scandals, and unsurprisingly given that they are public events, it was also *reputation* – of the municipal authority, its leaders, and (at a time when civic pride was important and competitive) the town as compared with others of its kind.

Scandals generally damage those involved. For this reason, and because they often seem symptomatic of wider heinous situations, they often become ammunition in broader political battles: immensely useful in damaging political opponents, and indeed entire 'regimes'. Governments may find them useful in smearing oppositions. Radicals often find scandals immensely serviceable in efforts to undermine traditional elites. Salford's SDF and ILP used the gas scandal in this way. More generally, Britain's early nineteenth-century radical press specialised in uncovering financial and sexual abuses amongst 'the idle classes'. Given this potential, scandals could and can help erode and de-legitimise entire local or national political classes.

As some of this may begin implying, scandals can also be damaging in more general and less contestable ways. If they are particularly likely to arise in liberal democracies because of the very openness of the communications process, they can also damage such regimes. Scandals can drive the search for ever-more stringent regulation beyond what is functional. This may be the case where they involve clashes amongst publicly desirable ends. Recent scandals surrounding organ-retention seem clear examples: a scandalised public, and even more scandalised relatives, however understandably, have threatened to produce a crisis in pathology, wherein the supply of organs for clearly beneficial medical research and training has been seriously endangered. The long-running, and equally understandable, nineteenth-century working-class outrage about compulsory smallpox vaccination (Durbach, 1998) is another example.

Scandals may increase public cynicism about politicians, politics or other areas of public life, for example reinforcing already common, and probably comfortable, beliefs that 'they're all in it for themselves'. This has been a clear legacy of recent scandals in many western democracies involving alleged corruption or misuse of public funds for party purposes. If scandals focus attention and debate upon undesirable situations, they can also distract from more serious problems. Politicians, beset by media-driven sexual scandal, can lose control of policy agendas many in the public might deem desirable at least to debate if not to enact. The later Clinton years provide a dramatic example. Moreover, as this suggests, scandal may erode the authority of political leaders and public authorities, and thus their ability to perform necessary duties. As some have suggested, these sorts of problems may have become particular features of western democracies in recent years, as media agendas, particularly those involving their watchdog role, arguably have become ever-more commercially driven rather than civic minded. What may enhance the problem is the fact that revelations of behaviour (particularly where it is sexual) deemed scandalous have become detached from what really scandalises, as distinct from titillates, large numbers of the public, and from questions of whether the persons concerned have the capacities to do the public job they are charged with. This, together with the increasingly hazy and constrained borderlines of the private lives of public people, may also impact upon political recruitment.

For further understanding, we may need to resort to Marxist notions of inner contradiction. The unhindered emergence of scandals testifies to the existence of healthy liberal democracy. Yet their multiplication potentially erodes its legitimacy, particularly as the demand for transparency begins building permanent apparatus for uncovering scandal,[1] and thus a sort of scandal-production industry. Such tendencies may be further enhanced by the close association between liberal democracy and thriving industrial and urban capitalism, with its capacity to produce increasingly desperate media competition. This is doubly so given the media's continued attachment to a concept of 'news' Lord Rothermere long ago identified as 'anything out of the ordinary' (quoted by Pound and Harmsworth, 1959: 110). Perhaps, whilst for much of the nineteenth and twentieth centuries, scandals were the means of properly cleansing politics, they have increasingly become the means of rendering relatively clean politics dirty looking, doubly so as media addictions have embraced not just news, but *bad* news. They may be rendering liberal-democratic politicians a threatened species.

Note

1 As apparently has been the case in parts of Australia. See Chapter 5.

References

Barker, A. (1992), 'The Upturned Stone: Political Scandals in Twenty Democracies and their Investigation Processes', Essex Papers in Politics and Government, University of Essex.

Birch, A. H. (1971), *Representation*, London, Pall Mall Press.

Doig, A. (1990), *Westminster Babylon: Sex Money and Scandal in British Politics*, London, Alison and Busby (W. H. Allen).

Durbach, N. (1998), 'They Might as Well Brand Us: Working-Class Resistance to Compulsory Vaccination', *Social History of Medicine*, 13: 1, 45–62.

Finer, S. E. (1966), *Anonymous Empire: A Study of the Lobby in Great Britain*, London, Pall Mall Press.

Garrard, J. (1988), *The Great Salford Gas Scandal of 1887*, Altrincham, British Gas North-Western.

Lee, Alan J. (1976), *The Origins of the Popular Press 1855–1914*, London, Croom Helm.

McCalman, Iain (1988), *Radical Underworld: Prophets, Revolutionaries and Pornographers in London 1795–1840*, Cambridge, Cambridge University Press.

Pound, R. and G. Harmsworth (1959), *Northcliffe*, London, Cassel.

'Public Affairs' (1990), BBC series presented by Charles Wheeler.

Ridley, F. F. and A. Doig (1995), *Sleaze: Politicians, Private Interests and Public Reactions*, Oxford, Oxford University Press.

Thompson, J. B. (2000), *Political Scandal: Power and Visibility in the Media Age*, Cambridge, Polity Press.

Weeks, J. (1981), *Sex, Politics and Society*, Harlow, Longman.

Williams, R. (1998), *Political Scandals in the United States*, Keele University Press.

2

Understanding the wave of scandal in contemporary Western Europe

Véronique Pujas

Political scandals have proliferated in democracies in recent years, particularly in Western Europe. Understanding this phenomenon requires close analysis of why previously tolerated practices are now considered scandalous. The wave of political scandal that has spread across different countries is not accidental; rather it reflects changes in power relationships within the public sphere. This chapter argues that scandal should be seen as a social construction, and that recent scandals in Western Europe have been the product of a shift in the balance of power within elite circles and of a change in the relative importance of democratic checks and balances.

Although much has been written on the proliferation of scandal in West European countries, to date there has been little or nothing in the way of investigation of the reasons for the explosion of public indignation at this particular point in time. Why the late 1980s and early 1990s and not before? To begin to address this question we have to understand that scandals result from conflicts of legitimacy involving four major arenas of the democratic polity: the political, judicial and media arenas, and the arena of corporate governance.[1] Understanding the emergence of these conflicts requires us to investigate tensions or 'strains' occurring within and between these four arenas. Only by analysing this complex process of interaction can we understand why scandal has emerged so widely in West European countries since the late 1990s, and why its implications for the future of these democracies are so important.

The limited amount of literature on the recent explosion of scandal in these countries usually focuses on corruption. The end of the Cold War is seen as stimulating the spread of capitalistic rules, and consequently growing bribery to win new markets. Meanwhile, various organisations that were involved in exporting the 'OECD mix' of economic and political institutions and policies through aid to developing and former socialist countries included anti-corruption policies as part of the globalisation package. Another thesis emphasises the significance of the apparent emergence of diffuse clusters of criminals believed to be profiting from new opportunities deriving from an increased international mobility of goods, capital and people (Stirling, 1994). For all these reasons, public awareness and anxiety about corruption issues has increased, thus stimulating a growing interest in the analysis of corruption scandals.

But none of these developments can by themselves explain the shift in public perceptions and attitudes that has taken place such that in a number of countries, political behaviour that was once considered 'white', is now considered 'black' (to use Heidenheimer's (1989) famous analogy) – that what was once tolerated is now rejected. This chapter argues for a structural interpretation, demonstrating that the recent wave of scandal has resulted from a simultaneous breakdown in the bargains that have hitherto governed relations between the political, corporate, judicial and media spheres. The consequent competition between them for influence and legitimacy has become the major driving force behind the emergence and exploitation of scandalised public opinion as a power resource. In the next section we show how scandal arises in particular contexts as a result of the mobilisation and manipulation of core values by strategic social actors. In the section after that, with particular reference to France, Italy and Spain, we consider why and to what extent the media, judicial, political and corporate fields are at the crossroads of public conflict, and demonstrate how strong tensions within and between them help explain the recent wave of scandals. We conclude with some reflections on the implications of widespread scandal for Western European democracies.

Understanding the emergence of scandal

We know that the same event or development can provoke a scandal in one country while failing to do so in another. We also know that the same set of political practices can provoke a scandal at one point in a given country's history, while failing to do so at some other point. This strongly suggests that scandal is a socially constructed phenomenon.[2] It emerges against the background of a specific set of norms and values and its public/collective impact involves the mobilisation of particular resources by social entrepreneurs or 'skilled social actors'.

Scandal only occurs if the denunciation of misconduct takes place in a sensitive context and is thus able to mobilise public opinion. Scandal is therefore the product of a social enterprise, which defines public opinion and persuades it that public order is being threatened. Public opinion is especially likely to be so persuaded in situations in which misconduct is no longer an isolated event but a widespread phenomenon, undermining – as in Europe in recent years – the legitimacy of the existing social and political order. The violation involved in this case is the betrayal of political confidence – confidence, that is, in the political institutions that link electoral mechanisms with representation of the public interest. The perception that the trust underpinning this relationship has been violated threatens a central pillar of democracy and throws into question the entire system of democratic governance.

We can hypothesise that four broad, interrelated sets of conditions must be fulfilled if scandals on the scale of those that have been witnessed in southern Europe and France in recent years are to occur. That is, there must be:

- a general atmosphere of mistrust;
- tensions between social, market-oriented and political values;
- recognition that a violation of standards has occurred, implying the active definition of events/facts as scandalous;
- a breakdown in the basic bargains regulating political relationships.

While the first two conditions may be characteristic of many societies, they do not necessarily produce scandal. The third and fourth conditions are critical, since they involve the active mobilisation of public opinion by skilled social actors. Such mobilisation is precisely what has occurred in a number of West European democracies with the erosion or (in Italy) the collapse of traditional bargains between politics, the judiciary and the media.

Underlying the emergence of scandal there is usually a clash or at least friction or 'strain' between *different sets of values*. If such 'strain' is absent, it is unlikely that denunciation of a certain type of political behaviour will trigger public disapproval. It is possible to theorise the value-strains from which scandals emerge. Using Smelser's (1962) terminology, 'strain' is defined here as a structural tension or 'latent state of conflict'. Most scandals are a public expression of internal and external strains in different areas of society. Societal principles in a state of friction or contradiction can be characterised as 'transversal strains', since they typically traverse social groups. But scandal may also be a product of heterogeneous social perceptions, varying from one group to another according to different sets of values.

Recognition that a *violation of standards* has occurred is influenced by the existing controls constraining and punishing deviant behaviour. But laws change and infringements and sanctions are re-evaluated over time. Without considering these factors, it is difficult to explain why once-tolerated behaviour is now rejected. When social relations are threatened by violations, the stigmatisation of crime becomes the occasion for expressing solidarity by opposing the perpetrator. This implies *the labelling and publicising of infringements*. Thus, scandalous conduct only exists in the public sphere: if an infringement were to stay secret, it could neither be defined nor condemned; because it is hidden, it cannot be apprehended. In other words, situations of infringement can only be subject to scandal where an ethical disequilibrium exists and where such disequilibrium is perceived by the public at large.

Most critically, however, the definition, labelling and publicising of a particular form of behaviour as scandalous requires purposive action and intervention. This has been crucial in all three of the polities from which we draw our principal examples in the following sections. Mistrust and tensions between values created the potential for the wave of scandals that overtook these societies; the breakdown of political bargains, and the *competitive* definition of behaviour as scandalous by skilled social actors were what precipitated them.

The competitive mobilisation of scandal

The breakdown of key political bargains

Rather than emerging from any one of the media, judicial, political or corporate arenas, scandal always results from conflict and co-operation between them. In many senses interdependent, these arenas are also in constant competition over relative power, influence and legitimacy in the public sphere. In complex societies, such conflicts of power and legitimacy are inevitable. How have traditional bargains between politics (parties and the state), business, the judiciary and the media broken down?

In France, Italy and Spain, the long-standing relationship between *politics and the media* has been undergoing a period of change, but with ambiguous results because the tradition of a free and independent press is still far from strong in these countries. Politicians and journalists find themselves in a state of structural interdependence. In societies where the media takes a central communicative role in structuring the public space (Gitlin, 1980; Lichtenberg, 1990; Turow, 1992), politicians and journalists are intrinsically linked by a common focus: the production of information and the interpretation of words/events (Bourdieu, 1994). Politicians have always tried to control the information available to journalists. This control can occur through direct censure or more indirectly and insidiously by disclosing certain facts in order to hide others. As discussed in greater detail below, political ownership of the press has also brought journalists within the sphere of political consensus, making them bulwarks rather than 'subverters' of the status quo. This old 'bargain' has broken down in various ways. Lack of ideological difference on social issues in the political sphere has led politicians to exploit the media to attack political opponents by denouncing them as corrupt. At the same time, new methods of 'political marketing', which force politicians to communicate through fixed codes, change the nature of the message and political competition. Specialists in communication deliver 'sound bites' aimed at media organisations; they create 'media events', which represent a new form of political propaganda (Sorrentino, 1995). These render transactions between politicians and the media much easier, especially because the liberalisation and privatisation of television has multiplied the opportunities for voicing denunciation and using scandal to delegitimise adversaries (Diaz Nosty, 1994). Thus, more than ever before, scandal is produced at the crossroads between these two arenas.

In the relationship between the *judiciary and the media*, traditionally judges have been governed by strict rules of secrecy and discretion and, unlike relations between politicians and the media, there has been little interaction, let alone interdependence. Consequently, this is less a case of a deal being broken than of a new interpenetration between these two spheres. This has had the effect of precipitating the decline of the traditional politics/media and politics/judiciary bargains. Thus, since the 1980s, more investigative and competitive media have forced greater transparency on a previously closed judicial profession. They have also given crusading magistrates a new power resource. This strain between the discretion necessary for the effective application of judicial procedures, and use of the media in order to publicise judicial actions, raises several problems (Leclerc, 1997). First, the treatment of judicial information by the media can be strongly criticised in some instances: the media have used judicial information to inform the public, though often reporting trials in a dubious and partial fashion (Commaille, 1994). The media also report scandalous events, thanks to the use of investigative techniques that imitate judicial procedures, often reaching the stage where it becomes difficult to distinguish between judicial/official and journalistic investigations. The widening role of the media, from merely reporting the news, to actually generating news themselves by conducting private investigations, at a time when investigating magistrates are also exploiting the press as a resource, creates ambiguities as to the status of information.

One effect has been a 'personalisation' of judicial activity, such that judges have been presented, first, as 'media heroes' and later as 'mentally disturbed',[3] leading to a closer proximity between the judiciary and ordinary citizens. This can detract from the supposedly impartial status of such figures and make them vulnerable to attack. The media have also tended to assume a new quasi-judicial function, claiming the right to judge what is and what is not fair in a given dispute. Intense media involvement in this respect has contributed to a growing incompatibility between demands for justice presented through the media, and the (necessarily slow) speed of legal proceedings. Judicial procedures are not adapted to fast-flowing demands, and especially not to the demands of the media (Bessin, 1998). This gap between the objectives of media and judicial pursuit of misconduct can also lead to unjust treatment in systems where scandal has become widespread. Media reports of legal proceedings are most likely to appear when the latter begin, and to focus on the personalities under investigation, who are not necessarily guilty, but are regarded with acute suspicion by public opinion. When proceedings come to an end, by which time public interest is likely to have waned, the media will rarely give prominence to the acquittal of those judged not guilty. This can have a damaging effect on personal reputations and also damage the integrity of the judiciary.

The strains between the *judicial* and *political spheres* relate both to their theoretical independence and to their social proximity. In other words, the traditional collusion between these elites has recently become conflictual in some cases. In terms of the principle of the separation of powers, the magistracy is an independent part of the constitution and considered politically impartial. In practice, however, in most democracies politicians have tried to exploit channels of influence allowing political interference in the activities of the judiciary, while politicisation of the judiciary means that application of the law may be politically motivated. As far as political misconduct is concerned, the magistracy's efficacy is, to a large extent, determined by its degree of independence from political authority. Political power has always tried to influence the judiciary, and magistrates, whether under direct political constraint or because of class collusion, have always attempted to manage these political pressures. Since the early 1990s, growing liberalisation seems to have changed the nature of judicial guardianship. In Italy, for example, conflict between members of the political class and the magistracy has become ferocious: witness that between the media tycoon and leader of *Forza Italia*, Silvio Berlusconi, and judicial investigators attached to the Milan Public Prosecutor's office. To speak of 'strain' in relation to this kind of open conflict is almost euphemistic.

Finally, as part of the wave of liberalisation, the strains produced by *economic and financial pressures upon business, politics, the judiciary and the media* explain an increasing number of scandals. Scandals linked to economic developments have been of two types. The first has involved economic and financial elites directly and has taken place as a result of corporate tax evasion and other fraudulent practices. The second has resulted from the increasing economic and financial pressures upon the media and politics.

Following the collapse of the Enron company in the United States in early 2001, there was increasing political and media attention given to 'business' or 'accounting' scandals. The 1990s and the beginning of the new millennium have been marked by the bankruptcy of new-economy companies like World Com, Global Crossin, Tyoc Qwest, Imclone Systems, Xerox and now Vivendi Universal. Each collapse has drawn attention to white-collar crime and corporate malpractice, with the result of undermining trust in stock exchanges as well as in the efficacy of market competition rules.

On the other hand, growing commercial pressures on the media explain the attention to news of a scandalous nature. Driven by the need for audience maximisation, the media attach great importance to any case or dispute involving high-profile VIPs. This has inevitably encouraged 'market-driven journalism' where the value of news items depends on their potential to create scandal.

As a consequence of expanding markets and globalisation, economic and financial news have in the meantime taken ever-more space within newspapers. Their higher visibility renders these sectors more exposed to dispute and potential scandal. Due to the development of financial news and public demand for this kind of information, the economic and financial sectors have been exposed as never before to the judiciary through high-profile legal proceedings. Self-regulation within the business sector no longer looks likely to ensure the legitimacy of corporate governance. As a consequence, a growing number of disputes land up within the judicial arena.

Finally, with regard to the political arena, the growing financial requirements of campaigning and propaganda activities raise problematic questions about the relationships between the business and political sectors. As illustrated by countries where private financing of politics is the norm, the influence of lobby groups on the political process is controversial. Elsewhere, the large number of scandals that have arisen from unclear, hidden or illegal agreements between politicians and business people suggests that public financing of political parties and campaign expenditure may offer but a partial solution. Expansion of the market sphere into the sphere of politics is likely to induce illegal behaviour whatever the funding regime.

Understanding the breakdown of these bargains requires further invest-igation of the changes occurring *within* each of the arenas themselves. The 'strains' within these arenas – greater competition among and within polit-ical organisations for financing; new competition in the media following liberalisation; conservative versus radical approaches to judicial prosecution; emphasis on market values and globalisation in all areas of society – have fuelled growing interaction and increasing friction between them. It is from the inter-play of these relations of interdependence and conflict that the social dynamic driving the recent scandals has in essence been forged.

The political arena: intensified competition
The political arena is the prime locus of scandal since it combines the repro-duction of democratic norms via the electoral process with the exercise and maintenance of power. Within the state machine, the possession of power is constantly placed in jeopardy by the fact of frequent elections. Consequently, problems of bribery, bureaucratic malpractice and the misuse of public power are frequently linked with the struggle to gain power (for example, through illegal party finance), or else with the struggle to conserve power (for example, through building networks of support via the corrupt distribution of public contracts). What is interesting about the late 1980s and 1990s is that the exposure of such practices has become a resource for parties seeking advant-age over political adversaries in the competition for power.

There has been much speculation about the *role played by the changing inter-national ideological climate in the explosion of scandals in recent years*. The fall of the Berlin Wall is frequently alluded to in the Italian case as a fundamental external cause of the crisis that afflicted that country's political class in the wake of the wave of scandals in the early 1990s (Ginsborg, 1996; Guzzini, 1994). The mechanism involved is assumed to be a change in the nature of domestic political competition due to the Italian Communist Party's transformation into a non-Communist party with a new name – an event which undermined some of the most basic political assumptions on which the post-war regime in Italy had been constructed. But on closer inspection it becomes clear that changes in the nature of political competition contributed – in combination with other developments – to the eruption of scandal in *all* of the countries considered in this chapter.

As already discussed, a scandal is created through a dispute over the definition of facts denounced as scandalous. Political actors are particu-larly active in this definitional debate: some are directly concerned with the accusations, because the issue which causes the scandal draws attention to a problem of public/political management for which they are in some way responsible. Others have to take a stand in the public dispute according to both their ideological beliefs and their position in the political arena. The capacity for scandal to disturb the status quo, and radically de-legitimise political actors in the eyes of the public, makes it a powerful weapon at the disposal of politicians, to be combined with other instruments of political competition. In all three of the countries of France, Italy and Spain, it is possible to demonstrate the contribution of intensified political competition to the emergence of scandals.

In the political arena, the heightening of tension and competition can derive from shifts in the political spectrum, the restructuring of political organisations, or changes in the balance of power. Elections are often the occasion for multiple accusations against politicians, since, by triggering a scandal, political mobilisation around the issue involved can put a candidate ahead of the field. This is especially likely to be so if on other issues the candidates are evenly matched. This was the case in the 1995 presidential elections in France when more than fifteen corruption cases were exposed in the media in the run-up to the elections. These involved members of the right-wing government, and several had to resign. Eventually the spiral of scandals reached the Prime Minister, Edmund Balladur, himself, who was competing directly with Jacques Chirac for the presidency. His chances of winning the election were destroyed when he was forced to explain his own sources of income from consulting for an informatics company.

A change in the configuration of political forces can instigate competitiveness amongst new players, as in the Italian case. Since the early 1990s, the nature of political competition has been totally transformed. Not only did the Communist Party transform itself into the Democratic Party of the Left while losing its hard-line rump, which became the far-left Communist Refoundation, but a new party, standing on a regionalist, populist, anti-Southern, anti-corruption platform, seriously threatened the already crumbling Christian Democratic Party (DC) vote in the North. The main reason for voting DC (to keep the Communists out of power) had already lost much of its potency. The Lombard (later Northern) League's meteoric rise tore the very fabric of the old party system. In the general election of April 1992, before the full extent of the misconduct underlying what became called the 'Bribe City' scandals was known, voters punished the old parties without yet destroying them. The emergence of new 'protest' parties like the Northern League (perceived to be outside the established 'partitocratic' system of power sharing) and *Forza Italia* (the new party created by businessman Silvio Berlusconi in early 1994) exploited the disclosure of corruption involving the ruling DC, thereby intensifying political competition still further.

Politicians often use corruption allegations as a political tool, taking advantage of the media's interest in them, but this in turn can lead to public scepticism. Both corruption involving politicians and the instrumental use of corruption accusations have eroded public confidence in government and undermined the legitimacy of political parties and their leaders. This has produced increasing apathy in many European countries. Indeed, as demonstrated by the re-election of Berlusconi in Italy in May 2001 as well as the re-election of President Chirac in France in April 2002, both involved in corruption trials, many voters do not bother to punish unethical behaviour by state leaders.

Finally, competition between national and international elites, particularly on the issue of corruption, creates new opportunities for scandals involving one or the other. For individual national governments, it can be a relief to delegate sensitive political issues to international institutions rather than have to grapple with them directly. The trans-national features of corruption lend support to the argument that the problem is best fought by strengthening international security. However, the combination of international measures to tackle the problem with national procedures of evaluation of such measures can be a source of dispute and potential scandal involving supranational institutions. For instance, the scandal leading to the dismissal of the Santer Commission in 1999 was largely due to the pressure exerted by certain national members of the European Parliament when they discovered mismanagement and nepotism within European institutions (Pujas, 2003). Equally, allegations about the 'high jacking' of billions of dollars of IMF support to Russia in 1997 were intended to undermine the legitimacy of the international ruling elite in charge of aid for development. In the meantime, national ruling elites are vulnerable to denunciation as never before by international organisations such as the Financial Action Task Force – whose blacklist of financial jurisdictions that fail to co-operate in the fight against money laundering exerts strong pressure on the national governments concerned. In short, under pressure from international organisations, the fight against corruption has become a legitimate issue to focus on, with national elites vulnerable to censure. This trend has opened up new opportunities for the outbreak of scandals.

The media arena: from institutional support to political opposition?
None of the tensions in the political arena discussed above would be scandalous without the transmission of information to the public via the media. This is an obvious but especially important point in countries such as Spain, France and Italy where the press has traditionally been anything but an active and independent critic of political behaviour.

Although scandal existed before the spread of the mass media, the first major French scandals, the Dreyfus Affair and the Panama Scandal at the beginning of the twentieth century, took place concomitantly with the growth of the mass-circulation press. In contemporary politics, the mass media are just as necessary a component in the triggering of a scandal. If information is concealed from the public, the infringement of standards cannot give rise to scandals. The media reveal such information, and fuel scandal by sensationalising it. Scandal, as a socially constructed phenomenon, is well adapted to media needs. The sensationalism of scandalous news, its surprising character, and the ease with which an event can be personalised (with a scandal it is easy to identify a guilty party and his or her accuser) are all ideal ingredients in the production of news stories. The definitional dispute and the labelling of the infringement involved in scandal make good copy. To a large extent, the public space is now coterminous with the media space (Habermas, 1978), given the media's strong agenda-setting effect on both the political and judicial arenas. Actors will naturally provide their own independent interpretations of the core issue, but their perception of the facts themselves will be mostly influenced by media presentation.

The likelihood that the media will fuel scandal depends on the way they are organised in a particular country and on the country's journalistic tradition. These have both been undergoing important changes in recent decades. Media competitiveness, their economic goals, ownership structures, and ideological proclivities are all pertinent to understanding their role as both democratic check and balance, and exploiters of scandal for their own purposes. Media competition has proved particularly important in recent years following liberalisation and privatisation in the sector. Intense competition has resulted in the predominance of audio-visual media in the production and dissemination of information. A new commercial logic has imposed its own criteria on cultural production and the result is the search for 'scoops' and evermore sensationalist ways of presenting events. In Spain and France, the entrance of new competitors and the increasing liberalisation of the media throughout the 1980s created a cleavage in journalism: between journalists as mediators of institutional news from official agencies on the one hand, and investigative journalism, seeking hidden information and aiming to bolster its audience or readership levels, on the other. Nevertheless, the general trend amongst mass media organisations around the world is towards concentration of the (visual, written and audio) packaging and of the (press, radio, television, cable and computer) channels of information. The globalisation and personalisation of the large companies producing information – such as Berlusconi's Fininvest, Lagardère and Dassault in France, or Rupert Murdoch's B Sky B – undoubtedly undermine journalistic independence and the media's capacity to be a watchdog.

The media's relationship with political parties and government will vary according to country and determine the role they play in the struggle against misconduct. For example, Italian newspapers have traditionally provided ideological support for particular political forces and until recently were not prepared to play key roles in the denunciation of systemic corruption in that country. By the early 1990s, however, they had become outlets for information provided by anti-corruption judges about trials in progress, and the newspapers and magazines of the *Espresso-Repubblica* group in particular were used almost as instruments of prosecution, provoking accusations that this was undermining the legality and legitimacy of the legal process. In Spain, the emergence of *El Mundo* in 1989 provided a vehicle for denouncing PSOE by systematically exposing information regarding the corruption of the socialist elite and its abuses of power over fourteen years. This newspaper introduced for the first time in Spain a form of investigative journalism interested in hidden information and the exposure of misconduct. However, this was not exactly impartial and independent. Behind *El Mundo*, political and financial lobbies and the friendship between its director and the leader of the opposition *Partido Popular* influenced the editorial line of the newspaper and focused its attention overwhelmingly on affairs weakening the legitimacy of PSOE. In France, where the management of television channels is regularly subject to political deals and pressures, the newspaper, *Le Monde*, occupies a special place. Its foremost investigative journalist, now editor-in-chief, Edwy Plenel, has been important in defining 'affairs', such as Botton/Noir, as scandals.[4] Meanwhile *Le Monde* has been accused by two investigative journalists (Péan and Cohen, 2003) of pursuing political scoops in its coverage of sensitive news in 2002.

The judicial arena: new notions of independence and investigation
The judiciary is a key actor in the production of scandal for three main reasons. First, the judicial arena has two general functions: to produce rules and to act as the guardian of the social order through the imposition of sanctions. The law determines the standards of what is legal and illegal. So law and its infringement will play a large part in determining whether denunciation leads to scandal. Given that illegal acts committed by public agents are usually breaches of criminal law, the eventual punishment of politicians guilty of misconduct is closely tied to the procedures of criminal prosecution. In turn, the prosecution – and eventually incrimination – of particular forms of misbehaviour will depend on how the law of criminal procedure is managed and deployed in any particular country. For instance, freedom of information legislation and laws on 'defamation' and/or the 'presumption of innocence' have a significant impact on the possibilities open to investigative journalists – as is demonstrated by the contrast in the styles of press coverage typical of the Anglo-Saxon tabloids, on the one hand, and the shy Southern European newspapers, on the other. In France in 2001, rules relating to the presumption of innocence were used to prosecute twelve journalists for publishing articles investigating matters of public interest, including political scandals.

Second, when a violation takes place, informants expect both formal and symbolic sanctions to be applied. Formal sanctions operate by means of the legal recognition that a crime has been committed; symbolic sanctions operate through trial and punishment and are experienced by the community at large as a form of catharsis. This latter aspect is related to the visibility of scandal. Although, as noted, the media are themselves able to generate information through their investigative capacity, most of the information they deal with comes from official sources. Therefore, when scandalous behaviour enters into the purview of the higher echelons of the judicial arena, it is often the product of intense media scrutiny. By dealing with misconduct in formal and 'rationalised' terms, above the fray of partisan argument and debate, the legal process gives greater visibility to the potential scandal, because the media feels empowered by the judicial 'framing' of the violation to deal with other aspects of the scandal outside the courts.

Third, the judiciary's institutional practices and professional competence affect the probability of scandal. Public prosecutors perform a crucial function in ensuring the legal accountability of politicians. They are the 'natural' adversaries of the corrupt and of corrupters. But the effectiveness of judicial intervention depends on the quality of legislation. For example, legal definitions will heavily influence the capacity of prosecutors to assemble evidence (as vividly shown, for example, by the difficulties that are often involved in securing convictions for 'corruption', owing to variations in the way that term is legally defined between one country and another). And as far as crimes committed by politicians are concerned, the efficacy of the judiciary is also heavily influenced by the degree of its independence from political authority. Open recruitment to its ranks – through competitive examinations open to those who have a university degree in law – ensures higher levels of judicial autonomy than are possible in countries where recruitment is through the less open procedures of co-optation. In the Southern European democracies, where the more open procedures apply, the success of the *Mani Pulite* (Clean Hands) and other investigations led to heightened levels of intervention by magistrates in the political sphere through the development of autonomous strategies of communication with citizens. In Italy especially, in the fight against terrorism and the Mafia, magistrates have taken a proactive stance and new legislation has bolstered their powers. Judicial probity has been in stark contrast with the involvement in criminal activity of numerous members of the political class. As a result, the judiciary has won direct legitimacy for its activities with public opinion (Giglioli, Cavicchioli and Fele, 1997; Pizzorno, 1998).

The likelihood that denunciation and criminal investigation will result in prosecution depends on the specific organisational features of the judicial system in question – as can be seen by comparing France and Italy. In France, public prosecutors have considerable discretion in exercising their powers to prosecute, something that they will do or not, depending on their evaluation of the nature of the offences before them. In Italy, on the other hand, while public prosecutors are obliged by the Constitution to investigate all allegations of wrong-doing brought to their attention, the Ministry of Justice has no institutional means of influencing them: the judiciary govern themselves through a free-standing *Consiglio Superiore della Magistratura* (Higher Council of the Judiciary). Thus, while in France, magistrates have often been accused of trying to hush up 'affairs' in accordance with their political preferences, in Italy, politicians (and some independent commentators) have accused the most zealous anti-corruption magistrates of waging a political war against the right-wing establishment.

While this view may be exaggerated, it is true that a different type of judge has entered the Italian judiciary since the 1970s, and the changing social profile of the profession has been crucial in the burgeoning prosecutions of corrupt politicians and therefore in the proliferation of scandals. Mass education opened the universities to the lower classes, and the protest cycle of the late 1960s influenced the political attitudes of a whole generation. In the legal profession, a new generation of so-called *giudici ragazzini* (child judges), refusing deference to the political authorities began a series of investigations into administrative violations. In 1992, the disclosure of Mario Chiesa's misconduct (the first in the long series of *Tangentopoli* ('Bribe City') revelations) had an explosive effect because of the accumulation of evidence linked to the affair and its revelation in the press. Neither newspaper editors nor the political class could control the flood of allegations and indictments, and senior politicians, previously considered 'untouchable', were now prosecuted almost as routinely as other people for the abuses of power and the other crimes they had committed. This was a new development in the history of justice in these countries.

The economic and financial arena: towards monopoly and contested legitimacy
One of the major shifts represented by the wave of private-sector corruption scandals that took place in 2001 and 2002 was the sudden awareness that the exposure of malpractice and irregularities could also undermine the legitimacy and stability of financial markets and institutions. In the early 1990s, analysts had deplored the fact that in the study of corruption there was an overemphasis on the political dimension and an underemphasis on the collusive roles of financial and economic actors. In contrast, most attention in the new millennium is apparently being directed at the corruption that is taking place through the mechanisms and channels of international finance – and that represents a novel trend in the processes of globalisation and the spread of principles of western capitalist democracy (Boltanski and Chiapello, 1999).

A number of specific circumstances in recent years have given rise to a heightened sensitivity to such corrupt practices as money laundering, false accounting and tax evasion. These include the collapse of internet stocks at the end of the 1990s, allegations of fraud against financial institutions such as European Clearstream (known as the black box of the global financial system) and Enron's bankruptcy in late 2001. Corruption is no longer seen as an issue limited to the politics of weak states; it is also understood to result from abuses and unaccountable management by financial institutions.

The Enron case and its European consequences have increased awareness of the possibility of illegal collusion between lawyers' organisations, auditing companies (in this case Andersen Consulting) and banks to manipulate the accounts of the companies with whom they work, thus providing false information to world-wide financial markets. The Enron scandal also brought to light the weakness of checks and balances within financial institutions; the lack of effective control by state agencies such as the American Securities Exchange Commission, and the complicit silence of 'ratings agencies', fund management companies and specialised financial journalists. The interdependence and collusion between ruling elites, from the legal, media or state fields, is directly highlighted by scandals involving commercial enterprises.

Moreover, *editorial freedom and investigative journalism* are threatened by the deepening financial crisis affecting broadcasting in several West European countries, and which, in Italy and France, has led to major struggles between public and private broadcasting networks. In Italy, where Silvio Berlusconi has still not resolved the conflict of interests between his position as owner of the Mediaset broadcasting conglomerate and his position as head of government, broadcasting pluralism continues to be jeopardised by the Prime Minister's potential capacity to control what is seen by 90 per cent of television viewers. In France, under pressure from Jean-Marie Messier – the media tycoon and head of the global media corporation, Vivendi Universal – the governing body of the pay-TV channel, 'Canal Plus' has dismissed the network's chairman, Pierre Lescure, founder of the 'French cultural exception'. Financial imperatives have clearly superseded professionalism and independence.

General considerations on the role of scandals in democracies

Governance in major areas of the public sphere has been more strongly contested in the 1990s than at any time since 1945. In principle, one result should be the reduction in levels of corruption and greater faith in ruling elites. Unfortunately, the main protagonists of democratic political systems – political parties and their leaders, business elites, but also judges and journalists – are currently suffering from a serious crisis of legitimacy, and this appears to be undermining the strength of democratic institutions in general. Moreover, as argued at the outset of this chapter, recent corruption scandals have been cause and effect of a growing awareness of corruption and corruption-related issues. Both phenomena are linked to the ideological changes and the processes of liberalisation that have swept the globe and most particularly the countries of Western Europe. Thus many questions are still open. Do political scandals illustrate disillusionment with what the instruments of public policy can achieve in general, or with certain political practices in particular? Does the coincidence between the wave of scandals, political globalisation and the imposition of a unique regime model, democracy, reflect the superiority of that model or its limits? The study of scandals is an opportunity to question democratic governance and explore in depth its historic weaknesses.

Notes

1 The concept of 'arenas' refers to the competition within and between sectors where problems evolve. Here we examine the effect of these arenas on both the evolution of problems and the actors who influence definitions and perceptions of such problems. See Hillgartner and Bosk (1988).

2 On the notion of scandals and 'affairs' as socially constructed phenomena, see Charles (1997); Garrigou (1993); Sabato, Stencel and Richter (2000); Thompson (2000); Yanai (1990).

3 These are the words of Silvio Berlusconi as reported in the *Guardian*, 5 September 2003.

4 The Affaire Botton/Noir related to the financing of political campaigns and the personal advantages given by the former mayor of Lyon, Michel Noir, a leading

member of the Gaullist Rassemblement pour la République, to his daughter-in-law who was involved in show business. Benefits included the distribution of gifts to obtain broadcasting rights and the use of financial funds from a pharmaceutical company, which eventually led to its bankruptcy. Pierre Botton, a businessman, infiltrated the political and media worlds through gift-giving and later used his television channel to promote the rise of Noir.

References

Bessin, M. (1998), 'La temporalité de la pratique judiciaire: un point de vue sociologique', *Droit et Société*, 39, 331–43.

Boltanski, L. and E. Chiapello (1999), *Le nouvel esprit du capitalisme*, Paris, Gallimard.

Bourdieu, P. (1994), 'L'emprise du journalisme', *Actes de la recherche en sciences sociales*, 101/2, 3–9.

Charles, C. (1997), 'Naissance d'une cause. La mobilisation de l'opinion publique pendant l'affaire Dreyfus', *Politix*, 16, 11–18.

Commaille, J. (1994), 'L'exercice de la fonction de justice comme enjeu de pouvoir entre Justice et medias', *Droit et Société*, 26, 11–18.

Diaz Nosty, B. (1994), 'Mario Conde et l'oligopole mouvant', *Médias Pouvoirs*, 35, 113–19.

Garrigou, A. (1993), 'Le scandale politique comme mobilisation', in F. Chazel (ed.), *Action collective et mouvements sociaux*, Paris, Presses Universitaire de France.

Giglioli, P. P., S. Cavicchioli and G. Fele (1997), *Rituali di degradazione. Anatomia del processo Cusani*, Bologna, Il Mulino.

Ginsborg, P. (1996), 'Explaining Italy's Crisis', in S. Gundle and S. Parker (eds), *The New Italian Republic: From the Fall of the Berlin Wall to Berlusconi*, London, Routledge.

Gitlin, T. (1980), *The Whole World is Watching*, Berkeley, University of California Press.

Guzzini, S. (1994), 'La longue nuit de la Première République, l'implosion clientéliste en Italie', *Revue Française de Science Politique*, 44: 8, 979–1001.

Habermas, J. (1978), *L'espace public. Archéologie de la publicité comme dimension constitutive de la société bourgeoise*, Paris, Payot.

Heidenheimer, A. J. (1989), 'Perspectives on the Perception of Corruption', in A. J. Heidenheimer, M. Johnston and V. T. LeVine (eds), *Political Corruption: A Handbook*, New Brunswick, Transaction Publishers.

Hillgartner, S. and C. L. Bosk (1988), 'The Rise and Fall of Social Problems: A Public Arenas Model', *American Journal of Sociology*, 94, 53–75.

Leclerc, H. (1997), 'Justice et médias, un affrontement nécessaire', *Medias Pouvoirs*, 1, 225–79.

Lichtenberg, J. (ed.) (1990), *Democracy and the Mass Media*, Cambridge, Cambridge University Press.

Péan, P. and P. Cohen (2003), *La Face cachée du Monde*, Paris, Mille et Une Nuits.

Pizzorno, A. (1998), *Il potere dei giudici. Stato democratico e controllo della virtù*, Roma, Laterza.

Pujas, V. (2003), 'The European Anti-Fraud Office (OLAF): A European Policy to Fight Against Economic and Financial Fraud?', *European Journal of Public Policy*, 10: 5, 781–800.

Sabato, L. J., M. Stencel and S. R. Richter (2000), *Media and Politics in an Age of Scandal*, Oxford, Rowman and Littlefield.

Smelser, N. J. (1962), *A Theory of Collective Behaviour*, London, Routledge.

Sorrentino, C. (1995), *I percorsi della notizia: La stampa quotidianna italiana tra politica e mercato*, Bologna, Baskerville.

Stirling, C. (1994), *Thieves World*, New York, Simon and Schuster.

Thompson, J. B. (2000), *Political Scandal: Power and Visibility in the Media Age*, Cambridge, Polity Press.

Turow, J. (1992), *Media Systems in Society*, New York, Longman.

Yanai, N. (1990), 'The Political Affair: A Framework for Comparative Discussion', *Comparative Politics*, 22: 2, 185–97.

3

Political scandals and political development in the United States

Robert Williams

Political scandal is a relatively new subject for academic inquiry, but there is a significant and growing literature (Markovits and Silverstein, 1988; Thompson, 2000; Welch and Williams, 2003; Williams, 1998) as well as numerous accounts of the origins, unfolding and consequences of particular scandals. The 'scandal database' has greatly expanded, but it is not clear whether this accumulation of data has significantly improved our understanding of political scandals. Basic questions about their character and causation, role and importance remain difficult to answer. It is even possible that the apparent increase in political scandals in recent years has inadvertently helped to create a 'data fog' in which it has become more, rather than less, difficult to discern shapes, trends, structures and patterns.

Accounts of individual scandals are important and necessary, but they do not yet seem to have produced much in the way of plausible comparative or historical generalisations. The suggestion here is that, in order to understand political scandals, they must be contextualised. They need to be located structurally within distinctive governmental systems, and they also need to be connected to wider processes of social and political change and development within particular societies. It is not only a question of what implications or consequences scandals have for politics and government, but of how social and political processes help generate and structure political scandal. The aim of this chapter is therefore to locate political scandal within a broader understanding of American political development, history and culture. Political scandals in the United States did not begin with Watergate, nor will they end with whatever scandal tomorrow's headlines bring. Public interest in, and concern about, political scandals is by no means an exclusively modern phenomenon, but was also clearly evident in earlier periods of American history.

Before embarking on an attempt to situate American political scandals in their historical, institutional and cultural context, it is necessary to sketch the nature of the phenomenon. It would be preferable to be more precise, but political scandals are hard to define, classify and measure. There is no settled method of gauging their relative importance or of assessing whether they have become more or less important than they once were. There is also room for debate about their impact on political development: are they superficial phenomena, 'the froth on the political cappuccino' (Williams, 1998: 131), or are they influential, even decisive, events? The upsurge of academic interest in political scandals suggests either that they have grown in importance or frequency in recent years or that political scandals generally have been subject to some historical revisionism.

It follows that some caution is necessary in approaching the subject. Judgements can only be tentative and provisional, but some specificity is possible. Scandal is conventionally defined by reference to notions of disgrace and damage to reputation. Scandalous conduct is conduct bringing discredit to an office or position. A scandal becomes a political scandal when it involves politicians or public officials. It may involve conduct that, in purely private settings, would be commonplace, but, because it occurs in a public setting, can destroy careers and bring down governments. What ordinary citizens do in their private lives and what they demand of their political leaders are not always the same. It is thus not the conduct itself, but its association with the holder of a public role and the expectations attendant on that role that create the possibility of political scandal. The illegality of some conduct, for example theft or corruption, is an obvious source of political scandal. However, scandals can also be generated by conduct that is condemned by public opinion rather than public law, for example adultery.

Allegations of misconduct are at the root of political scandal, but that does not mean that scandal is synonymous with misconduct. Allegations of misconduct are a necessary but not sufficient condition for the outbreak of a political scandal, and the relevant questions are: who makes the allegations, and who responds to them? Political scandal, by definition, depends on public awareness, and there can be no awareness without some means of identifying possible misconduct and sharing that knowledge with a wider audience. It follows that political scandals have both political and media dimensions. The media do not simply report on political scandals, because publicity is essential to the very nature of scandal. Misconduct without publicity can never constitute a scandal. It is not possible retrospectively to 'discover' a scandal. If the misconduct is not publicised at the time it takes place or shortly thereafter, there cannot be a scandal. Thus, President John F. Kennedy's reckless sexual liaisons – for example – appear to provide ample material for a major political scandal, but they were not reported and therefore no scandal occurred.

This is not to imply that political scandals are whatever the media say they are, or that they are simply 'invented' by the media. The combination of alleged misconduct and media reporting are the basic elements of political scandal, but for 'take off' to occur political scandals require additional dimensions, notably an attentive audience and a process of political contestation. Thus the scale and importance of a political scandal cannot be measured solely in terms of the gravity of the alleged misconduct because other considerations, such as the breadth and depth of media coverage, the receptiveness and interest of the public and the roles and positions adopted by particular political institutions and political personalities, all need to be taken into consideration. In practice, there is little consensus on what differentiates major from minor scandals. It is possible, for example, to characterise the Clinton–Lewinsky scandal as either a gross trivialisation of political debate or as a morally and politically import-ant effort to arrest the undisciplined excesses of amoral politicians and to restore moral accountability to the White House.

Political scandals exhibit a range of defining characteristics, and they dis-play many different forms of political conflict. Disputation occurs about what happened, and the significance of whatever happened. There is also dispute about the motives of the accusers, the response of the public and the responsib-ilities of different institutions to resolve it. Alleged misconduct may be defended as perfectly legitimate, or at least as commonly accepted behaviour, or excused as trivial and irrelevant to the larger purposes of politics. The media may be blamed in their roles as both definers and messengers of political scandal. They may be accused of conducting personal vendettas, being blindly partisan or incurably corrupt, or of simply 'muckraking' and lowering the tone of political discourse. Public 'outrage' at a political scandal may be characterised as synthetic, unrepresentative, disproportionate and based on limited information and understanding. The representatives of different polit-ical institutions may dispute about whose responsibility it is to detect and expose misconduct, to pursue the criminal prosecution of wrong-doers, to broaden or narrow the inquiries, to debate public policies relevant to the misconduct and to change laws and procedures.

A brief examination of some apparently similar episodes in American polit-ical history can help illuminate the salience of these interactions of politics, media and public. But it is important to remember that just as accounts of particular contemporary scandals are deeply contested by both participants and observers, so too were earlier scandals. Further, historical eras strongly associated with political scandal and corruption are frequently subject to the process of historical revisionism, which argues that the particular period was not as bad as it has conventionally been depicted.

Scandalous eras in American history

We first examine the Gilded Age in nineteenth-century American history. This era, whose boundaries and character are still disputed by historians, is normally linked to the excesses of post-Civil War politics and lasted until around 1890. The term 'Gilded Age' is derived from the eponymous novel of Mark Twain and Charles Dudley Warner, published in 1873, which depicted the period as mired in corruption, dishonesty, deception and greed. The news-papers of the period were filled with sensational accounts of scandalous behaviour by politicians. Much nineteenth-century politics was intensely personal and the French commentator, Alexis de Tocqueville, lamented the tendency of journalists to 'assail the character of individuals, to track them into private life and disclose all their weaknesses and vices' (quoted by Summers, 2000: 827).

The Gilded Age witnessed many political scandals, notably the Credit Mobilier scandal of 1872 in which senior politicians were bribed with railroad shares, the Belknap scandal in 1876 involving bribery of a cabinet member, and scandals in revenue collection and the allocation of mail-delivery franchises. The attendant publicity helped create the impression that this was a golden age of scandal arising from endemic corruption in government. This impression was created by newspaper coverage and the observations of authoritative critics such as James Bryce (1888).

But in exploring the incidence and significance of political scandal, it is important to note that commentary and reportage are rarely disinterested. Party politics in the Gilded Age was intensely competitive and fiercely partisan. It was based on a bitter contest for 'spoils' – for the advantages given by possession of office in terms of licenses, jobs, franchises, regulations, subsidies and tax evasion – rather than on any fundamental ideological division between Republicans and Democrats. The principal sources of party funding were bribery and 'kickbacks' together with levies imposed on government employees. It was not possible to dispense government influence, favours and jobs without winning elections and, in the struggle to win elections, political campaigning became progressively more negative and unscrupulous. The size of the stakes in terms of patronage can be demonstrated by the near doubling – from 51,000 to 100,000 – in the numbers employed in the federal bureaucracy between 1871 and 1881. The political parties were evenly matched in terms of their electoral support, and the very closeness of elections encouraged both electoral malpractice and accusations of vote buying and ballot rigging.

In the Gilded Age, party politicians were very willing to accuse their opponents of misconduct, partly because it helped to give them the moral high-ground and they could be sure such charges would be widely reported, and partly because of the imperative need to enhance party funds by gaining access to the resources of government through election victory. Once in power, allegations of misconduct could still be used to ensure that the opposition was weakened and on the defensive. The party in control of the Senate or House of Representatives was able to use the investigative authority of congressional committees to hold hearings and publish reports about the alleged misdeeds of opposition politicians.

It was noted earlier that political scandals are not merely or solely about politicians. They are public events, dependent for their existence on the media publicising allegations that raise public awareness and concern. But it would be a mistake to see the media in the Gilded Age as impartial, dispassionate, detached observers of events, committed to rigorous journalistic standards, and single-mindedly seeking truth. The reality was that the newspapers of the time were also intensely partisan. Both daily and weekly papers were dedicated to the cause of partisan advantage, and could find no fault with their own party and nothing right with the opposition party. According to Calhoun, 'Their "news" pages as well as their editorial columns served up mixtures of vituperation, trumped-up charges of fraud and corruption and downright falsehoods about the opposing party' (Calhoun, 1996: 187). Kaplan even argues that 'Partisanship was a public and ubiquitous phenomenon that defined the very essence of nineteenth-century American journalism' (Kaplan, 2002: 1). This was not surprising because in effect newspapers were dependent on party funding, and editors and journalists are rarely anxious to bite the hand that feeds them.

The combination of closely contested elections fought by determined political parties supported by their own intensely partisan media supporters was matched by an electorate which was also strongly partisan and highly mobilised. Politics was a subject of keen interest to many people; voter turnouts reached record levels in this period and the partisanship of politicians reached down into the mass public.

Given the prominence of these features of political life in this period, its subsequent characterisation as one of hitherto unparalleled corruption and scandal is unsurprising. There certainly were lots of allegations of misconduct, which were widely and loudly reported, and excited substantial sections of the population. This does not necessarily imply that there was a lot of misconduct, that the allegations were fairly reported or that the public was well informed. Political scandal was an important weapon on the battleground of politics and, if the other side used it, you were forced to retaliate. Meanwhile, if they refrained from using it, you could always get your attack in first and secure a possibly decisive political advantage.

As the need and opportunity for political parties to make use of 'kickbacks' and levies on employees declined, as newspapers' financial dependence on parties lessened and as the public's information increasingly came from new and divergent sources, the climate of political scandal also changed. In short, significant changes to party organisation and competition, as well as to the economics of newspaper publishing, help create different incentives and constraints for the generation of political scandal. The nature and extent of public involvement in and perception of potential political scandal also changes when it receives information from different, conflicting sources rather than relying on a local, relentlessly partisan viewpoint.

The Gilded Age was succeeded by the Progressive Era (1890–1913), which offers a very different example of how American political development shaped the incidence and form of political scandal. The characteristics of progressivism are well known: it was moralistic, it valued efficiency and specialised expertise, and it was technocratic and anti-party in spirit. Politics became less competitive as the Republicans gained ascendancy. As election outcomes became more certain, party organisation declined and the incentive to engage in scandal mongering was reduced. Yet, paradoxically, there was an upsurge of political scandal, partly because the progressive reform movements outside the two-party system grew in importance. From 1881 onwards, the federal civil service's reputation as a bastion of patronage had been destroyed by waves of civil service reform that saw merit replace party patronage for most civil service posts.

While the changes in party organisation and practice helped change the incentive and opportunity structure for scandal, there were parallel changes in the mass media, which produced new and less obviously partisan sources of misconduct allegations. Newspapers became much less dependent on party subsidy as the rapid growth of the commercial economy boosted advertising revenues and allowed the severing, or at least loosening, of party affiliations. While parties had been able to claim solid mass allegiance from blocks of votes, newspapers and other journals found it more difficult to take independent stances.

The development of popular magazines as a new, national medium of mass communication had a significant impact on public awareness (Schneirov, 1994). Newspapers had been locally owned with parochial priorities. The new magazines, which flourished in the early years of the twentieth century, gave a national profile to reform movements and, in effect, helped nationalise what had hitherto been local concerns. But political scandals were shaped not only by new forms of media, but also by a new breed of journalist concerned to make news and set political agendas, rather than simply report events. Such journalists saw themselves as independents, and journalism began establishing itself as an autonomous profession. In the nineteenth century, university schools of journalism were almost unknown; by 1915, thirty-nine universities taught journalism. Codes of ethics for journalists began to develop and the National Press Club was formed in 1908, signifying that journalism was now a respectable, even high-status, occupation.

The activities of the new breed of journalists were pejoratively labelled 'muckraking' by Theodore Roosevelt, who likened them to the muckrakers of Bunyan's *Pilgrim's Progress*. The epithet is believed to have been provoked by reaction to the 'Treason in the Senate' series published in 1906 in William Randolph Hearst's *Cosmopolitan* magazine. The main newspaper magnates, Hearst and Joseph Pulitzer, helped foster a better-informed and less-parochial newspaper readership. And those journalists termed 'muckrakers' increasingly accepted the label as a badge of honour.

Political scandals are generated by political, media and public developments. The partisanship of party and press in the Gilded Age promoted political scandal, but, during the Progressive Era, new political forces and developments in media forms and journalistic practice interacted to ensure that alternative scandal-production processes were in operation. Reform movements dedicated to tackling egregious political corruption in states and cities were not new, but they found a more accessible and better-informed public for their message and, in turn, the formation of a national public opinion was facilitated by the new media.

This chapter has thus far been concerned to identify some key features of American political development, which generated political scandal, and to help us understand the place of political scandal in American politics in particular periods. Thus evenly matched and highly competitive parties competing for patronage spoils helped to increase the incidence of scandal. But so did reform movements and a new, less-partisan, media, dedicated to uncovering political misconduct. The mass media are rarely passive observers but often take sides in political contest. At different times, they may support one party against another or 'good governance' against corrupt machine politics. The general public may be politically mobilised in a partisan cause, as many were in the Gilded Age, or become informed citizens concerned at the apparent moral decay of the political class.

Thus, although the common elements of political scandal – competitive politicians, allegations of misconduct, an effective mass media and a concerned public – remain constant, there is scope for considerable change within each element and in the ways in which they interact with each other. This latter point is particularly important when we consider the political and institutional consequences of periods of extensive political scandal. When there has been an increase in the number or scale of political scandals, this has often prompted some form of institutional or procedural reform, designed to prohibit or restrict the misconduct that led to scandals. One consequence has been to refashion the political architecture and to shift concerns about misconduct from one institutional space or process to another, for example the creation of the office of Independent Counsel, which moved the focus away from the executive branch to a judicial process.

Where there were frequent electoral scandals, as in the Gilded Age when electoral procedures were largely unregulated, it generated numerous electoral reform proposals, some of which were implemented. The introduction of, for example, the secret ballot and stricter voter registration requirements helped reduce the scope for electoral scandal. Similarly, Progressive Era reforms, which eroded the position of city bosses, helped limit the scope for political corruption in local government by substituting professional managers for politicians.

Scandal and American political culture

The character of political scandals in the United States is shaped by the political culture in a variety of ways, not least by preceding waves of political scandal and reform. Although it is a common response of participants and commentators to try to explain current scandals in terms of their predecessors, one danger is that insufficient attention is paid to the ways in which politics, the media and public opinion have changed. Political scandals can, therefore, by implication, be helpful in pinpointing important phases in American political development, and the most obvious example is the Watergate scandal.

The relationship of Watergate to American political development is not straightforward. It has clearly had many effects on politics, the mass media and public opinion. We note here only those most important to the incidence of political scandal. First, it became legitimate for members of Congress to

question publicly the integrity of the White House, and encouraged the legislature to take a prominent role in holding successive presidents to account
for alleged misconduct. Congressional politicians who witnessed the virtual
canonisation of Senator Sam Ervin, Chair of the Watergate Committee, were
not slow to appreciate the political benefits of prime-time televised investigations of White House scandals. The initial reluctance of senior members
of Congress to serve on the Watergate Committee was influenced by their
assessment of the political fallout likely to follow an unprecedented and probably unsuccessful challenge to presidential dignity and authority. The resignation of Richard Nixon was therefore an historic event, which emphasised
the potential of political scandal to shape public events and determine political fortunes. Thus, when the next major presidential scandal emerged in
the 1980s, there was an unseemly scramble in both the Senate and House of
Representatives to serve on the joint congressional committee investigating the
Iran–Contra scandal.

The mass media were slow to react to the first Watergate disclosures. There
seems to have been a reluctance, shared with Congress, to think the worst of
President Nixon, who, after all, had been re-elected by a record margin in 1972.
But as the Department of Justice investigators gradually picked up the trail
leading to the Oval Office itself, the role of one newspaper, *The Washington Post*,
also became very prominent. The *Post* itself became news and its reporters,
Bob Woodward and Carl Bernstein, were increasingly seen as 'white knights'
illuminating the darker side of presidential politics. The age of the 'investigative reporter' had dawned, and many people believed that these new celebrity
journalists had double-handedly unmasked a scandalous conspiracy against
the American public (Bernstein and Woodward, 1974). Thus both the role and
status of the mass media were different after Watergate. Perception and self-
perception had changed.

The impact of Watergate on public opinion was also striking. The televised
hearings on Capitol Hill were avidly watched by millions. And, as the scandal
unfolded, President Nixon's approval ratings slid to unprecedented levels.
The public visibly cared about this political scandal. Discussions of the decline
in public trust in government and politicians are often linked to Watergate,
suggesting perhaps that the scandal symbolised the end of an era of deference
and respect in American politics. But opinion poll evidence suggests that the
decline in public trust and confidence in government was already noticeable in
the 1960s and, while Watergate seemed to exacerbate the situation considerably, it was not the origin or the sole cause. Contemporary public opinion is
now deeply sceptical about the efficacy of political institutions and the
motives and trustworthiness of politicians of all parties, and is more willing to
believe the worst.

Thus our understanding of contemporary political scandals in the United
States needs to take into account the fact that many politicians are now convinced of the potential political benefit of making scandal allegations, and
that the mass media know that publicising political misconduct can improve

ratings, sell newspapers and win Pulitzer Prizes. And scandals are played out before a public which is better informed about them by a variety of media forms and technologies, and which is deeply suspicious of most things political. It is perhaps not surprising that these political and social developments have created a culture receptive to the generation of political scandal.

If the resignation of President Nixon over Watergate was an important landmark in the history of American political scandal, the unsuccessful impeachment of President Clinton in 1998 was even more remarkable. Nixon resigned to avoid almost certain successful impeachment and criminal prosecution. Yet the Clinton impeachment proceeded, even though the prospects of success were never high. As the first president to face impeachment since Andrew Johnson in the 1860s, Clinton spent much of his time in the White House dealing with a series of political scandals. It was almost as though, once Clinton became enmeshed in the Whitewater scandal, there emerged a scandal-production machine that kept finding new allegations for him to address.

It was noted earlier that high-profile political scandals often generate structural and procedural reforms that have important consequences for the contexts in which subsequent political scandals occur. After Watergate, the political architecture of the American state was significantly changed in ways likely to make it more probable that the misconduct of politicians would be subject to formal inquiries. When the president of the United States breaches the trust of the American public as spectacularly as President Nixon did, trust in all politicians is likely to decline. The response was to create new institutions, like the Special Prosecutor or Office of Independent Counsel, to provide new ways of calling politicians to account (Williams, 1999). President Nixon's decision to dismiss the first Special Prosecutor, Archibald Cox, as part of what became known as the 'Saturday Night Massacre', convinced many of the need for an independent means of investigating the executive branch. This desire was embodied in legislation as part of the 1978 Ethics in Government Act, which took oversight responsibility for the independent counsel away from the president and gave it to a judicial panel.

But, while the new independent counsel office was to play a major role in the political scandals of the Clinton presidency, it was simply part of a culture of mistrust that saw the FBI test the integrity of members of Congress by offering them bribes in the ABSCAM[1] scandal. The politicians who helped pass the new laws and create the new institutions presumably hoped such measures would help restore public confidence, but their impact was to ensure that political conduct was more closely monitored than ever before (Roberts and Doss jr, 1997). Together with the increased vigilance of the mass media and their greater willingness to intrude into what had previously been private matters, political life became a scandal minefield and politicians were forced to tread very carefully.

Politicians who failed to recognise that the scandal climate had changed or who were unable to change their behaviour (for example, Senator Robert Packwood and arguably Bill Clinton) were likely to find themselves embroiled in scandal. Misconduct that was once largely ignored if not formally condoned, such as improper use of the congressional frank, breaches of employment and earnings rules and sexual harassment, now became serious matters and rich sources of political scandal, which helped bring down some senior politicians.

Since passage of the law establishing the office of the independent counsel, a succession of presidents (Reagan, Bush and Clinton) have been caught, to varying degrees, in the scandal trap. The independent counsel is effectively a legalised political scandal hunter, who can explore personal and private matters, as well as the discharge of public duties, to find evidence of scandalous behaviour. One lesson of Watergate is that scandal hunters need independence from the White House in order to do their jobs. Without such independence, they risk summary dismissal when they stray into sensitive territory. With independence, no skeletons are safe in their closets, because, given sufficient time and resources, they will be located and rattled in public.

Legalising and institutionalising presidential scandal hunters create new difficulties for those charged with scandal management and avoidance. There are a variety of strategies available for deployment, but almost by definition we only know the less-successful strategies, because we know there was a scandal. An entirely successful scandal-management strategy should presumably be impossible to detect. The most popular techniques include plausible denial, where there is an attempt to focus blame and attention on the unauthorised and unknown actions of subordinates. This was used at several stages of the Watergate scandal until the scandal hunters arrived at the door of the Oval Office. It was also used in the Iran–Contra scandal, where Oliver North and John Poindexter accepted responsibility to protect President Reagan.

The famous Watergate question was 'what did the President know and when did he know it?', and this proved difficult for an activist president like Nixon to answer without incriminating himself. In Iran–Contra, the question became 'did the President know anything and when did he forget it?' Reagan's denials had greater political credibility because his limited attention span and inability to recall names and detail was already well known before he was afflicted with Alzheimer's. Plausible denial may be linked with other strategies: for example, 'stonewalling', where the president denies any wrongdoing, refuses to respond to questions and blocks the efforts of journalists, independent counsel and other investigators to acquire further information. Thus the claim is made that the president has done nothing wrong, but if some misconduct did occur he did not know about it or authorise it; in any case, there are sound constitutional and legal principles, such as executive privilege, which justify refusal to co-operate with investigators. Another approach is to impugn the motives of those making the allegations. The Clinton White House, for example, attempted to divert public attention and criticism away from their own conduct by identifying themselves as 'victims' of a 'vast right-wing conspiracy' (Brock, 2002). Allegations of scandal are thus sometimes met with counter-allegations. To the Clintons, the scandal wars dominating their administrations were waged by political opponents who could not accept political defeat at the ballot box.

Political scandal in the United States is characterised not merely by allegations and counter-allegation but also by escalation. As noted above, the
Clintons in effect accused their critics of trying to mount a constitutional
coup d'etat. Successive political scandals have raised the stakes and increased
institutional and legal capacities to identify emerging scandals. Presidents,
Speakers of the House, prominent Senators and State Governors have all been
brought down by political scandal, and politicians, journalists and voters
understand its power in modern America.

Contemporary American politics is closely contested. The results of the
presidential election in 2000 and recent congressional election results point
to a polity where partisan support is evenly divided. In such an environment,
the political incentives of scandal mongering are compelling. In the mass
media, broadcasting has given way to 'narrowcasting', with a profusion of broadcasting outlets catering to particular segments of public taste and opinion.
The internet has mushroomed and access to it is now extremely widespread.
Controlling the news agenda has therefore never been more difficult for political decision makers. There is less deference and respect among the public toward
politics and politicians, and politicians themselves are increasingly willing
to criticise colleagues and the political institutions they inhabit. New media
forms such as 'phone-ins' and the 'shock jocks', like Rush Limbaugh and Gordon
Liddy, engage large audiences in scandal debate and help keep scandals alive.
Where mainstream journalism was once authoritative, even magisterial in
the case of the *New York Times* and *Washington Post*, it is now outflanked by
'infotainment' and by ideologically committed journals and websites.

But the political architecture essential to scandal production has changed
again, because the independent counsel statute is now in abeyance. With a
Republican in the White House and Republicans controlling both Houses of
Congress, it is unlikely to be revived. If the Democrats had gained control of
Congress, it seems probable that the embarrassments of the White House over
their relationship with bankrupt corporations would have developed into more
determined legislative efforts to involve President Bush in major scandal.

Thus, while some of the ingredients of extensive scandal production are
in place in contemporary American politics, others are missing. Deprived of
control of the Justice Department, the FBI, the independent counsel and congressional investigations, the ability of Democrats to make scandal mischief
is correspondingly reduced. The ideologues of the far right in the media and
think-tanks, who featured so prominently in the Clinton scandals, are now
quiescent because their man is in the White House and they have no obvious
liberal counterparts. But these different elements of scandal production are not
frozen in time. They have changed in the past and will change in the future.
Political circumstances will change and, as they do, the form and intensity of
political contestation will also change. The character of the mass media has
changed profoundly on several occasions since the Gilded Age, and doubtless
further changes will occur, which will affect the ways in which scandals are
'discovered' and reported.

The audiences for scandal are changing, not least because they have been exposed to prior scandals. Thus, there is an increasing sophistication among the public, which allows discrimination between authentic and synthetic scandals. Even at the height of the Clinton scandals, his approval rating as president remained high. The implication here is that, while scandals may disrupt a politician's career and absorb much of his or her time and resources, they need not prove terminal or even seriously damaging. The social values of the audience for scandal may change so that scandal allegations involving adultery or homosexual conduct no longer have the resonance with the electorate it was once supposed they did. Such developments create new difficulties for politicians eager to use political scandal as a weapon of first resort. If allegations go unreported or, if reported, fall on deaf ears, the reputations of the accused may themselves be scrutinised.

Conclusion

It was argued at the beginning of this chapter that political scandal has largely resisted comparative analysis. It was suggested that a more fruitful line of inquiry is to examine a specific political system longitudinally, that is to say to compare successive scandal eras over time within a defined political culture. The above analysis has shown that, while the 'ingredients' of political scandal – political misconduct (or allegations thereof), media coverage, political contestation and public awareness and concern – are constant, the nature of each of these ingredients, and the dynamics of their interrelationship, change over time. The American party system was initially forged in the years after the American Civil War and its character was changed by democratisation, industrialisation, urbanisation and by political and social reform. Opportunities for political misconduct have also changed over time, and depend critically on the range of government responsibilities and the mechanisms for political scrutiny and oversight. The media has developed in parallel with the polity; but here we have seen a proliferation of media outlets and forms, and waves of partisanship giving way to claims of neutrality and objectivity. These in turn have succumbed to the current wave of partisanship. But this is not the past repeating itself because the new partisanship of the media is more ideological than institutional and not tied to party by financial purse-strings, as it was in the Gilded Age. And the audiences for scandal are now better-educated and able to access diverse print and electronic sources of information.

As links between politicians, parties, the media and the public change, so too will the dynamics of political scandal. This analysis has shown that American political scandals are the product of distinctive patterns of American political, social and media development. In terms of the research agenda for students of political scandal, it seems the gap between accounts of individual scandals and the aspiration for a general theory of political scandal is too great to bridge. But a first step towards closing the gap is to compare political scandals over time within a specific political context so that the analytical and contingent variables are kept within reasonable bounds. Only when we have a set of country-specific longitudinal studies of political scandal can we begin to understand what they have in common. In the meantime, political scandal will continue to shape, and be shaped by, broader patterns of American political development.

Note

1 'This stands for "Abdul Scam". An FBI agent dressed up and pretended to be an Arab sheikh called Abdul, while "scam" is the American word for a deception/fraud/ confidence trick' (Williams, 2003: 78).

References

Bernstein, C. and B. Woodward (1974), *All the President's Men*, London, Secker and Warburg.

Bryce, J. (1888), *The American Commonwealth*, London, Macmillan.

Brock, D. (2002), *Blinded by the Right: The Conscience of an Ex-Conservative*, New York, Crown Publishers.

Calhoun, C. W. (1996), 'The Political Culture: Public Life and the Conduct of Politics', in C. W. Calhoun (ed.), *The Gilded Age: Essays on the Origins of Modern America*, Wilmington DE, SR Books.

Kaplan, R. A. (2002), *Politics and the American Press: The Rise of Objectivity, 1865–1920*, Cambridge and New York, Cambridge University Press.

Markovits, A. S. and M. Silverstein (1988), *The Politics of Scandal: Power and Process in Liberal Democracies*, New York, Holmes and Meier.

Roberts, R. N. and M. R. Doss Jr (1997), *From Watergate to Whitewater: The Public Integrity War*, Westport, CT Praeger.

Schneirov, M. (1994), *The Dream of a New Social Order: Popular Magazines in America, 1893–1914*, New York, Columbia University Press.

Summers, J. H. (2000), 'What happened to Sex Scandals? Politics and Peccadilloes, Jefferson to Kennedy', *Journal of American History*, 87, 825–54.

Thompson, J. B. (2000), *Political Scandal: Power and Visibility in the Media Age*, Cambridge and New York, Polity Press.

Welch, S. and R. Williams (2003), 'Political Scandals in the United States: Outline of an Analytical Framework', paper presented at the PSA American Politics Group Conference, University of Reading, 3–5 January.

Williams, R. (1998), *Political Scandals in the USA*, Edinburgh, Keele University Press.

Williams, R. (1999), 'The Persecution of the Presidency? The Role of the Independent Counsel', *Parliamentary Affairs*, 52, 291–305.

Williams, R. (2003), 'Political Corruption in the United States', in M. J. Bull and J. L. Newell (eds), *Corruption in Contemporary Politics*, Basingstoke, Palgrave Macmillan.

Part II

What scandals are and how they unfold

4

A journalist looks at political scandal[1]

Chris Moncrieff

Political scandals are the life-blood of Fleet Street and a source of dismay, frustration and fury for politicians. Such scandals usually embrace at least one of the four ingredients – often more than one – which bring joy to a journalist's heart: sex, royalty, religion and money. When political scandals break, the wrath of Westminster descends on the media, and often, I regret to say, some reporters use as a 'defence' (where I think no defence is needed) of their story the excuse that it is in the public interest. There is no doubt that it may be in the public interest. But, if reporters are honest, they will tell you that a political scandal sets their adrenalin running, simply because it is a good story. Politicians deride these stories as gossip and trivia; and sometimes they are just that. But what is so wrong about that? Politicians, just like everybody else, are as entranced by scandal as journalists. As often as not, though, a political scandal can have dire consequences, leading even to the fall of a government or the destruction of a huge political figure. When the Commons is debating defence or foreign affairs, the whips, very often, have to trawl the bars, the dining rooms and even the lavatories to virtually frog-march MPs into the Chamber to ensure that the debate does not collapse for lack of speakers, which it otherwise would. But when MPs are debating such as, say, the Profumo affair, which had the added ingredient to all the others, namely espionage, the Chamber is full to bursting point; standing room only. What is true, however, is that the Fleet Street attitude to scandals over the past fifty years or so has dramatically transformed.

A prime example of the timidity of Fleet Street in years gone by was the Abdication crisis, and the scandal of King Edward VIII and the American divorcee, Mrs Simpson. In those days the so-called Establishment included the Fleet Street editors. The King's liaison with Mrs Simpson was well known to them, as well as to members of the government. But the editors were part of the conspiracy that kept it out of the public domain. It took an unwitting remark by the then Bishop of Bradford and an astute Press Association reporter to bring the scandal to light. Even then, there was a succession of telephone calls between the papers, provincials and nationals, as to whether they 'dare' use it. Such an attitude is unthinkable today. Any Fleet Street editor who tried to suppress such a story would be sacked on the spot. The full story of that scandal is as follows: the bishops – or most of them – knew all about Edward's lover, the American divorcee Mrs Wallis Simpson; the Cabinet knew and, most surprising of all, the Fleet Street editors knew. Yet for reasons of propriety – can you imagine propriety entering the equation now where newspapers are concerned? – and the tendency of the Establishment to stick together, not a whisper of this appeared in the newspapers. It was, I am glad to say, the Press Association which first broke the story, largely as a result of an indiscretion by the then bumbling Bishop of Bradford, Dr A. W. F. Blunt. But even when it appeared on the Press Association wires it was handled with the utmost nervousness by the papers, both national and provincial. Papers were ringing each other up, asking whether they were going to be bold enough to use the PA story. It is a situation which could not happen today. Inhibition is not a quality easily found in Fleet Street any more.

It was a bizarre story involving the cloistered Bishop Blunt who clearly had not logged into the ecclesiastical grapevine, where the scandal was on every primate's lips. Blunt had prepared a diocesan speech in which he had gently and indirectly criticised the King for not turning up at Church except on special occasions and insinuated that the King lacked grace. These criticisms, although pretty daring, were innocently made. Blunt had not heard about Mrs Simpson. But when it was mentioned to him, in a whispered conversation by another Bishop, at a gathering before the one at which Blunt delivered his speech, Blunt came to the view that, since his comments bore no relation to that scandal, he would still go ahead and deliver the speech.

The mind boggles at the naivete of the man. A reporter called Charles Leach reported the speech, which that evening was splashed all over the *Bradford Telegraph and Argus*. Leach, a PA correspondent, thought he had better send it to the PA and the other then national news agency, Exchange Telegraph, or Extel as it is known. He wired the story to Extel first, but for some unaccountable reason the sentence about the King needing grace was omitted, so that version of the speech was largely innocuous. Then he filed it to the PA, where, unusually, there was a delay in disseminating the report while PA executives considered its massive implications. Ultimately, it went out intact with all the relevant controversial elements included. Fleet Street mistakenly assumed the Bishop was referring to Mrs Simpson and that the King's secret was out. But this was merely a gaffe by an ill-informed bungling bishop. The subsequent nervousness of Fleet Street to use the story was based on the momentous consequences that its publication would provoke. Even so, it was bewildering. It was actually a leading article in the *Yorkshire Post*, which, according to contemporary accounts, dealt 'soberly but portentously but ultimately censoriously' with what the paper described as rumours but what in truth were well-known facts in Fleet Street. Even the *Yorkshire Post* did not decide to go ahead with its editorial until its editor, Arthur Mann, had consulted on the phone with the editors of the *Birmingham Post* and the

Manchester Guardian, both of whom also decided to comment. Other provincial papers were quick to follow suit, but Fleet Street remained disgracefully timid. Finally, after reading the *Yorkshire Post* editorial, some decided to take the plunge, waiting another astonishing twenty-four hours before deciding to comment on the issues. So it was the Bishop of Bradford who unthinkingly lit the match that caused one of the biggest constitutional conflagrations in Britain of the entire twentieth century.

Nowadays there are no such inhibitions. The fact that a scandal could be so overwhelming that it might topple a government or create some other constitutional crisis would not even be considered by an editor as a reason for suppression – if anything it would have the reverse effect. Nor would an editor worry about the possible subsequent knuckle rapping by the Press Complaints Commission. The routine Fleet Street attitude is: act now and answer the questions after the deed is done. You have no idea how galling it is for a newspaperman to have a world-beating story and have to keep it to himself. The possibility of legal action may enter into an editor's considerations before he publishes a story like this, but sometimes a risk is taken even with that possibility. If ever a politician sought advice from me, I would give him this 'health warning': namely, the moment you enter the House of Commons you should kiss goodbye to your private life. And if you are still inclined to have a little bit of dalliance on the side, well forget it, or face the risk of a public shaming.

But exposure does sometimes have its plus side. When the world heard about Paddy (Pantsdown) Ashdown's illicit amours, his personal stock immediately went up – if not in the eyes of his good lady wife, at least in the opinion polls. There was another such case in the nineteenth century. When Palmerston was in power he was cited as co-respondent in a divorce action after having forged a relationship, when he was seventy-nine years old, with a Mrs O'Kane. This inevitably gave rise to the joke: 'She was Kane, but was he Able?' However, when his rival Disraeli, himself something of a sower of wild oats, heard about this liaison, he said it was a pity it had come to public knowledge because it would mean that Palmerston would sweep the country at the next election. Disraeli's fears were justified. Palmerston did just that.

David Lloyd-George was one British statesman whose scandalous life style, in both the areas of sex and corruption, largely escaped the microscopic attentions of the press. His amours with what has been described as 'streams of ladies' were not of a romantic but rather a clinical nature, for which reason he was nicknamed 'The Goat'. He has been compared in his lustful activities to Edward VII who allocated a pew for his mistresses at his Coronation, known as 'the loose box'. But these were all mere trifles compared with Lloyd-George's sale of honours, anything from peerages downwards, with the OBE – known cynically as the Order of the Bad Egg – specially created for Lloyd-George's nefarious activities. The press of the time seemed to be unbothered by this blatant corruption – which, of course, gave rise to the ditty, 'Lloyd-George Knew My Father' – which is not entirely surprising since The Goat judiciously gave away, gratis, free and for nothing, honours to the newspaper barons of the day, thus ensuring their silence. The scandal of the newspaper hush-up was as great as the scandal itself. But the amazing thing is that nobody, least of all the newspapers, appeared to bother about it too much. The issue is even referred to as a joke in one of P. G. Wodehouse's Jeeves books, with Bingo Little referring to a peerage 'costing the deuce of a sum. Even baronetcies have gone up frightfully nowadays, I'm told' (Wodehouse, 1924: 43).

It could be argued that honours are still sold today, although the connection between the gong and the cash laid out is far more subtle. Someone who gives large sums to a political party may well do so in the belief that one day they will be called to an investiture at Buckingham Palace. But nowadays, the press is far more censorious, probing and, some may say, far more sanctimonious than it was all those years ago. No amount of pressure, certainly not cash, nor even threats can these days deter a newspaper from printing a story of a scandal involving a top political figure. Yet it still seems possible to cause politicians to change their minds if certain blandishments are on offer. We have seen recently the subterfuge – in my view legitimate – used by the *News of the World* – the fake Sheikh – to expose the activities of the Countess of Wessex and her public relations company. It is sometimes necessary for the press to take what might be called as a euphemism 'unorthodox action' to expose cover-ups and the like. But before we get too sanctimonious ourselves about this, whatever some journalists may say about doing things for the public interest, our main, overriding instinct is to get a good story. We are in the business of selling newspapers, and if by any chance we do some good along the way that is the bonus; but the true, hard-bitten newspaperman – something I aspire to being myself – wants a good story over and above everything else. As the *Sun* columnist Richard Littlejohn said recently, one of the jobs of the reporter is to sit at the back of the hall and throw bottles.

The most astonishing scandal of recent years was the liaison between John Major, when he was a government whip, and Edwina Currie. How they kept that secret over a period of four years remains a mystery and does not reflect well on the so-called bloodhounds of the parliamentary lobby at the time, of whom I, shamefully, was one. One marvels now how Major, when he was Prime Minister, kept such outward cool, because he must have feared that Currie – no shrinking violet – might blow the gaff at any moment. Ultimately, of course, she let the cat out of the bag. When it was put to her that she had done this for money, she retorted that if she had really wanted to make serious money out of it, she would have published it during his premiership. Major's response, probably a wise one, was to issue a brief statement of deep regret, and keep out of the public eye for a few months to let the whole affair blow over.

What made it all the more remarkable was that his premiership was bedevilled by sleaze. Almost every Sunday, you could discover in the *News of the World* that another Tory had been caught, to put it vulgarly, with his trousers down. The only respite (for the Tories, that is) was when the Labour MP Dennis Skinner, known as The Beast of Bolsover, was caught having an affair. The

News of the World had an inspired headline for this story: 'The Beast of Legover'. There was David Mellor, then Heritage Secretary, and his liaison with an out-of-work actress; Tim Yeo also had to resign from the Tory government after his affair with a Conservative councillor led to the birth of a child. There were half a dozen others.

These indiscretions, which had a cataclysmic effect on those involved, usually came to light with a tip-off to Fleet Street by a political enemy, followed up by what could be described as a 'stalking' operation by the newspaper concerned. This was very much how the then Foreign Secretary, Robin Cook's liaison with his secretary, later to become his wife, became public property. But there are other ways of bringing a scandal to light – and that is by creating the scandal yourself. There was a prime example of this in the last, seedy years of the John Major regime. The *Sunday Times* was suspicious that a number of MPs – although they did not have any names – were only too ready to table questions in the Commons, if they were paid to do so, usually by business interests. So they set up a trap. A reporter, posing as a businessman, offered ten Labour and ten Conservative MPs £1,000 each to ask a specific parliamentary question. Two of the Tories rose to the bait, Graham Riddick and David Treddinick. They were both ultimately suspended for 'offences' – and I put the word in quotation marks – which many other MPs felt sympathy about. To my surprise, little was made at the time of the element of entrapment adopted by the newspaper in using what can only be described as an impostor who tried to trick MPs into breaking the rules. It is also worth pointing out that the paper attempted the trick on several MPs before they found any gullible enough to fall for it. Some time earlier, a judge had stopped a murder trial and released the accused because of a so-called honey-pot entrapment of the suspect by a pretty woman police officer. The kind of entrapment successfully attempted by the *Sunday Times* would probably, on that precedent, not have stood up in a court of law.

The sleaze marking that period of Conservative rule undoubtedly played an important part, although not an absolute one, in the subsequent demise of the Major regime and the stunning successive general election victories by Labour in 1997 and 2001. Tony Blair entered 10 Downing Street with a promise to be purer than the driven snow. Sleaze, we were confidently told, was a thing of the past, now that the Conservatives had been routed at the polls. But surprisingly quickly after Labour's sweep to power, there was a major problem, and it got dangerously close to Downing Street, something which never happened during eighteen years of Conservative government. It was so serious, in fact, that Mr Blair found it necessary to make a fulsome apology on television, stressing that he was, in effect, 'a regular sort of guy' who would never do anything that was not on the straight and narrow. This was the 1997 case of Formula One racing and tobacco sponsorship. Labour, in that year's election manifesto, had promised (or threatened, whichever way you care to look at it) a ban on tobacco sponsorship of sporting events. The Blair government had not been in power for many weeks when it was put about – despite the apparently blanket nature of the manifesto pledge – that Formula One racing would be exempt from this ban. This seemed odd, given the government's stated desire to cut down on the nation's smoking habits, which was the point of the ban in the first place. Needless to say, newspapers started making inquiries and, thanks to their investigations, it was discovered that one Bernie Ecclestone, regarded as the King Pin of Formula One, had donated £1 million, no less, to the Labour Party. This really was the stuff of scandal. When the story leaked out, the Labour Party were compelled to hand the money back and Blair went on the television – grotesquely over made-up for some reason – to make what amounted to a grovelling apology during an interview with John Humphrys. And, although the newspapers waxed lyrical about this scandal, the Conservative Opposition in the House of Commons inexplicably failed to capitalise on it. They were probably still in a sense of shock following the calamity that overwhelmed them at the 1997 election. But it was a serious omission on their part because this was an element of sleaze that went right into 10 Downing Street – far worse than any which played an important role in that Tory election defeat. The government could be said to have got away with murder in that case. And had it not been for the hawkish eyes of the press, it would never have been uncovered, because Her Majesty's Opposition disgracefully barely batted an eyelid.

We have seen recently the subterfuge (in my view legitimate) used by the *News of the World* – the fake Sheikh – to expose the activities of the Countess of Wessex and her public relations company. The next example of scandal involved a celebrated, or probably more appropriately a notorious, paedophile court case in the 1970s. A very senior member of the Establishment, one who had reached ambassadorial rank, was implicated in the case, although he was not in the dock. But his name cropped up throughout the trial – or would have done had the judge not ordered him to be referred to as 'Mr X', or some such disguise, whenever he had to be mentioned. To those listening, it became obvious as the trial wore on that this high-ranking diplomat was involved in the unsavoury activities being put before the court. Afterwards, there was something of an outcry about this cover-up, which seemed to be – and indeed was, as we discovered later – the Establishment protecting its own. Most journalists covering the case were aware of the man's identity, but publishing it would have amounted to contempt of court and almost certainly an open-ended jail sentence. So, what I did was to find a friendly MP who would table a House of Commons motion using this man's name and asking why his involvement in the affair had been covered up. I waited up at Westminster all night to get hold of the parliamentary document bearing the crucial words. As soon as they appeared – remember House of Commons documents and their contents bear absolute privilege – we circulated the name on the PA wires and the Establishment's little secret was a secret no more. It turned out this man had a history of paedophilia, and afterwards engaged in more of it, was subsequently jailed and eventually died. If anyone asks me if I feel ashamed at doing that, well, the answer is a resounding, 'No!'.

I was also personally 'used' – although I make no complaint about that: far from it – by the Thatcher government in the scandal of the Law Officer's letter during the Westland Helicopter crisis of 1986. It was this latter incident which nearly caused the downfall of Margaret Thatcher and probably would have done had not Neil Kinnock, then Leader of the Labour Opposition, made such a hash of his speech during the Commons debate on the issue. This letter certainly led to the spectacular resignation from the Cabinet of the Defence Secretary Michael Heseltine – he actually flounced out of a Cabinet meeting and stormed down Downing Street, if you recall – and the subsequent but less dramatic resignation of the then Trade and Industry Secretary, Leon Brittan. The background was that the entire Cabinet, with the exception of Heseltine, wanted this ailing West Country helicopter company to be rescued from its financial difficulties by an American aid package. Heseltine opted for a European package, and, despite the unwritten but normally strictly adhered-to rules of Cabinet unanimity, he publicly campaigned for his point of view against the rest of his Cabinet colleagues. Needless to say, Margaret Thatcher was incandescent with rage. But Heseltine still continued. However, the government wheeled into action its dirty tricks department, which engaged in a subterfuge against one of its own members, which amounted to a Grade A scandal – although for once no sex or corruption was involved. It was simply an attempt, by foul means or fair, to blacken Heseltine's character – Thatcher could not bear the sight of him – and to utterly destroy his case.

What had happened was that Heseltine had written to the Attorney General to seek a dispassionate and uncritical assessment of the pluses and minuses of his proposal and those of the rest of the Cabinet's alternative proposal. This, subsequently, the Solicitor General did – the Attorney General was ill at the time. He answered all Heseltine's points apolitically as a law officer. In other words, the Solicitor General wrote his reply strictly in legal terms. There was not even a whiff of political input in his missive. What happened was that a copy of this letter fell into the hands of Leon Brittan, who instructed one of his press officers, Colette Bowe, to telephone me at the House of Commons, with selective extracts from the Law Officer's letter to Heseltine. Needless to say, those 'selective extracts' comprised only the minus points about Heseltine's proposal. They completely ignored the plus-points as they did the minus points of the rest of the Cabinet's proposal. To say that Heseltine was hopping mad about this is to under-estimate his fury when I told him. He hit the roof – and three days later, on January 9, he hit it again, storming out of the Cabinet without a by-your-leave. But equally furious was the Solicitor General himself who had been grossly betrayed by a government colleague. To make public at all a law officer's letter would have been bad enough. But it was unthinkable that selective parts should have been put into the public domain. With hindsight, I am astonished that the Attorney General and the Solicitor General did not themselves storm out of office. I believe they very nearly did – and that probably *would* have been curtains for Margaret Thatcher.

There can have been little doubt that 10 Downing Street and almost certainly Mrs Thatcher herself were involved in this scandal. Leon Brittan, a ferociously ambitious minister, would scarcely have risked all by doing it off his own bat without instructions, indeed orders, from Number 10. When Sir Bernard Ingham, Margaret Thatcher's press secretary for nearly all her premiership, retired at around the same time as she was removed from power, I asked him for the true story of this leak. But he hedged around it and failed to enlighten me at all. I was hoping, when his memoirs, *Kill the Messenger* (1991), came out, that they might shed some light on it. But I was disappointed again. Nor were Margaret Thatcher's any more revealing. As far as I can see, Downing Street decided to fudge their own involvement in this affair and distance themselves from it. I imagine that we will have to wait for the thirty-year rule to expire, when we can see confidential Cabinet papers before we shall know the real truth about this murky affair. I hasten to add that I am not moralising or preaching about this. I was over the moon to be the recipient of a story that had enormous repercussions and which, but for the failure of the Labour Opposition in the Commons, would have generated even more momentous repercussions, possibly the downfall of Margaret Thatcher herself. Indeed, that was what she feared. Just before she entered the Chamber of the House of Commons for what looked like a make-or-break debate, she was overhead whispering to a colleague: 'I may not be Prime Minister by six o'clock tonight'. And, as I say, thanks at least in part to the incompetence of Neil Kinnock, who completely fluffed his lines, she survived.

Perhaps the greatest purely political scandal of the twentieth century involving sex, national security and espionage – meat and drink for newspapers – was the Profumo affair of 1963. John Profumo was Secretary of State for War, and the Conservatives were on their last legs – almost literally – as they approached thirteen years in power. It was the seediness of this scandal, with its undertones and overtones of decadent orgies involving models – the word which was the euphemism for prostitutes at the time – in a sumptuous country mansion, implicating members of the nobility and self-indulgence on the grossest possible scale, which ultimately finished the Conservatives off. In a way the demise of the Conservatives in 1964 (although by only the narrowest of margins) was similar to their 1997 defeat – although the latter, as we all know, was a rout. But the Tories had been in office for eighteen years by 1997 and the welter of sleaze which characterised the final few years of this era was probably the factor which transformed what might otherwise have been a manageable defeat into an overwhelming one.

As ever, the newspapers played a major role in the uncovering of the Profumo scandal, although they were inhibited somewhat after Profumo's statement in the House in which he denied, falsely, that he had slept with the model Christine Keeler and threatened to issue writs on anyone who said or suggested otherwise.

Before I get into the mainstream of this huge affair, let me briefly dwell on one small incident, which gave reporter Christopher Morris, now on Sky

News, a sensational scoop for the *Daily Mail*. Christine Keeler had left Britain when the hue and cry began and flitted across to Spain. The general but mistaken view in Fleet Street was that she was in Cadiz, down in the South. So some of Fleet Street's finest journalists hired cars in Madrid and headed South in hope of tracking her down. Christopher Morris was one of these. And as he and a photographer left the suburbs of Madrid at the start of the long journey, which they presumed lay ahead, their Spanish driver was waxing lyrical about a beautiful dark-haired English girl who was staying with his family in their modest pension in the city. At first Morris and his friend took little notice, but then they suddenly expressed not so much interest as avid curiosity. Could this be, they asked themselves, Christine Keeler? At first they dismissed the idea as too ludicrous for words, a coincidence simply too good to be true. But gradually they were convinced. They suddenly ordered the driver to turn round and take them to his home. It was a huge gamble and the driver was totally mystified by these new instructions. Morris and his colleague were biting their nails, fearful they had made a terrible mistake. But when they returned to their chauffeur's modest home they found, indeed, they had Christine Keeler to themselves. She was as shocked as they were elated. And it was, in a sense, a double whammy, because the rest of Fleet Street were bowling down to Cadiz in what would turn out to be a complete wild goose chase. It was, as I say, a sensational scoop. I do not know what odds a statistician would have put on that happening, but I reckon it would have run into six figures to one at least.

The Profumo affair suddenly reached the headlines, although nervously, when a man called John Edgecombe, a petty criminal and film extra, fired shots at the door of a house where Keeler was staying at the time. He was a former boyfriend of hers. There were rumours of wild parties at Cliveden involving Cabinet ministers, call-girls, procurers and most significantly of all, Eugene Ivanov, a naval attaché at the Soviet Embassy in London. His grand title was a cover for his real job: spying. The fact was – although at first fiercely denied by Profumo – that he had had sex with Keeler, who was also sleeping with Ivanov. The implications of the Secretary of State for War sharing a prostitute with a Soviet spy were horrendous. But the patrician Prime Minister, Harold Macmillan, naively believed Profumo's lies. The papers were by no means so naive. Keeler was whisked off to hide herself in Spain during the Edgecombe trial, for fear, one assumes now, that she would compromise a lot of distinguished people if let loose in the witness box. It was probably very judicious of them to do that, although in the long run it probably did not make a lot of difference as the whole sordid story did eventually emerge. It was gripping stuff, which had, as I have mentioned, all the key elements which contribute to selling newspapers.

But the newspapers were trapped by what most journalists believed then and still believe now are draconian laws of defamation. But there are ways round these problems and what most of the newspapers did at this stage of the proceedings was to write stories about the disappearing model Christine

Keeler, without any reference to any involvement with John Profumo. And then write another story printed side by side with the first one about Profumo – written with great care and crawled over by the libel lawyers before appearing in print. These two stories, which to all intents and purposes had no connection, were nevertheless printed side by side on the front pages of most newspapers. The un-stated connection was their juxtaposition on the front pages. Readers could and did draw their own conclusions – and the conclusions they drew were correct, although these stories were 'safe' from a legal point of view. It was an ingenious way of frustrating the libel laws, and it all turned out to be true.

In the couple of months between Profumo's lying and threatening statement to the Commons and his subsequent admission that it was all a lie, I was given the task of following Profumo, who was usually with his beautiful wife, the actress Valerie Hobson, around the country on his official engagements, to see, along with other reporters on the same mission, whether Profumo would 'crack' in public. But he never did, not until he was questioned in private by the government whips, and as far as I can recall he barely spoke to this bedraggled travelling circus, of which I was a particularly bedraggled component, throughout that period.

One of the people who greatly helped the press throughout this astonishing affair was a Labour MP (he eventually became a minister in Harold Wilson's early administrations) called George Wigg, a shifty, sneaky untrustworthy individual (now dead), the carrier of tales to Harold Wilson. Anyway, George Wigg used every opportunity available to him to make insinuations about Profumo, although he of course had to be careful, too, about the libel laws, except when speaking in the House of Commons itself where there is absolute privilege. But even then he was likely to be stopped by the Speaker for referring to matters which were probably out of order in relation to what was being debated at that particular time. But he once brilliantly, I have to say, managed to get his message across. It was during a Commons committee debate about, of all things, a new type of sewage machinery. George Wigg said they could not conduct their business properly unless they had before them a model of the sewage machinery. That request was, of course, denied him, probably because no such model existed. But then, devilishly, he began to talk about missing models and would Spain be the best place to get hold of one. 'The trouble with this House,' he said, '[was] that we can never get to the truth of anything unless we have the models available. Where is this model?', he inquired. 'We need to have one in our midst immediately.' Everybody, not least the Committee chairman, knew what he was talking about but could not call him to order because, very cleverly, he had, to all intents and purposes, kept strictly in order. That committee contribution by George Wigg made all the front pages. We thought afterwards that it is not often that you go into a Commons Committee meeting expecting to come out with a front-page splash! This was an amazing story, which destroyed John Profumo, a man already tipped as a future Prime Minister.

He never uttered a word about the events afterwards but threw himself into good works, which earned him a CBE in 1975. It also destroyed the lives of others, notably Stephen Ward, the osteopath, who committed suicide, and Christine Keeler herself, who is still alive, a sad but rather dignified woman. I said that Profumo made no reference subsequently to the events which so dramatically brought him down. But he did, in fact, write a letter to a journalist, Matthew Parris, who in 1995 sought some information from him for a book he was writing, partly devoted to this affair. The journalist wanted to hear Profumo's own side of the story, which has never really been aired. But Profumo wrote back to him:

> Since 1963 there have been unceasing publications, both written and spoken, relating to what you refer to in your letter as 'the Keeler interlude'. The majority of these have increasingly contained deeply distressing inaccuracies, so I have resolved to refrain from any sort of personal comment, and I propose to continue thus. I hope, indeed believe, you will understand and acquit me of any discourtesy. (unpublished letter, shown to author)

What that means, I assume, is that Profumo will eventually follow his wife into the grave without ever having given his side of these remarkable events. That, sadly, will leave a great and unfillable gap in one of the most intriguing scandals of modern times. The Profumo affair was not only a personal tragedy for a whole host of people. It also spawned – not just in Britain but around the world – a veritable orgy of press speculation and innuendoes about tenuously related matters. It sparked off what is today termed 'a media frenzy', which needs to be nourished. In the United States' papers the scandal was being described as 'the sordid side of London's high society' and produced in the US papers stories, mostly uncorroborated rumour, of the most racy goings on in the upper reaches of society.

But one story which stuck, and which has not really been resolved to this day, is the allegation of the mysterious man in the mask. The story first saw the light of day in the *Washington Star* and was greedily pounced on by the papers in Britain and elsewhere. The claim was made by Mandy Rice-Davies, a bubbly blonde and a dominant figure in the Profumo affair. This is how the *Washington Star* reported the latest piece of juicy gossip.

> At Scotland Yard's request, Mandy cut short a continental holiday last month and came back to Britain. Newspapers said she was helping to uncover a top people's call-girl ring involving dozens of girls. Mandy herself said on June the First: 'I can say that probably a number of well-known people will be involved.' Mandy has talked of one gay little party she went to – that use of the word gay is not used in its modern connotation – where the host who opened the door wore nothing but his socks. 'Then', she said, 'there was a dinner party where a naked man wearing a mask waited on table like a slave. He had to have a mask because he was so well known.' (20 June 1963, p. 3)

You can imagine the flurry that caused. MPs, who always pretend they are above such frivolities and only interested in policies not personalities, were involved in a sordid guessing game. They assumed the man in the mask was one of their own. All sorts of names were bandied about, most of which failed to get into the newspapers because of the obvious libel risks if the name was wrong. One such name was Duncan Sandys, a prominent Cabinet member who subsequently became a peer and has since died. But there was no evidence at all. The *Daily Express* was the first which dared to allude to the story in this country. They quoted another unnamed guest at this bizarre party. It read:

> As the slave handed us cocktail snacks the guests abused and reviled him. He was obviously enjoying it. I was told by the host that the man arrived first at the party. He undressed and put on a mask before the other guests arrived. The host revealed his true identity to me. I could hardly believe it. I left after a few minutes. (21 June 1963, p. 1)

Then, three days later, the *Daily Mirror*'s front page screamed: 'Prince Philip and the Profumo Scandal'. Under the headline was a denial of a 'foul rumour' linking the Queen's husband to the affair. It is, of course, an old trick of the newspaper industry – a trick that still thrives today – to name someone in relation to a sordid story, by way of denying that person was ever involved. Some may regard these tactics as of dubious merit since, in this particular case, Philip's name had scurrilously been mentioned only in the hothouse of the bars of Parliament, with not the slightest inkling in the wider world, and the rumour was certainly untrue.

But if I may digress for a minute: newspapers have got into very hot water indeed, plus a considerable financial outlay, where their reports have been challenged successfully by people not even named in them. One celebrated – or rather notorious – example concerned a splash in the *Sunday Mirror* on 11 July 1964. This is what the paper said: 'Peer and a Gangster: Yard Probe Public Men at Seaside Parties'. And the front page of the newspaper alleged that Scotland Yard was investigating a homosexual relationship between a peer and a London thug. The following Sunday the same paper again splashed the story, claiming it had a photo: 'The Picture We Must Not Print', the paper trumpeted. In fact, a photograph did exist. It was of Ronnie Kray, who was a homosexual, and Lord Boothby together in Boothby's flat. But, according to contemporary sources, by not printing it the paper inflated its importance. Even so, I was in the House of Commons at the time and I do not recall anybody knowing who this 'mystery peer' was, even though the paper, somewhat sanctimoniously you might think, described the picture as 'of the highest significance and public concern'. Subsequent events suggested that that description of it all was not in the slightest degree valid. It was Boothby who in effect blew his own cover. He wrote an outraged letter to *The Times* on 31 May 1964, explaining everything. Kray, he conceded, had been to his flat to discuss a business arrangement, but nothing came of it and no deal was struck. Before he left, Kray, who enjoyed being photographed with the rich and famous, requested to have his picture taken with Boothby. The picture was accordingly taken. Later Boothby was to claim he had no knowledge of

Kray's gangster connections – he must have been the only man in the world who was so ignorant – and the sexual innuendo was also rebutted. However, the *Sunday Mirror* acknowledged there was no truth in the allegations and Boothby received what must have been the most spectacular apology in Fleet Street's history. It was a front-page splash, like the original allegations. The paper's editor was sacked and Boothby was paid £40,000 in compensation. I still wonder how it was that a paper so meekly forked out so much money to a man whose name, in this connection, was unknown to the world at large. But clearly it was the case that the *Mirror* feared much greater expense if the matter had gone before a court, which Boothby plainly would have done if the paper had not caved in so quickly. When political scandals occur, newspapers always have to be wary about breaking codes of conduct in relation to privacy and also about breaking the law of trespass.

Most politicians, of whom Tony Blair is currently a prime example, make great show about protecting their families from press attentions, which is fair enough. However some of this so-called protection seems to be somewhat over the top. For instance, Blair has been almost obsessed with stopping press photographers taking pictures of the baby. Once there was a huge complaint from Downing Street because pictures were taken of the Prime Minister carrying the infant along a public place. I think most people treated that complaint with the derision it deserved. However, when it comes to public and political scandals, when a politician gets into hot water, they invariably assume double standards about their families. Politicians are only too ready to use – I would go so far as to say 'exploit' – their families when it comes to photographs, for instance on their general election literature. In other words they use their families to help them get elected into Parliament. However, when there is trouble brewing, suddenly the politicians' families are supposed to be 'off limits'. Most journalists – and I count myself among them – take the view, which some people might regard as unfair, but which I do not, that if a politician exposes his family on his election addresses, then that family can be regarded as fair game when things go wrong. Sometimes politicians will do it themselves during a crisis, and wheel out their families for public viewing.

This happened, notoriously, when David Mellor, the former Secretary of State for Heritage (he called it the 'Ministry of Fun'; I call it the 'Ministry of Free Tickets') was caught up in a sex scandal involving an out-of-work actress. He was alleged to have been wearing a Chelsea football strip at the time, a sartorial detail that has never been officially confirmed. When things got hot for Mr Mellor, when the paparazzi were dogging his every footstep, he chose the line of least resistance and produced his entire family at what looked like a farm gate, demonstrating to the world at large that here was a family in total unity. To be frank, it looked terrible. It was contrived, the smiles were false and most people were amazed that a man of Mr Mellor's undoubted intelligence could for a minute have thought anybody would take this picture seriously. It was so crudely contrived that even Mr Mellor's mother-in-law rapped his knuckles over it. The rest is history. Not long after this – incidentally,

Mr Mellor had to resign from his Cabinet post – he left his family. And at the subsequent general election he lost his seat. It has always been a source of wonder to me that politicians, not only Mr Mellor, believe that such pictures will be regarded by the newspaper reading public at large as spontaneous. Their naivete is breathtaking. The pictures just look like what they are: cynically contrived.

Another example of this was over the BSE scandal a few years ago. The then Minister of Agriculture, John Gummer, arranged a photo-opportunity (a euphemism for 'show me in the nicest possible light') of him looking suspiciously as though – although it cannot be true – he was force-feeding a beef-burger down the gullet of his offspring. Mr Gummer is an intelligent man, so I am baffled that he should have dreamt up this ludicrous image. Perhaps he was the victim of his ministerial spin-doctors – a body to be avoided at all costs. Whoever was to blame for this, the effect is to make the politician involved look even more ridiculous than he normally does. This is a case of politicians in trouble using the press to make fools of themselves, to put it bluntly.

Another massive political scandal, which brought about the downfall of one of the most talented and amusing politicians of his day, was the Jeremy Thorpe affair. He was, when the scandal started to emerge into the daylight, leader of the then small but voluble Liberal Party in the House of Commons. If Thorpe had belonged to any other party, he would surely have been a candidate for Prime Minister, such an outstanding political figure was he. It was, not for the first time and almost certainly not for the last time, the press which gradually started to unearth this scandal, which involved allegations of conspiracy to murder, homosexuality, blackmail, and even teeth-marks on Thorpe's desk in the House of Commons.

The whole affair had an extremely bizarre beginning. A sharp-eyed political reporter, perusing the daily list of parliamentary questions that have been tabled, spotted a strange one. The MP, Sir Robin Maxwell-Hyslop, from the West Country, had asked what the police were doing about the case of a dog, called Rinka, which had been shot dead on Exmoor. The question looked innocent, but it was to have horrendous consequences, which few people could have envisaged at the time. The reporter contacted Sir Robin who indicated to him that there was far more to this question than simply a dead dog on Exmoor. The story appeared, but it was written, naturally, in a very guarded manner, spattered with qualifying get-out phrases like, 'It is understood . . .' and 'It is alleged . . .'. But the very caution with which the story was written immediately alerted the world to the fact that there was a lot more here than met the eye.

It all revolved around a claim by one Norman Scott, a male model, and incidentally the owner of the dead dog, that he was in fear of his life because he was writing a book about an alleged homosexual affair between himself and Mr Thorpe. An airline pilot called Newton was given a two-year prison sentence for shooting the dog, claiming that he had done so because Scott was blackmailing him. Thorpe denied the whole story, but he and three other men were eventually tried for conspiracy to murder Scott. They were all subsequently acquitted. But it marked the end of Thorpe's political career. He had already lost his North Devon seat to the Conservatives in the run-up to the trial and emerged from the affair a broken and sick man. But it was once again the press that played a massive role in uncovering this scandal. The more newspapers inquired into it, the murkier it seemed to become. The affair was complicated and serpentine. But there was a bombshell when Newton, the pilot, came out of prison – all this was well before the trial started. Newton went straight to the London *Evening News*, which paid him £3,000 for the story which was head-lined: 'I was paid to kill Scott'. Then, the *Sunday People* capped that by paying Newton a further £8,000 for secret photographs, allegedly showing Newton being paid the £5,000 hit-man fee by a businessman, who ultimately finished up in the dock with Thorpe. But then – here was the media being involved again – Thorpe disastrously held a press conference to deny any suggestion of a murder plot, which was now the rumour buzzing round Westminster. He admitted to reporters at one of the tensest press conferences I have ever attended, that even if he had had a 'close, even affectionate' friendship with Scott it had been non-sexual. Then a BBC reporter, Keith Graves, asked the question which had to be asked but which most reporters, me included, were too nervous to ask. It was whether he had ever had a homosexual relation-ship. Thorpe was furious. He replied: 'If you do not know why it is improper and indecent to put such a question to a public man you ought not to be here.' But that was it. Thorpe had put his own sexuality back on the agenda. At the trial, the judge ripped Scott apart in his summing up. 'A crook, an accom-plished liar, a fraud, a sponger, a whiner, a parasite, spineless, neurotic and hysterical.' Marvellous front-page headline words and the papers had a feast with them the following day.

And although the Jeremy Thorpe case involved allegations of grave crimes – allegations that were all thrown out – in many cases, I have to say, what amount to petty peccadilloes by politicians, are somehow grotesquely blown up out of all proportion. I refer to conduct which in 'ordinary' people would barely raise an eyebrow. It was Bernard Shaw who summed it up beautifully when he said that Britain had produced thousands of blameless greengrocers but never a blameless monarch. I myself am as guilty as any on this issue. When what looks like being a marvellous story begins to emerge, journalists, me included, tend to lose a sense of proportion. We regard politicians as fair game if they step out of line. They are constantly preaching at us, so, if they err, then they get what they deserve. Time and again you get MPs delivering moral-istic speeches in the House of Commons, and then jumping into a mistress's bed the following day. It deserves exposure. Some editors defend their muck-raking tactics – and there is sometimes nothing wrong with muck-raking – by saying that what is uncovered is in the public interest. Well, most people are not so naive as to believe that is the truth, the whole truth, and nothing but the truth. Most newspapers regard themselves as being part of the entertainment industry and editors would probably earn more respect if they admitted that their inquiries were aimed not so much at performing a public service, as producing a humdinger of a story adding thousands to circulation. There was a Conservative MP called David Ashby who lost a bitter, even traumatic, libel action against the *Sunday Times*. The case revolved around Ashby's sexual proclivities and had the effect of polarising, indeed poisoning, the relationship between himself and his wife. Afterwards Mr Ashby summed it all up in one bitter sentence: 'For the press it was sport but for me it was my very soul.' One can hardly fail to be moved by those words of a man who was, as a result, financially ruined and his family torn asunder. It is possibly a dreadful thing to say, but I still cannot divorce myself from the journalists' buzz that politicians are fair game even for the machinations of Fleet Street.

Note

1 This is an edited transcript of the keynote speech delivered by the author at the conference, 'Political Scandals, Past and Present' held at the University of Salford, 21–23 June 2001. We have produced it more or less as given because of the insight it offers into the journalist's world, particularly into their fascination and delight in scandal and gossip.

References

Ingham, B. (1991), *Kill the Messenger*, London, HarperCollins.
Wodehouse, P. G. (1924), *The Inimitable Jeeves*, London, Herbert Jenkins.

5

'Keeping the bastards honest': Australia and the investigation of political scandal[1]

Jenny Fleming

Australia is no stranger to political scandal. Its history is littered with examples of misappropriation of public funds, vote buying, bribery, conflicts of interest and administrative corruption (Tiffen, 1999). While British political scandals arise out of politicians' sex lives and espionage (or a mixture of both), and France and the US 'more closely associate scandal with more serious criminal actions' (Barker, 1992: 4, 27), in Australia the dominant characteristic of the political scandal is the probity of politicians, that is, the perceived abuse of political power for personal gain.

This recurring motif in Australia's political scandals has raised particular concern in the past two decades as accountability and transparency in public life have come to dominate the way we think about governance and political activity. A number of official inquiries have exposed political corruption and serious misconduct within the country's political institutions (for example, Fitzgerald, 1989; Wood, 1997; see also Tiffen, 1999: 93–113). Following these inquiries and the accompanying public outrage, a number of strategies have been put in place to ensure conformity and encourage accountability and transparency in public life. It is hoped that these strategies will reduce levels of political transgression and subsequent scandal and counter declining public confidence in politicians (Fleming and Holland, 2001; Jackson and Smith, 1995; McAllister, 2000; Walsh and Richardson, 1995).

This chapter is concerned with political scandal in Australia, how it emerges and how it develops and unfolds. It looks at the role of the media and that of independent oversight bodies in the perpetuation of scandal. The chapter examines the emergence, in Queensland, in the late 1980s, of a political scandal that continued to reverberate well into the 1990s. The scandal was such that a government was brought down and parliamentarians and senior public figures imprisoned. The inquiry that followed, its subsequent findings and its institutional solution combined to change the way government was conducted and the way its activities would be monitored. The introduction of external, independent oversight bodies whose mandate extended to members of Parliament and local government officials has changed the nature of political scandal in Queensland. The investigative activity of such bodies has ensured that political transgressions are now almost inevitably played out in the public arena. They are less likely to be covered up, swept under the carpet or glossed over by spin-doctors. As a result the original scandal is inevitably heightened.

In the search for alternative means of investigating political misconduct and 'keeping the bastards honest', the creation of external independent oversight bodies has had an unintended consequence. Given the scandalous findings of the Fitzgerald Inquiry, the operations of the institution established to monitor Queensland's public life were always going to attract media attention. Any investigation involving politicians or senior public figures would ensure a 'scandal' regardless of the substance or veracity of the allegations. In short, the very existence of the investigative body made scandals ever-more likely to emerge. Indeed, as this chapter demonstrates, the institution itself became the subject of scandal.

Further, with the usual, predictable and enthusiastic attention of the media to all things political, the scandals 'develop a life and momentum of their own which are hard to extinguish or deflect' (Williams, 1998: 1). The ramifications of this for the standing of politicians and political institutions generally are discussed at the end of the chapter. Before turning to the original scandal and the sequence of action and events that followed, some grasp of the term political scandal is needed.

What are political scandals?

Markovits and Silverstein (1998: 6) argue that the defining feature of political scandal is 'a violation of due process' in the pursuit of power in a liberal democratic system. Lowi (1998: viii) makes a distinction between a 'substantive' or initial scandal and a 'procedural scandal' whereby the original scandal is overshadowed by the 'cover up' that follows the initial allegations. This is a particular feature of political scandal. Others have noted the indisputable presence of 'moral transgression' in any discussion of scandal but have added several caveats to define the term more explicitly. Thus scandal involves transgressions of society's values, norms and moral codes and has an element of secrecy (Thompson, 2000: 13–14). Most agree that what constitutes scandal is a 'function of time and place and culture-bound' (King, 1984: 4), and that it involves both the scandal and the response to it (Tiffen, 1999: 11). In Australia's case, William's (1998: 6–7) definition of political scandal is perhaps helpful as an initial starting point:

> A political scandal involves a departure or lapse from the normative standards that guide behaviour in public office. It may or may not involve unlawful conduct . . . It is thus not the conduct itself but its relation to a public role and the attendant expectations of that role which matter. Scandals involve damage to reputation and conduct which is perceived to disgrace a public office or position in society.

Yet a scandal is not merely a lapse or departure from accepted values. A scandal evolves. It is carried by its own momentum, with regular influxes of new information and suitable proclamations of indignation from prominent public figures and the media. A key but not essential element is also the potential for an individual or group of individuals to be discredited publicly. The more powerful the individual or group the more interesting the scandal. A political scandal becomes important to the political process when it involves 'intense and extensive media coverage, committees or commissions of inquiry and the appointment of special prosecutors or independent counsel' (Williams, 1998: 9). The political scandal in Queensland incorporated all these elements and provides a classic example of how scandals emerge and unfold in response to the dynamics of the political environment.

The emerging scandal: the Fitzgerald Inquiry

In 1987, the state of Queensland in Australia had been governed by a conservative rural-based National–Liberal coalition for thirty years. Unlike other Australian states it had no upper house of review; parliament met infrequently; the political opposition was irrelevant and seemingly powerless against the state's 'gerrymander' system; senior police officers were extremely influential in the highest political circles; trade unions were abhorred; public protest was illegal, and the state's media were passive (see Whitrod, 2001: 141, 155). In May of that year, the national broadcaster televised a documentary airing allegations that Queensland's police force was engaged in illegal activity. In the absence of the Premier, the Deputy Premier established an official inquiry, which it was suggested would run for approximately six weeks.

Queenslanders had few expectations about the impact of the latest inquiry into police corruption. In the previous twenty-five years there had been four such inquiries, all characterised by what Lewis (1999: 122) calls 'illusions of action'. Each time, the government had effectively 'neutralised' the inquiries – through 'limiting the terms of reference', establishing 'bureaucratic committees' to consider their findings, and effectively ignoring and/or rejecting recommendations (Prasser cited in Lewis, 1999: 122). These previous unsatisfactory outcomes did not bode well for yet another inquiry, regardless of whether or not the Premier was out of Australia at the time.

Public sittings for the inquiry began in July and the Police Commissioner took the stand. He told the inquiry that he had been instructed by police ministers and the Premier that policing vice (prostitution, gambling) was to be given a low priority and run in a 'tolerable manner'. Other senior police officers confirmed his story. The inquiry, which eventually ran for two years, unfolded like a soap opera. The long-standing inappropriate relationship between the government and its police force was exposed. Several senior police officers resigned after confessing to taking bribes and running what were known as SP (special price) betting scams. The illegal running of brothels and massage parlours was revealed, as were money laundering and protection rackets (Lewis, 1999: 124).

The Fitzgerald Inquiry also exposed anomalies in political donations, the exaggeration of ministerial expenses, unacceptable public sector employment practices and deliberate manipulation of the electoral system. Many of the key individuals known to have played a central role in corruption were given conditional indemnity (Fitzgerald, 1989: 127–45). By the end of the Inquiry, the Premier had resigned in disgrace as had the Police Commissioner (he was eventually tried for corruption and jailed for fourteen years); four ministers were in jail and others were awaiting investigation. A change of government for the first time in thirty-two years was virtually inevitable (see Dickie, 1989).

The Queensland media, once noted for its 'attitude of timidity' and inclination to 'report other peoples' lies' rather than 'engage in real investigative journalism' and face the state's strict defamation laws (Grundy, 1990; Dickie, 1990), had feasted well on one of the biggest political scandals in Queensland's and Australia's history. Daily newspaper reports from the inquiry, hourly television bulletins, current affairs programmes, regular public rulings and remarks from the Commissioner himself, and significant academic interest, all ensured that the foundation for continuing scandal had been laid.

The apparent solution: the Criminal Justice Commission

The misuse of the state's political institutions evoked an institutional response from Commissioner Fitzgerald. This, it could be argued, was characteristic of a Westminster approach, where the use of institutions and rules is traditionally perceived as the solution to policy problems. Among other proposals, Fitzgerald recommended the establishment of an independent body, the Criminal Justice Commission (CJC), 'permanently charged with monitoring, reviewing, co-ordinating, and initiating reform of the administration of criminal justice' (Fitzgerald, 1989: 308). The CJC was to be accountable to a bi-partisan Parliamentary Criminal Justice Committee (PCJC) whose function was to monitor and review the operations and expenditure of the newly created Commission. It reported directly to Parliament (Lewis, 1999: 144).

The CJC's mandate extended to members of the state's Legislative Assembly, the Parliamentary Service, the Executive Council and local government members and officials. Recognising the potential for conflict between the newly established body and the parliamentary machinery that would establish it, the report emphasised the need for the 'exclusion or reduction of party political considerations and processes from the decision-making process' with respect to the CJC:

> executive authority and connection with the CJC must be limited to what is necessary to finance it, provide administrative and resource needs, and that necessary for public financial and other accounting purposes. For those purposes, and not otherwise, a Minister should be responsible for the CJC. (Fitzgerald, 1989: 309)

Yet it was the capacity of this newly established independent commission to investigate and review the parliamentary executive that 'marked [it] out for a troubled existence in post-Fitzgerald Queensland politics' (Wanna, 1991: 223).

The relationship between the inaugural Chair of the CJC, Sir Max Bingham, appointed by a government disgraced by scandal, and the newly elected Labor government was under constant strain. Perceiving the CJC as an unconstitutional interference with the traditional Westminster system of government, where ministers are held accountable for their departments solely by Parliament, the new Labor government resented the fact that the CJC reported directly to Parliament, bypassing the 'authority and influence of the executive' (Lewis, 1999: 152). In 1991, the CJC announced its intention to use its powers to investigate the ethical behaviour of ministers and parliamentarians in the use of travel entitlements.

The sign of things to come: the travel entitlement investigation

The CJC's first investigation was conducted retrospectively and involved prominent political figures, some of whom were now ministers in the new Labor government. The government was publicly committed to ethical reform and the implementation of Fitzgerald's recommendations. It was a government the CJC should have been able to rely on for support. It was not to be. The investigation took over a year to complete (CJC, 1991) largely because of the reluctance of Labor politicians to be investigated by an external and independent body.

The protracted and public nature of the inquiry ensured that the original parameters within which the 'travel entitlements scandal' developed were considerably enhanced by the continued focus on the role of the CJC as a new 'accountability' institution and the government's response to its inquiry. Some of the initial delay was due to the Auditor General's insistence that the CJC produce an authority from the Supreme Court prior to his releasing documentation. Under the Criminal Justice Act, the Auditor General was not bound by the Financial Administration and Audit Act and according to the Commission his 'well-intentioned' caution was costly and time consuming (CJC, 1991: 10–11).

Parliamentarians spoke publicly about what they perceived as the CJC's illegitimate foray into the way elected officials conducted their affairs. Rumours that Bingham had received many 'distinctly menacing' telephone calls advising him of the vulnerability of the Commission if the investigation continued (Walker, 1995: 173) fuelled what was until then a relatively minor scandal involving parliamentarians, many of whom were associated with the previously disgraced Conservative government.

To add to the public interest, thirty-seven members of the new parliament refused voluntarily to relinquish travel records and other documentation to the CJC on the grounds that information would be leaked to the media. As a result, the CJC had to exercise its legislative powers to obtain the information it required (CJC, 1991: 51–3). Not only was there a disinclination to proffer information, there was also some reluctance to attend hearings. Of thirteen members called to an investigative hearing, one had to be officially summoned by the Commission (CJC, 1991: 54). Under the Criminal Justice Act, a witness may object to answering questions on the grounds that it may incriminate him/her. If such an objection occurs, the information furnished is 'not admissible in evidence against the person or witness in civil or criminal proceedings in a court'. Of the fifteen individuals questioned, seven chose to take advantage of this protection (CJC, 1991: 55) much to the public's outrage. Media coverage of these incidents did much to augment the seriousness of the scandal.

Given the volume of travel claims, the CJC restricted its investigation to daily travelling allowances. But the lack of records and documentation was a problem: records had not been kept and where there had been notations there was too little information to investigate. No one wanted to talk to the CJC, rendering the investigative body incapable of effective investigation (Fleming, 2001: 131–2).

Legal experts advised the CJC that the lack of guidelines and paperwork relating to travel entitlements would diminish the likelihood of successful criminal proceedings. As a result, anonymous case studies were used in the report rather than names (CJC, 1991: vii–viii). But in the public arena, names were soon attached to cases. Several ministers were forced to resign and relations between the CJC and politicians became extremely sensitive (Walker, 1995: 173–80). Politicians from both sides of Parliament decried the 'unprofessional, subjective, sloppy, judgmental, and pathetic travel entitlements' report (cited in Lewis, 1999: 155).

A political power game was played out in the press as the government sought to assert its authority and remind the CJC of its vulnerability. The deteriorating relationship between the government and the CJC illustrated the difficulties for an external oversight body investigating its master. More significantly, its early investigative attempts demonstrated how its controversial existence and the public manner in which its inquiries were conducted would shape and determine the nature of the investigation and, inevitably, the ensuing scandal.

The adverse findings of the report on parliamentary travel entitlements, coming so soon after the revelations of the Fitzgerald Inquiry, undermined the government's dismissive comments about the CJC's handling of the investigation. If there was any intention to act on what the CJC had perceived as the government's intimidating threats, the investigation's findings, the high media profile of the CJC and its apparently strong community support ensured that any 'government action was kept in check by the weight of public opinion' (Lewis, 1999: 155).

At the end of the day, the scandal became the relationship between the Labor government and the institution established to monitor and investigate political transgressions. The issue of travel entitlements paled into insignificance, as the CJC itself became the main player. Five years later in its inquiry into another alleged political transgression, this time dealing with a Conservative government, the CJC once again found itself part of the problem rather than the solution, engendering another scandal of far greater proportions.

The Mundingburra by-election: the saga continues

In February 1996 a by-election was held in Mundingburra in North Queensland. Given the marginal Labor win a few months earlier, the election would decide whether or not the Labor government retained office. The Queensland Police Union (QPU), an organisation cited by Fitzgerald in 1989 in connection with its unseemly influence and inappropriate relationship with the National–Liberal coalition government (1989: 280), campaigned in the election for more police, using television and newspaper advertising to promote its cause and taking advantage of contemporary law-and-order debates. The by-election delivered state government to the coalition that had been at the centre of the Fitzgerald Inquiry nine years earlier.

Within weeks of the new government taking office, a member of the QPU revealed publicly that the organisation had signed a Memorandum of Understanding (MoU) with the soon-to-be-appointed Police Minister and the incoming Premier limiting the power of the CJC in its dealings with the state's police service and giving the QPU more influence in the management of the Queensland Police Service. Given the findings of the Fitzgerald Inquiry and its observations about the unacceptable relationship between the QPU and the parliamentary executive, the media and the political opposition insisted that the new Police Minister forward the MoU to the CJC for further investigation. Seven years on, the reverberations of the Fitzgerald Inquiry were about to be publicly revisited.

Obliged to investigate, the CJC engaged a retired Supreme Court Judge from another Australian state, Ken Carruthers QC, to conduct an inquiry into the events that had led up to the signing of the MoU. Each major player, including the Premier, the Police Minister and the Police Union executive, had independent counsel. It was the beginning of another major scandal involving the CJC, its relationship with the government and the nature of its business. Once again, the substantive scandal would be lost in the procedural scandal involving the government's response to the allegations.

Throughout the Carruthers Inquiry (CJC, 1996),[2] the government attacked the CJC, particularly once Carruthers began to speculate publicly on the inappropriate activities of the Premier, Rob Borbidge, and the Police Minister, Russell Cooper. The government appeared to retaliate by reducing the CJC's operational budget by $2.7 million, or approximately 10 per cent. As a result, a number of staff were laid off (CJC, 1996–97: 3). The government's action was a reminder of the oversight body's political vulnerability. For the government the unethical conduct of one or more of its members was not the only issue at stake, the loss of government was a real possibility.

Midway into the inquiry, a parliamentary member of the coalition accused one of the CJC's senior officials of leaking sensitive information to the federal parliament. On the basis of these allegations the government announced, somewhat farcically, an inquiry into the CJC and the allegations – an inquiry that would include an investigation of Carruthers' Inquiry. Carruthers resigned in protest and the CJC was obliged to rely on two barristers to collate the existing evidence to provide a report. As the MoU had not given anyone concerned any tangible benefits, the barristers absolved the Premier, the Police Minister and the Police Union executive of any illegality (CJC, 1996). In many ways it was an anti-climax to what had been the sequel to Fitzgerald and the travel entitlements investigation of 1991. Yet the scandal that was developing was just emerging.

The government's attack on the CJC continued. The inquiry into the CJC became known as the Connolly–Ryan Inquiry after its investigators. The choice of Peter Connolly was surprising. The former Liberal parliamentarian and Queensland Supreme Court judge had acted as advisor to the Police Minister on the MoU some months earlier. Connolly's overtly political comments in the press, and his erratic behaviour and sporadic outbursts during the hearings, prompted the CJC to commence Supreme Court action to stop the inquiry on the grounds of bias (Smith, 2000). The Court found in favour of the CJC and the inquiry was terminated in August 1997.

The investigation had taken over eighteen months. The government's attempts to conceal, deny, justify, mitigate and shift the onus of responsibility for its behaviour contributed to the scandal that unfolded so dramatically in Queensland in this period. Played out in the public arena, once again the resulting scandal became more important than the original indiscretion. Once again the politicians had placed themselves in an unfavourable light. Enraged by the CJC's ability to investigate individuals in the Queensland parliament seemingly without restraint, and undaunted by the public's sense of outrage, the government deemed it an auspicious time to provide some legislative restraint on the organisation it had created from the Fitzgerald blueprint.

And still the story unfolds: the Criminal Justice Amendment Act

In September 1997 the coalition introduced a Bill to amend the Criminal Justice Act. The Bill strengthened the PCJC's role, increased ministerial control over the organisation's budget and introduced a permanent commission of inquiry in the shape of a PCJC Commissioner. Once again there was considerable moral outrage because of the perception that the government was using its political power for personal gain. The media, the political opposition and the public generally particularly resented the perceived attack on the CJC's independence (Clair, 1997; Hansard, 1997; Homel, 1997).

Under the new legislation, the PCJC assumed a more significant directive and decision-making role. Its monitoring and reviewing powers were extended to include the issuing of mandatory guidelines and policy directions to the CJC.

It could now order the CJC to initiate and pursue specific investigations into any conduct or activities of CJC members or staff. The all-party Scrutiny of Legislation Committee, the Labor Opposition, the CJC's Commissioner, Frank Clair, and the Queensland Law Commission all expressed concern about the PCJC assuming an 'executive role . . . in circumstances where it itself is not accountable to the parliament . . . through the processes of ministerial responsibility' (Hansard, 1997: 3885–6, 4012). The Law Society put it more bluntly and observed, 'to give the power of direction to the parliamentary committee would enable politicians to use the CJC to target persons or groups in the community' (Hansard, 1997: 4013).

Moreover, the PCJC would now handle all complaints against the CJC and exercise a power of veto over legal practitioners working on behalf of the organisation. It would be able to inspect and copy all operational material (including that gathered using listening devices) for information purposes, and would have the power to order the CJC to surrender confidential information when requested.

The Act directed that the CJC obtain the minister's approval for any changes relating to wages, allowances, conditions of employment, promotion and salaries. The minister could now legitimately request details of proposed and actual expenditure by the Commission. Clearly, under the proposed legislation, the minister was in a position whereby s/he could exercise considerable control over the CJC's exercise of its investigative powers. As Frank Clair (1997) pointed out: 'this legislation has the potential to destroy the effective operation of the CJC. It will be impossible to recruit persons of integrity and ability to serve under such conditions, impossible to ensure that the hard decisions are made in future without fear, favour or an eye to avoiding unfair investigation.'

For an organisation designed to be independent of political intervention, the proposals were undeniably intrusive and were considered scandalous in the context of the state's recent political history.

The final indignity: the Office of the Parliamentary Criminal Justice Commissioner

The legislation established the office of a Parliamentary Commissioner (PC) as a standing Commission of Inquiry. Its comprehensive powers included the power to audit records and activities of the CJC and to investigate complaints against the CJC referred to it by the PCJC. Its investigations however could only be triggered by a request of a bi-partisan majority of members of the PCJC.[3] The PC would have full access to information, including the records of the discredited Connolly–Ryan Inquiry. Under the legislation, information held by the CJC could be directed back to the PCJC by the PC for re-evaluation. Given the history of the Connolly–Ryan Inquiry and the Supreme Court's judgement of bias, this seemed singularly inappropriate.

The CJC was concerned about the loss of legal rights of CJC Commissioners and staff generally. In a submission to the Attorney General, the CJC pointed out that the legislation left it with little entitlement to judicial review or other legal rights that would protect it from excessive enthusiasm on the part of the PC (Homel, 1997).

The PC could decide whether the CJC was exercising its powers appropriately or even whether matters already under investigation were 'appropriate to be investigated by the CJC'. The PC could also, on the advice of the PCJC, target the CJC for what could be a purely political investigation. As one CJC part-time Commissioner observed, 'the investigation of government politicians will be very difficult' (Homel, 1997).

This was obviously the government's intent. The government itself did little to persuade observers otherwise. The Minister for Transport questioned the independence of Carruthers during parliamentary debate and suggested that the Carruthers Inquiry 'was a vendetta against the coalition'. The opposition welcomed the minister's interjection because, 'that is precisely the view which has prompted the government to bring in the legislation . . . the CJC [would] pay a very high price for [its] audacity in investigating Premier Borbidge and Police Minister Cooper' (Hansard, 1997: 3880–2). Whatever the reasoning, the legislation clearly restricted the CJC's activities, diminished its credibility as an independent organisation and severely impeded its ability to investigate politicians. In Labor's words, the CJC had been 'neutered' (Hansard, 1997: 3919). The scandal had come full circle.

Labor was re-elected to the Queensland parliament in 1998. There was no attempt to restore the CJC to its former standing. The new government had other priorities and had no wish to re-ignite the CJC story. In January 2002, the CJC merged with the Queensland Crime Commission,[4] and the Crime and Misconduct Commission was created. Under the provisions of the Crime and Misconduct Act 2001, the new Commission focuses on reducing major crime in Queensland, reducing 'the incidence of misconduct in the Queensland public sector' and generally raising the standards of integrity in the public service.

Conclusion

What do these stories tell us about how and why scandals unfold? Thompson (2000: 266–7) has suggested 'the best way to respond to political scandals is to create more openness and accountability in government'. Yet, as this chapter has demonstrated, openness and transparency can have unintended and unwelcome consequences. The history of the CJC, in an environment of public disenchantment with political institutions, suggests several conclusions about political scandal in Australia.

First, its controversial existence ensured that any issue the CJC investigated, especially when explicitly associated with political institutions and politicians, was likely to become a scandal. The fact that the CJC was involved rendered the matter scandalous so far as both public and politicians were concerned (regardless of the salience of any allegation). The CJC's job was to identify and investigate inappropriate behaviour. Its investigations were followed diligently by the media and academics alike and ensured the visibility of issues that previously may have had little impact on the public agenda. Freedom of information legislation and easier access to public information (for example via the Internet) makes media coverage easier, more thorough and continuous. In the manner of a good soap opera, the public is fed titbits of information on a regular basis. Letters to the editors of local newspapers and responses to talk-back radio indicate the level of interest excited by such scandal and by the media's efforts to perpetuate and fuel such interest.

Why the particular scandal originating in 1987 with the Fitzgerald Inquiry managed continuously to unfold in the way it did is more complex. First, the concept of independent external oversight bodies is considered controversial. They are conceived, in true Westminster tradition and in the midst of political crisis and a rush of enthusiasm, as a solution for accountability and transparency in public life. In a political environment embracing reform no one can disagree with its fundamental logic. Yet, as their investigators move to identify political transgression and investigate the activities of politicians, enthusiasm wanes and hostility emerges. It is bi-partisan hostility. It is not confined to Labor or non-Labor political parties, but is a common response to the notion that an external watchdog should have the autonomy to question the motives of elected parliamentary representatives, a notion fundamentally at odds with politicians' understanding of the Westminster tradition of parliamentary responsibility. So the very idea of independent scrutiny provokes confrontation and discord.

Second, the CJC's existence and autonomy, the parameters within which it operated and the ways in which governments systematically sought to evade its authority when under scrutiny, provided the basis for fresh scandals whenever it embarked on an investigation into alleged parliamentary transgressions. So much so that often the original transgression became less scandalous than the environment that developed around the CJC in its attempts to investigate it. This conundrum besets external independent oversight bodies like the CJC. The mechanism established to police and investigate political transgression inevitably becomes the focus of controversy and the cause of further scandals. The mechanism of probity becomes the feeder of scandal. Thus scandal evolves.

What are the repercussions for political life of the continuous friction and scandal that accompanies efforts to increase the level of probity in politicians? It was mentioned earlier in this chapter that politicians are increasingly seen as self-serving; more concerned with feathering their own nests than fulfilling their fiduciary duty to act as trustees for the people (McAllister and Wanna, 2001: 7–35). They are a group of people whose value systems are perceived to be increasingly at odds with those expected by the community. Indeed, it has been argued that the creation of institutions like the CJC was a specific attempt 'to shape and constrain the behaviour of individuals and perhaps the values of political actors' (Lewis and Fleming, 2003).

In an environment where there is declining public confidence in political institutions and those that serve them (Fleming and Holland, 2001; Mancuso, 1998; McAllister, 2000; Rosenthal, 1998; Walsh and Richardson, 1995) each new scandal confirms the prevailing view that the honesty and ethics of parliamentarians is 'only slightly better than those of car salesman' (Roy Morgan, 1998). Reforms that seek to reverse the trend, and raise the bar simply accelerate the decline in public confidence. At its simplest, even crudest, it is people that count, not institutions, and the politicians have not been willing to meet public expectations.

Notes

1 'Keeping the Bastards Honest' was the widely cited political slogan of the Australian Democrat Party in the 1980s. A minority party, often holding the balance of power in the Senate, the slogan reflected the Party's perceived role.
2 The following account is drawn from Fleming (2001).
3 The original Bill suggested that the majority decision would only need to come from government members of the PCJC. The Opposition successfully amended the clause at the Committee stage.
4 The Queensland Crime Commission was established by the Crime Commission Act 1997 to investigate major and organised crime and allegations of paedophilia.

References

Barker, A. (1992), 'The Upturned Stone: Political Scandals in Twenty Democracies and their Investigation Processes', Essex Papers in Politics and Government no. 92, University of Essex.

Criminal Justice Commission [CJC] (1991), 'Report of an Investigation into Possible Misuse of Parliamentary Travel Entitlements by Members of the 1986–1989 Queensland Legislative Assembly', Brisbane, CJC.

CJC (1996), 'Report of an Investigation into a Memorandum of Understanding between the Coalition and the QPUE and an Investigation into an Alleged deal between the ALP and the SSAA', Brisbane.

CJC (1996–7), 'Criminal Justice Commission Annual Report Summary', Brisbane.

Clair, F. (1997), 'Clair condemns move to reincarnate the Connelly-Ryan inquiry', Criminal Justice Commission Press Release, 12 October, cited: http://cjc.qld.gov.au/cjc/1210medi.shtml.

Dickie, P. (1989), *The Road to Fitzgerald and Beyond*, St. Lucia, University of Queensland Press.

Dickie, P. (1990), 'The Media: A Lot to Answer For', in S. Prasser, R. Wear and J. Nethercote (eds), *Corruption and Reform: The Fitzgerald Vision*, St. Lucia, University of Queensland Press.

Fitzgerald, G. E. (1989), 'Report of a Commission of an Inquiry Pursuant to Orders in Council: Commission of Inquiry into Possible Illegal Activities and Associated Police Misconduct', Government Printer, Brisbane.

Fleming, J. (2001), 'Conduct Unbecoming: Independent Commissions and Ministerial Adversaries', in J. Fleming and I. Holland (eds), *Motivating Ministers to Morality*, Aldershot, Ashgate.

Fleming, J. and I. Holland (eds) (2001), *Motivating Ministers to Morality*, Aldershot, Ashgate.

Grundy, B. (1990), 'Who Sets the News Agenda: The Turkeys or the Chooks?', in S. Prasser, R. Wear and J. Nethercote (eds), *Corruption and Reform: The Fitzgerald Vision*, St. Lucia, University of Queensland Press.

Hansard (1997), *Queensland Parliamentary Debates*, Brisbane, Government Printer.

Homel, R. (1997), *Political Control of the Queensland Criminal Justice Commission*, Brisbane, CJC.

Jackson, M. and R. Smith (1995), 'Everyone's Doing It! Codes of Ethics and New South Wales Parliamentarians' Perceptions of Corruption', *Australian Journal of Public Administration*, 54: 4, 483–93.

King, A. (1984), 'Sex, Money and Power: Political Scandals in Great Britain and the United States', Essex Papers in Politics and Government no. 14, University of Essex.

Lewis, C. (1999), *Complaints against Police: The Politics of Reform*, Sydney, Hawkins Press.

Lewis, C. and J. Fleming (2003), 'The Everyday Politics of Value Conflict: External Independent Oversight Bodies in Australia', in I. Holland and J. Fleming (eds), *Government Reformed: Values and New Political Institutions*, Aldershot, Ashgate.

Lowi, T. J. (1998), 'Introduction', in A. S. Marcowitz and M. Silverstein (eds), *The Politics of Scandal, Power and Process in Liberal Democracies*, New York, Holmes & Meier.

Mancuso, M. (1998), 'Politicising Ethics: Scandal and the American Experience', in N. Preston and C. Sampford with C. A. Bois (eds), *Ethics and Political Practice: Perspectives on Legislative Ethics*, Sydney/London, Federation Press/Routledge.

Markovits, A. S. and M. Silverstein (eds) (1998), *The Politics of Scandal, Power and Process in Liberal Democracies*, New York, Holmes and Meier.

McAllister, I. (2000), 'Keeping Them Honest: Public and Elite Perceptions of Ethical Conduct among Australian Legislators', *Political Studies*, 48: 22–37.

McAllister, I. and J. Wanna (2001), 'Citizens' Expectations and Perceptions of Governance', in G. Davis and P. Weller (eds), *Are You Being Served? State, Citizens and Governance*, Sydney, Allen & Unwin.

Rosenthal, A. (1998), ' "Appearance" as an Ethical Standard: Its Consequences for US State Legislatures', in N. Preston and C. Sampford, with C. A. Bois (eds), *Ethics and Political Practice: Perspectives on Legislative Ethics*, Sydney/London, Federation Press/Routledge.

Morgan, Roy (1998), 'Politicians Fall to Low Levels of Honesty and Ethics', Roy Morgan Research Centre, Finding No. 3088, May, cited www.roymorgan.com.au/polls/1998/3088/index.html.

Smith, F. (2000), Forbes Smith, Chief Investigator, Criminal Justice Commission, Personal Interview with Jenny Fleming, 7 May 2000, Brisbane.

Thompson, J. (2000), *Political Scandal: Power and Visibility in the Media Age*, Cambridge, Polity Press.

Tiffen, R. (1999), *Scandals, Media, Politics and Corruption in Contemporary Australia*, Sydney, University of New South Wales Press.

Walker, J. (1995), *Goss: A Political Biography*, St Lucia, University of Queensland Press.

Walsh, K. A. and N. Richardson (1995), 'Politicians: How Low Can They Go?' *Bulletin*, 12 September, pp. 14–17.

Wanna, J. (1991), 'Parliamentary Commissions of Review: The Criminal Justice Commission and the Electoral and Administrative Review Commission', in R. Whip and C. A. Hughes (eds), *Political Crossroads: The 1989 Queensland Election*, St Lucia, University of Queensland Press.

Whitrod, R. (2001), *Before I Sleep: Memoirs of a Modern Police Commissioner*, St Lucia, University of Queensland Press.
Williams, R. (1998), *Political Scandals in the USA*, Keele, Keele University Press.
Wood, J. R. T. (1997), 'Royal Commission into New South Wales Police Service', Final Report, Vols. I, II, III (May 1997), Sydney, New South Wales, Government Printer.

6

Payments for no political response? Political corruption and tribunals of inquiry in Ireland, 1991–2003

Gary Murphy

Introduction

'Corrupt influence', stated Edmund Burke in his famous 'Speech on the Plan for Economical Reform' in February 1780, 'is itself the perennial source of all prodigality, and of all disorder; which loads us, more than millions of debt; which takes away vigour from our arms, wisdom from our councils, and every shadow of authority and credit from the most venerable parts of our constitution'. Corrupt influence has been a salient feature of Irish political life throughout the 1990s and at the start of the twenty-first century. It has taken the form of financial donations to political parties, and such donations have produced a plethora of tribunals. As we shall see, the impact of the resulting scandals and of the tribunals remains uncertain, even though the latter have been very effective in forcing the corrupt activities into the open.

Until the establishment in 1991 of the Hamilton Tribunal on the beef industry, judicial inquiries had for two generations been employed, not for investigating corruption, but to investigate a range of natural calamities.[1] Tribunals of Inquiry are in essence amongst the last legacies of British to Irish law under the Tribunals of Inquiry (Evidence) Act of 24 March 1921 (O'Neill, 2000: 201). They have quite an array of powers and are equipped with the full armoury of High Court powers to compel the attendance of witnesses, the production of documents, and the making of such orders as are deemed necessary to carry out their functions. Principal among these are to establish the facts about issues of 'urgent public importance'. The remit of the 1991 Beef Tribunal was explicitly political in that it was established to examine allegations of government favouritism towards certain companies in the beef processing industry. Its creation was a prerequisite for the continued survival, under Charles Haughey, of the then governing coalition of Fianna Fáil and the Progressive Democrats. Some months after Mr Haughey's enforced resignation in 1992, the Tribunal's proceedings created a rupture in the coalition because of the belligerent language used by the then *Taoiseach*, Albert Reynolds, who, in giving evidence, challenged the testimony of his cabinet colleague, Progressive Democrat leader, Desmond O'Malley. This precipitated a general election that produced yet another Fianna Fáil-led coalition, this time with the Labour Party. When it finally reported in 1994, the Tribunal uncovered evidence of massive tax fraud, official connivance in systematic abuses of EU export rebates and reckless ministerial decision making. Although it was exhaustive in detail it was so opaque that almost any construction could be put on it (O'Halpin, 2000: 184–5). The Tribunal of Inquiry as a method of investigation did, however, suffer a dramatic decline in popularity with the Beef Tribunal. The latter took three years to deliver its report, saw seven different applications for judicial review made to the High Court and Supreme Court, cost approximately £20 million and ultimately failed to deliver a clear result in the form of punishment, condemnation or significant policy change (see O'Toole, 1995).

The McCracken Tribunal

The Tribunal of Inquiry was, however, to make a stunning comeback only two years later, with the establishment of the McCracken Tribunal, whose remit was to inquire into the so-called 'Dunnes Payments'. The immediate origin of both it and the subsequent Moriarty Tribunal into payments to politicians lay in a rather mysterious and often squalid family dispute about control of the most famous supermarket group in Ireland, the billionaire retail outfit Dunnes Stores. This arose after the Chairman of the company, Ben Dunne, was arrested in Florida in July 1992 on allegations of possessing cocaine, having been found by local police in a hotel room with quantities of the drug and in the company of a local prostitute. It was also reported, though subsequently denied by Dunne, that he had tried to commit suicide by jumping from a seventeenth floor balcony. Following this dramatic episode involving one of Ireland's leading businessmen, there came into the public domain a dispute, which had been going on in private for some years between Dunne and his sister Margaret Heffernan, over ownership of the Dunnes Stores group (Smyth, 1997). During this often-rancorous dispute, it emerged that a whole host of payments had been made to a variety of politicians. In the light of this, the *Oireachtas* established the Tribunal as the best way both to establish facts and to command public confidence in terms of openness and accountability.

The McCracken Tribunal dealt with the initial flurry of allegations about financial links between the Dunnes Stores group and two senior politicians, the former *Taoiseach* and leader of Fianna Fáil, Charles Haughey, and the former Fine Gael minister, Michael Lowry. The Tribunal proved remarkably successful in eliciting information from both Irish and offshore financial institutions in its search for secret payments. It uncovered a host of payments from Ben Dunne to politicians of various parties. Haughey's opulent lifestyle was exposed as existing largely on the donations of wealthy businessmen. He at first denied before the Tribunal that he had received any financial contributions from Dunnes Stores. However, when faced with hard evidence that £1.3 million from

Dunnes had found its way to him while *Taoiseach* between 1987 and 1991, he belatedly acknowledged its receipt. It also emerged that, practically throughout his political career, Haughey's financial and tax affairs had been handled by a close friend and practising accountant, Des Traynor. The latter controlled the so-called Ansbacher accounts, a complex and extensive tax-avoidance system, traces of which the Tribunal and a separate departmental investigation into the Dunnes Stores group had uncovered. Of this, some £40 million was held in a Cayman Islands bank. The Tribunal also discovered that a commercial firm, Celtic Helicopters, run by one of Haughey's sons, had benefited from funds in these accounts (Keena, 2001: 235–44).

For his part, Lowry was disgraced when it emerged during the course of the McCracken proceedings that his refrigeration company had had only one real customer: Dunnes Stores. After resigning from ministerial office in December 1996, but crucially before the end of the McCracken Tribunal, he made a personal statement to the *Dáil*, stridently denying that he had done anything wrong, engaged in any abuse of office or held any offshore bank accounts. Following the appearance of the Tribunal's report, in September 1997, showing quite clearly that he had several such accounts, he had to offer this rather surreal apology:

> With the benefit of hindsight I now accept that the words I used and the example I gave were most unfortunate and conveyed a misleading impression. I fully accept responsibility for that. However, I categorically assure this House that it was not my intention to mislead. I offer my full and sincere apologies to the *Ceann Comhairle* and to all Members of the House then and now for having misled them in any way. (*Dáil* Debates, 10 September 1997)

The importance of the McCracken Tribunal lay in its clarity, efficiency and unequivocal conclusions about payments to both Haughey and Lowry. It also cast much new light on the performance of the Revenue Commissioners in relation to tax avoidance, specifically with regard to the Ansbacher accounts. Both general and political reaction to the Tribunal was positive, with the then *Tanaiste*, Mary Harney, declaring that her faith in tribunals had been restored by McCracken. In that context, Fianna Fáil felt obliged to agree to a further tribunal into the affairs of Haughey and Lowry after the June 1997 general election, which saw them enter into coalition with the Progressive Democrats led by Harney.

Rather bizarrely, however, the major political parties agreed it would be improper to determine who else held money in the secret Ansbacher accounts, even though these were patently illegal and implied large-scale tax evasion (O'Halpin and Connolly, 1999: 141). Nevertheless, only a few months later, on a tide of rising public anger, the Fianna Fáil–Progressive Democrat government set up an official investigation into the Ansbacher accounts. This initially took the form of the *Tanaiste*, Ms Harney, announcing that she was appointing Gerard Ryan (an accountant and senior civil servant from her own Department of Enterprise, Trade and Employment) to investigate possible breaches of company law by Celtic Helicopters in the wake of details contained in the McCracken report. This was later expanded into a full Revenue Commissioner investigation, when evidence linking a host of wealthy individuals to the Ansbacher accounts emerged at the Moriarty Tribunal hearings into payments to politicians. The final Ansbacher report issued in July 2002 revealed that some of those who hid their money in the Cayman Islands had been appointed to State boards to serve the public interest. The names listed included former directors of Aer Lingus and Bord Fáilte, the author of the influential Culliton report on industrial policy, and a former director of the Central Bank (Keena, 2003).

The McCracken Tribunal was very successful in tracking down payments to Michael Lowry and Charles Haughey from Dunne. Nevertheless, its conclusion that 'there was no political impropriety' on the part of Lowry and that 'there appear[ed] in fact to have been no political impropriety' on the part of Haughey (McCracken, 1997: 70, 73) seemed to imply that the covert payments to both individuals had had no effect on their political behaviour. This was despite the fact that the Tribunal castigated Haughey, stating that it was 'quite unbelievable' that he would not have known of the illegal off-shore accounts and consequent tax evasion, and that much of his evidence was 'unacceptable and untrue'. Moreover, it stated quite bluntly that no *Taoiseach* 'should be supported in his personal lifestyle by gifts made in secret to him' (McCracken, 1997: 52, 72–3). The conclusions of the McCracken Tribunal did, however, force the *Oireachtas* to establish a further tribunal to examine whether business interests might have secured favourable policy decisions from Lowry or Haughey during their respective ministerial careers.

Payments to politicians and the Flood Tribunal

The payments-for-no-political-response defence was reiterated by the *Taoiseach*, Bertie Ahern, in July 2000 when campaigning in the Tipperary South by-election. He maintained that the 'vast majority of donations to Fianna Fáil are not made in expectation of either favours or special access'. However, when asked by the chairman of the Flood Tribunal in May 2003 why land developers were giving councillors money, long-time Fianna Fáil local councillor and current Senator, Don Lydon, was forced to admit: 'I believe that they hoped to influence (them). That's my firm belief. They did it then, they did it before, they do it now' (*Sunday Tribune*, 18 May 2003).

The 1990s therefore saw the Irish body politic awash with controversy. Allegations of wrongdoing involving political and business interests prompted the establishment of several Tribunals of Inquiry. From the so-called Beef Tribunal of 1991–4 to the current Tribunals of Inquiry into planning irregularities (Flood) and payments to politicians (Moriarty), revelations about the increasingly muddy links between business and politics have created something of a crisis of confidence in Irish political life. Both the Flood and Moriarty Tribunals have enjoyed spectacular success in uncovering complex networks of covert financial payments to politicians and government officials, and if they have not yet proved definitively that money bought public policy favours at local or national levels they have increasingly posed the question of why else businessmen would contribute so lavishly and so discreetly to certain individuals (O'Halpin, 2000: 191). Yet both Tribunals have come under sustained attack from a variety of political, media and academic spokespersons. Since their establishment in late 1997, they have been criticised as exercises in futility, and dismissed as expensive wastes of time and public money (Cullen, 1999; Corcoran and White, 2000). Yet, as we have seen, both the Hamilton Tribunal of Inquiry into the beef processing industry and the McCracken Tribunal of Inquiry into payments to politicians revealed that certain large businesses regularly make substantial contributions, particularly at election time, to political parties they consider sympathetic to them. And before Lydon's appearance at the Flood Tribunal, no politician of any hue would have admitted that those who fund the political process do so in the expectation of a return on their investment.

As a result of the evidence given to the Flood Tribunal by the political lobbyist and former government press secretary, Frank Dunlop, that fifteen Dublin county councillors had received payments totalling £112,000 in connection with the re-zoning of a giant shopping centre in west Dublin, both Fianna Fáil and Fine Gael initiated major internal inquiries into payments to politicians. On 19 April 2000, after some sensational evidence by Dunlop, both *Taoiseach*, Bertie Ahern, and leader of Fine Gael, John Bruton, announced they were appointing high-ranking committees to ascertain whether any party members had received illicit payments while serving as county councillors. Those who had would face sanctions, including possible expulsion from their respective parties. This followed the admission by Dunlop at the Tribunal that he had made payments, ranging from £500 to over £48,000, to unnamed county councillors around the time of the local elections in June 1991. He said the money had later been reimbursed by his client, the developer of the Quarryvale centre, Cork-born entrepreneur Owen O'Callaghan (*Irish Times*, 20 April 2000). It was in many respects a stunning victory for the much-maligned Flood Tribunal.

The latter (sometimes known as the Planning Tribunal) was established under the chairmanship of Justice Feargus Flood by the *Oireachtas* in October 1997.[2] It was set up to investigate the planning history of 726 acres of land in north county Dublin. These were the subject of a letter written by the developer, Michael Bailey, to James Gogarty, then of Joseph Murphy Structural Engineering (JMSE), in June 1989. Gogarty alleged the former Minister for Foreign Affairs, Ray Burke, had received payments amounting to £80,000 from JMSE and Bailey in connection with the lands. Burke said he had received £30,000, which was a normal electoral expense. The Tribunal's terms of reference were widened in June 1998 following the disclosure of a further payment of £30,000 to Burke in 1989, this time by Rennicks Manufacturing Ltd. The Tribunal was also empowered to investigate all improper payments made to politicians in connection with the planning process. Under this provision, it is still investigating allegations made by the UK-based Irish property developer, Tom Gilmartin, about payments, including a claim that he gave the former EU Commissioner, Pádraig Flynn, £50,000 in 1989. Flynn is due to appear before the Tribunal to answer questions about missing funds donated to his party.

The Tribunal has also been spectacularly successful in showing that the former Dublin assistant city and county manager, George Redmond, the most important planning official in Dublin for over a quarter of a century, was literally in the pockets of a number of wealthy builders. 'I was the Council; I had the powers', he rather magisterially declared when he first entered the witness box in September 1999.[3] He was soon humbled by the Tribunal lawyers and Justice Flood, who warned him to reflect on the credibility of his claim that his opulent lifestyle was funded from his civil servant's salary. When threatened with up to two years in jail for misleading the Tribunal, he finally admitted that he had received huge amounts of money from a variety of builders and landowners. Subsequently convicted of failing to make numerous tax returns, he was convicted of corruption in November 2003 and sentenced to twelve months imprisonment.

After this initial success, Flood and his legal team pushed on and had their reward with Dunlop's breathtaking evidence of 19 April 2000. Dunlop had initially been a reluctant witness and, in the earlier part of his evidence, had strongly denied ever making cash payments to councillors in return for votes on re-zoning issues. However, the Tribunal's discovery of a bank account in his name, from which £250,000 had been paid out at around the time of the Quarryvale re-zoning, led to a reassessment of Dunlop's evidence. Cautioned by Justice Flood to reflect on his previous testimony in the light of the existence of this account, Dunlop bared his soul in a momentous day's evidence.

The political parties respond

For both major political parties, Dunlop's evidence had the potential to create enormous difficulties, and both responded with alacrity. Fianna Fáil announced that its Standards in Public Life Committee, put in place as part of its code of ethics agreed at its 1999 *Ard Fheis*, would be convened to explore whether any of its members were affected by Dunlop's allegations. Fine Gael, for its part, announced a three-person internal inquiry and vowed that any person against whom allegations of corruption were proved would be expelled. For its leader, John Bruton, those facing expulsion would be those councillors who 'received donations that cannot be shown to have been for legitimate party or electoral purposes' (*Irish Times*, 20 April 2000). The party also rather dramatically promised to introduce a new offence of bribery, punishable by a seven-year prison sentence. Whilst the political parties conducted their internal inquiries, Dunlop continued to give more sensational evidence. This reached a climax in May when he identified a further £75,000 he had paid to politicians in return for their support on re-zonings (*Irish Times*, 10 May 2000). Moreover it transpired that a further £250,000, which had passed through Dunlop's bank accounts, remained unaccounted for, and was thought to have been paid to politicians throughout the 1990s. This evidence resulted in Fianna Fáil extending its internal inquiry into whether any of its elected representatives accepted money for planning favours up to and including the Dunlop evidence.

Fine Gael was the first to conclude its internal review, which was presented to John Bruton on 12 May 2000. Its remit covered 'payments made to Fine Gael Representatives on Dublin Corporation and Dublin County Council by builders, developers or their agents since 20 June 1985 and the motives, circumstances and considerations thereto pertaining'.[4] Chaired by Senior Counsel, James Nugent, the report revealed that Fine Gael's deputy leader, Nora Owen, chief whip Seán Barrett, two other deputies, Michael Joe Cosgrave and Olivia Mitchell, and two senators, Therese Ridge and Liam Cosgrave, had all received donations from Frank Dunlop. The six Fine Gael *Oireachtas* members told the party inquiry that the donations were political contributions and had not influenced their votes. However, in the case of payments made to Senator Cosgrave, Councillor Cathal Boland and Anne Devitt, the leader of the Fine Gael group on Dublin County Council at the time of the Dunlop payments, the committee was unable to come to definitive conclusions. This resulted in John Bruton stating that he would seek to prevent all three politicians from standing for the party in any future *Dáil* election unless they provided more information on donations received from builders, developers or their agents (*Irish Times*, 13 May 2000). Amidst threats of legal action from the councillors, and vehement denials of any impropriety, the report left Fine Gael in rather a quandary. Even though the party was seen as proactive in investigating allegations, the final report left some members distinctly uneasy about why some of them had been singled out over others (Murphy, 2000: 195).

Fianna Fáil issued its report on 7 June. The Committee, chaired by the parliamentary party chairman, Dr Rory O'Hanlon, interviewed Fianna Fáil members of Dublin County Council who had been councillors during the period 1985–91, and from 1991 to the local elections of 1999. The purpose was to enquire 'whether Fianna Fáil councillors were in receipt of donations from Frank Dunlop and/or developers; whether Fianna Fáil councillors – who were in receipt of such donations – were thereby influenced in their voting, and whether Fianna Fáil councillors had any information about any corrupt activities in relation to planning matters'.[5] Running to 200 pages, the report revealed a whole host of payments to a variety of members but focused primarily on the Dublin West TD Liam Lawlor (Cullen, 2002: 140–68). Lawlor had received between £12,000 and £14,000 in donations before the early 1990s, and £38,000 in consultancy fees from Dunlop in 1994 and 1995. The report accused him of being unco-operative and contradictory about a series of payments made to him over a number of years by a variety of individuals. It stated that during questioning Lawlor had given conflicting accounts of dealings that a Czech-based company (The Irish Consortium SRO), in which he had a one-third share, had had with Frank Dunlop. Later Lawlor revealed in the annual register of members of *Dáil Eireann* that he was also a non-executive director of a company called Zatecka 14 SRO, based in Prague.[6] Lawlor, who had been embroiled in numerous planning controversies over a long career, resigned from Fianna Fáil, claiming he had done so because he did not want to distract from the workings of the government. The Dublin North TD, G. V. Wright, also came under scrutiny as the report revealed he had received £20,000 in donations, including £10,000 from Frank Dunlop, over a period from late 1991 to early 1994, when he had been the party whip on Dublin County Council. Wright insisted to the inquiry that all the donations he had received had been unsolicited. However, the property developer, Owen O'Callaghan, directly contradicted this claim when he issued a statement stating he had given £5,000 to Wright only after having been asked for an electoral contribution (*Irish Times*, 8 June 2000). The Fianna Fáil report ultimately declared that any councillor convicted of a corruption offence should be banned from holding public office for life, and maintained that councillors should not be allowed to act as consultants to property developers while serving on a local authority (Murphy, 2000: 195–6). Wright, however, suffered no penalty and was indeed comfortably re-elected at the last election. Moreover, while Liam Lawlor has done no fewer than three stints in jail, he still defiantly insists that the Tribunal has wronged him.

However, during the presentation of a variety of items of witness evidence at the Flood Tribunal in the spring of 2003, it emerged that both these reports were little short of cosmetic window dressing. The Tribunal has now categorically shown that Fianna Fáil councillors Tony Foxe and Don Lydon, and Fine Gael's Liam Cosgrave, son and grandson of two former leaders of the Irish State, failed to disclose full information both to the Tribunal and to their respective party inquiries. Lydon suggested that the Fianna Fáil inquiry into political payments had ignored its own terms of reference by concentrating only on allegations relating to Frank Dunlop. He further maintained that the inquiry had not carried out a complete trawl when interviewing councillors. When questioned at the Tribunal about why he had failed to disclose a number of political contributions to the inquiry set up to investigate payments to councillors by Frank Dunlop and/or developers, Lydon stated that members of the committee had told him the inquiry was only dealing with 'two or three things' and was not 'a general trawl' (*Irish Times*, 3 May 2003).

The Flood Tribunal has shown quite clearly that Liam Cosgrave misled the Fine Gael inquiry about the size and number of donations he had received from Frank Dunlop. Cosgrave admitted to the Tribunal that he had received almost £8,000 in election expenses from Dunlop, not the £3,000 he had declared to the Fine Gael inquiry. He maintained he had simply forgotten or underestimated the donations, again insisting that all payments he had received were legitimate political donations and had had nothing to do with the various re-zoning controversies that the Flood Tribunal was investigating. He went on to castigate the Fine Gael inquiry as 'sloppy' and 'sinister'. The Fine Gael inquiry said it was unable to come to a definitive decision in relation to the payments Cosgrave had received, something he described as 'the worst thing that has ever happened to me' (*Irish Times*, 4 April 2003). Dunlop has named Cosgrave as one of nine county councillors who allegedly took bribes in return for their votes on the re-zoning of land at Carrickmines in south Dublin, maintaining he gave Cosgrave £20,000 in payments, some of which were legitimate political contributions and some bribes. Cosgrave, who had complained bitterly about both the Fine Gael inquiry and the Flood Tribunal, was ultimately caught in the web of his own deceit. Having complained that both inquiries were sloppy, he relied on his own shoddy memory, a memory shown to have been seriously deficient in its recollection of monies given to him.

The Flood Tribunal and Ray Burke

In September 2002, the Flood Tribunal issued its second interim report, dealing mostly with Ray Burke. The question of political donations first came to haunt the Fianna Fáil–Progressive Democrat coalition government elected in June 1997 when Burke, then Minister for Foreign Affairs, was forced to resign the following October. Burke had been involved in various planning controversies since as early as 1974, and had at one stage been interviewed by the Gardai about a planning development at Mountgorry, county Dublin. Moreover, in the mid-1980s, he had been chairman of Dublin County Council, which carried out numerous re-zonings, usually against the advice of its own planning officials. No charges were ever brought against Burke in relation to any re-zoning questions. However, in September 1997, he admitted having received £30,000 in cash during the 1989 general election campaign at a meeting at his home with two property development figures, one of whom he had never previously met. He maintained there was nothing unusual or sinister in this and the money received was simply an election contribution, of which he passed on £10,000 to Fianna Fáil headquarters (Murphy, 1999: 285). The familiar argument that this was a case of 'payments for no political response' was used as Burke insisted that 'at no time during our meeting were any favours sought or given'.[7] However, it was clear his position was becoming increasingly untenable. In early October, the *Irish Times* revealed Burke had played a key role in obtaining eleven Irish passports for a Saudi-Arabian banker and his family in 1990 in return for investments. Burke had had enough. He resigned both as a minister and as a TD. He took the step, he said, because the 'ongoing public controversy' was preventing him giving his full attention to the Northern Ireland talks and ongoing developments in the European sphere. In his resignation statement Burke made clear that, in his view, he had been wronged: 'I want to clearly restate that I have done nothing wrong', he intoned to the rapt audience. The *Taoiseach* declared that an 'honourable man' had been 'hounded from office'. He then immediately acceded to opposition demands for the setting up of a judicial inquiry into planning in Dublin, and the Burke payment (Cullen, 2002: 102).

Since his resignation Burke has been embroiled in countless battles with the Flood Tribunal. He gave his first evidence in July 1999, and most of the second interim report, running to over 150 pages of text with another 250 pages of appendices, is devoted to him. After sifting through some at times turgid and evasive evidence from Burke, Mr Justice Flood ruled that Mr Burke had received corrupt payments from a succession of builders, including Michael Bailey, Tom Brennan and Joseph McGowan. He also ruled that Mr Burke, during his time as Minister for Communications in the late 1980s, had made decisions that were not in the public interest after receiving payments from Century Radio's main backer, Oliver Barry. This related to the establishment of Ireland's first national commercial radio station, Century Radio. Century was the victor in a national competition amongst four groups to provide the commercial service. The decision was made in January 1989 by the ten members of the Independent Radio and Television Commission set up by the Minister for Communications, Ray Burke, some four months earlier. It was dubbed Radio Fianna Fáil by some because of its connections in high places (Cullen, 2002: 170). In May 1989, four months after Century had won the commercial radio licence, its main backer, impresario Oliver Barry, gave £35,000 in cash to Burke at one of his departmental offices.

After it won the commercial radio licence, Century benefited to an extraordinary degree from direct interventions by Burke. He initially reduced the transmission fee payable by Century to the state broadcaster, RTÉ, for use of its transmissions mast, thereby saving Century some £636,000 over seven years. Not content with doing this once, Burke again reduced the fee, saving Century around £500,000 a year. Moreover, he capped RTÉ's advertising and attempted to introduce a host of other measures that would have seriously diminished RTÉ's ability to keep the huge audiences it had built up, to the benefit of Century (Cullen, 2002: 203–4). In the end none of this mattered as Century collapsed, but that was no fault of Burke who seems to have done everything humanly possible to ensure its success. This was too much for Justice Flood. In a devastating critique of the Century episode, he ruled that Barry's payment of £35,000 to Burke had had the effect of ensuring that decisions made by Burke in his capacity as Minister for Communications would reflect favourably on those paying him:

> The Tribunal is satisfied that Mr Burke's decisions . . . were all motivated by a desire on his part to benefit those who had paid monies to him, and that proposals on such issues would not have been advanced by Mr Burke at that time were it not for the fact that he had been paid £35,000. In all the circumstances the Tribunal concludes that the payment made to Mr Burke was a corrupt payment. (Flood, 2002: 65)

After these findings, the Flood Tribunal report became an instant best seller, with eager queues forming at the government publications office. It was to remain at the top of the best-seller charts for weeks.

Besides Burke, Mr Justice Flood found that Tom Brennan, the Bailey brothers, Tom Bailey's wife, Caroline, Joseph Murphy junior, and Joseph Murphy senior, Oliver Barry, James Stafford, Joseph McGowan, John Finnegan, Roger Copsey, Frank Reynolds, Tim O'Keeffe and John Bates had all obstructed the Tribunal's work. Its report has now been sent to the Director of Public Prosecutions, the Garda Commissioner, the Criminal Assets Bureau, the Revenue Commissioners and the Office of the Director of Corporate Enforcement.

The Moriarty Tribunal

For its part the Moriarty Tribunal has been most effective in uncovering a whole host of payments to Charles Haughey. This has been ongoing, while Haughey himself is facing criminal charges arising from his alleged obstruction of the McCracken Tribunal. Following a variety of comments, most notably by the *Tanaiste*, Mary Harney, that Haughey 'should be convicted' and 'spend time in prison', an indefinite stay was put on the trial by Justice Kevin Haugh in June 2000 on the grounds that Haughey could not get a fair trial (*Irish Independent*, 27 May 2000). The Moriarty Tribunal has proved remarkably successful in tracking down a complicated money trail leading to Haughey, and it is now estimated he received £8.5 million in donations over a sixteen-year period. But these revelations have not been the only source of controversy for Fianna Fáil at the Moriarty Tribunal. In late June 2000, it became embroiled in a dispute with the Tribunal over whether or not party members had co-operated fully with it. This related to a list of donors given by the party to the Tribunal and whether or not there was a second list or extract containing other donors. Fianna Fáil blamed the Tribunal for causing the controversy, with the Minister for Defence, Michael Smith, stating that it had given all its documents to the Tribunal and 'anything they missed was their fault' (*Irish Times*, 29 June 2000). The dispute, however, led to the appearance of the *Taoiseach* at the Tribunal. He tried to explain how a complaint from a donor, Mark Kavanagh, that he had not been given a receipt for a donation of £100,000 to Charles Haughey in 1989, had been withheld from the Tribunal. Fianna Fáil had not told the Tribunal about this payment, even though irregularities in its documentation had led to an internal party investigation in 1996. The *Taoiseach*, Bertie Ahern, had previously been caught up in controversy over revelations at the Tribunal that he had pre-signed all the cheques on the Fianna Fáil leader's allowance account in the period 1984–92 (*Irish Times*, 16 October 1999). Some of these cheques, the Tribunal discovered, had been made out to exclusive restaurants in Dublin and an expensive shirt shop in Paris.

It was also learned that John Ellis, Fianna Fáil TD for Sligo-Leitrim, was saved from bankruptcy twice by Haughey in 1989 and 1990, using money taken from the state-funded party leader's allowance. Meanwhile, a member of the *Dáil*'s Public Accounts Committee, the Fianna Fáil TD for North Kerry, Denis Foley, charged with investigating offshore tax evasion, was himself found to be the holder of an Ansbacher account. Foley's punishment turned out to be a fourteen-day paid suspension from the *Dáil*. Minister for State, Ned O'Keeffe, and backbench TD, Beverly Cooper-Flynn, were others to find themselves in difficulties during the course of the legislature. O'Keeffe was forced to resign as Minister in February 2001 for a breach of the Ethics in Public Office Act. Cooper-Flynn was expelled from her parliamentary party in 1999 after she voted against an amendment calling on her father, the EU Commissioner Pádraig Flynn, to respond to claims that he was paid £50,000 by developer Tom Gilmartin.

On the other side of the political fence, the Moriarty Tribunal has, however, become bogged down in investigating the award of the country's second mobile phone licence to Esat Digifone in 1995, during the rainbow government of Fine Gael, the Labour Party and the Democratic Left. A payment of $50,000 to Fine Gael from the winning consortium has been the subject of a detailed Tribunal investigation. The payment occurred while Michael Lowry, Minister for Communications at the time the licence was granted, was a trustee of the party. The Tribunal has uncovered a vast array of complex financial transactions, and wildly different accounts of what happened. What is clear at this stage is that two defeated parties for the licence are threatening to sue the state on grounds of ministerial interference in the awarding of the licence. Both Lowry and his civil servants making the decision have strenuously denied any impropriety. At the time of writing the Tribunal is continuing its investigations.

Yet scandal has most tainted Fianna Fáil. This is best illustrated by the so-called Sheedy affair in mid 2000.[8] The Fianna Fáil–Progressive Democrat coalition came under enormous strain when it appointed former Supreme Court judge, Hugh O'Flaherty, to the position of vice president of the European Investment Bank (EIB) on a salary of £147,000 in May 2000. O'Flaherty, long associated with Fianna Fáil, had been forced to resign from the Supreme Court on threat of impeachment by the government over his role in the Sheedy affair in 1999. Bertie Ahern was also involved when it was alleged he had made representations on Sheedy's behalf to the Minister for Justice, John O'Donoghue, to obtain day release for Sheedy. Nevertheless, the government had ridden out this particular storm until its shock decision to appoint O'Flaherty to the EIB post brought the Sheedy case back into the open. Serious divisions emerged between the coalition partners, with Minister for State at Foreign Affairs, Progressive Democrat TD, Liz O'Donnell, being most critical of the decision. Progressive Democrat Senator Helen Keogh was also deeply disturbed by the appointment and ultimately defected to Fine Gael. The problems this appointment created for the government were seen to most dramatic effect in the Tipperary South by-election of 23 June 2000. The left-wing independent candidate, Seamus Healy, won the election, with Fianna Fáil being relegated to third place – only the second time in the history of the state that this had happened at a by-election – with a dismal showing of 22 per cent in the first preference vote. It was an eloquent statement of dissatisfaction with the government, and was reinforced by the government's poor opinion poll showings. The government's satisfaction rating fell to below 50 per cent for the first time since the 1997 general election in an IMS poll on 15 June, while an *Irish Times*/MRBI opinion poll suggested that 68 per cent of voters believed the government had been wrong to nominate O'Flaherty as vice president of the EIB (*Irish Independent*, 15 June 2000; *Irish Times*, 16 June 2000). Nevertheless, with anything up to two years to a general election and with no evidence that any of the revelations at the various Tribunals were having much of an effect on the government's popularity, the result of this by-election was likely to have little long-term significance for the government come a general election (Murphy, 2003: 11–12).

Conclusion

For all these revelations, then, the resulting scandals seem to have had very little impact in terms of public *behaviour*, whatever the public's *thoughts* might be. The Fianna Fáil–Progressive Democrat government became the first in over thirty years to be re-elected and Fianna Fáil, despite being the most tainted with corruption, came extremely close to achieving an overall majority. Corruption rarely surfaced as an issue at the May 2002 general election. In contrast to the media coverage of the various Tribunals, which focused heavily on the sleaze being uncovered, Fianna Fáil's internal research findings showed that the public was in no way antagonistic to the party (Collins, 2003: 23). Public corruption has been defined as 'the breaking, for the sake of financial or political gain, of the rules of conduct in public affairs prevailing in a society in the period under consideration' (Tanzi, 1998). Justices Flood and Moriarty have most certainly shown that such rules were broken in the Ireland of the 1990s. From Charles Haughey's charvet shirts to Ray Burke's sale, for 4.8 million euros, of a house he received from its builders for free, the words of Edmund Burke that corrupt influence is itself the perennial source of all prodigality hold true. These scandals and the corruption underlying them have proved extremely useful as a means of highlighting abuses of power. They also provide us with the opportunity for legal and other types of innovation. In the Irish case in the last decade, this has meant the Tribunal of Inquiry. However, as of the summer of 2004, it is estimated that at the current rates of progress, the Flood Tribunal will finally end in 2020 and the Moriarty Tribunal a decade earlier – twenty-three and thirteen years respectively after they were established. To this end the never-ending Tribunal of Inquiry might not be the best way to investigate such abuses. Other avenues need to be looked at as the Minister for Justice Michael McDowell has vowed to do. However, the scandals that have emerged from the Flood and Moriarty Tribunals, as well as from McCracken, have provided us with crucial insight into the way modern Ireland has governed itself in the recent past. In the rush to bury Tribunals, that should not be forgotten.

Notes

1 The Tribunal of Inquiry is a parliamentary body set up by the *Dáil* as a whole, as distinct from the government, to investigate matters of urgent public importance.
2 The proceedings of the Flood Tribunal can be accessed at www.flood-tribunal.ie
3 Proceedings of the Flood Tribunal from 20 September 1999.
4 The full report of the Fine Gael Committee of Inquiry could once be accessed on the Fine Gael web site at www.finegael.ie/main.htm, and could be seen through the News Releases section. It has since been removed.
5 The full report of the Fianna Fáil committee on standards in public life could once be accessed on the Fianna Fáil web site at www.fiannafail.ie/report/index.htm. It has since been removed.
6 Register of Interests of Members of Dáil Eireann, 1 February 1999 to 31 January 2000. The Register of Interests is a list of the financial interests of TDs and Senators. It includes all shares, donations and consultancies.
7 See *Dáil Debates*, vol. 480, col. 617–18, 15 September 1997.
8 'This occurred in November 1998 and concerned the unorthodox early release of a prisoner convicted of dangerous driving causing death. An inquiry by the Chief Justice led to the resignation of two judges and a court official. One of these was Judge Hugh O'Flaherty of the Supreme Court' (Collins and O'Shea, 2003: 177).

References

Collins, N. and M. O'Shea (2003), 'Political Corruption in Ireland', in M. J. Bull and J. L. Newell, *Corruption in Contemporary Politics*, Basingstoke, Palgrave-Macmillan.

Collins, S. (2003), 'Campaign Strategies', in M. Gallagher, M. Marsh and P. Mitchell (eds), *How Ireland Voted 2002*, London, Palgrave.

Corcoran, M. P. and A. White (2000), 'Irish democracy and the Tribunals of Inquiry' in E. Slater and M. Peillon (eds), *Memories of the Present: A Sociological Chronicle of Ireland 1997–1998*, Dublin, Institute of Public Administration.

Cullen, P. (1999), 'Flood's Exercise in Futility Begins Again', *Irish Times*, 22 November.

Cullen, P. (2002), *With a Little Help from my Friends: Planning Corruption in Ireland*, Dublin, Gill and Macmillan.

Flood, F. (2002), 'The Second Interim Report of the Tribunal of Inquiry into Certain Planning Matters and Payments', Stationery Office, Dublin.

Keena, C. (2001), *Haughey's Millions: Charlie's Money Trail*, Dublin, Gill and Macmillan.

Keena, C. (2003), *The Ansbacher Conspiracy*, Dublin, Gill and Macmillan.

McCracken, B. (1997), 'Report of the Tribunal of Inquiry' (Dunnes Payments) Stationery Office, Dublin.

Murphy, G. (1999), 'The Role of Interest Groups in the Policy Process', in J. Coakley and M. Gallagher (eds), *Politics in the Republic of Ireland*, 3rd edition, London, Routledge and PSAI Press.

Murphy, G. (2000), 'A Culture of Sleaze: Political Corruption and the Irish Body Politic 1997–2000', *Irish Political Studies*, 15, 193–200.

Murphy, G. (2003), 'The Background to the Election', in M. Gallagher, M. Marsh and P. Mitchell (eds), *How Ireland Voted 2002*, London, Palgrave.

O'Halpin, E. (2000), 'Ah They've Given us a Good Bit of Stuff . . . : Tribunals and Irish Political Life at the End of the Twentieth Century', *Irish Political Studies*, 15, 182–93.

O'Halpin, E. and E. Connolly (1999), 'Parliaments and Pressure Groups: The Irish Experience of Change', in Philip Norton (ed.), *Parliaments and Pressure Groups in Western Europe*, London, Frank Cass.

O'Neill, B. (2000), 'Political and Legal Issues Arising out of Recent Tribunals of Inquiry', *Irish Political Studies*, 15, 201–12.

O'Toole, F. (1995), *Meanwhile Back at the Ranch: The Politics of Irish Beef*, London, Vintage.

Smyth, S. (1997), *Thanks a Million, Big Fella*, Dublin, Blackwater Press.

Tanzi, V. (1998), 'Corruption Around the World', IMF Staff Papers, 45: 4, Washington, IMF.

7

Sex, lies and audiotapes: the Watergate and Monica Lewinsky scandals in American politics[1]

Eric M. Uslaner

In the first two centuries of the American Republic, only one President (Andrew Johnson) was impeached by the House of Representatives. In the past quarter of a century, we have witnessed a second impeachment (Bill Clinton) and the resignation of another President who was about to be impeached (Richard M. Nixon).

I shall investigate public support for impeachment in this chapter. There is a presumption that the only two impeachment cases in the twentieth century must have a lot in common. Both revolved around allegations (shown to be true in each case) that Presidents had lied and tried to cover up their false-hoods. Tape-recorded conversations proved essential to discovering the truth for both Nixon and Clinton. Yet the two impeachments were otherwise very different, and public attitudes reflect these dissimilarities. This is a tale of two scandals, one starting out as a partisan battle but becoming more of a criminal investigation and the other commencing as a partisan conflict and becoming an ideological holy war. In the Nixon impeachment, there was no debate over whether the offence was criminal. In the Clinton impeachment that was just about all people were debating.

The stories of Nixon and Clinton are well known. Prior to the 1972 Presidential elections, burglars rifled the headquarters of the Democratic National Committee. The burglary was clearly an attempt to disrupt the campaign of Democratic Presidential nominee George McGovern. A security guard notified the police and the perpetrators fled. Nixon initially called the break-in 'a third-rate burglary', of no real consequence. Ultimately, some of his top aides admitted that the planning of the crime and the financial sup-port for it had come directly from the White House. While the President did not take part in designing the break-in, he did know about the plans and the financial support for the burglary.

Initially, Republicans charged Democrats with seeking political advantage. Press reports (especially in the *Washington Post* using an anonymous source, 'Deep Throat') linked senior administration officials to the burglary and several resigned. Then the President refused to turn over materials to the

(Republican) Special Prosecutor he himself had appointed. Nixon ordered the Special Prosecutor to be fired, but his replacement (Leon Jaworski) was no more favourable to the President. The House Judiciary Committee was marked by partisan rancour. The Senate Judiciary Committee, led by conservative Democrat, Sam Ervin, and Republican, Howard Baker, conducted its investigation in a bipartisan manner. In April 1974 Nixon initially refused to comply with the Special Prosecutor's demand that he turn over the tape-recorded conversations with his aides. By this time, the impeachment battle was all but over. The House Judiciary Committee voted articles of impeachment in late July 1974, but the pressures for resignation from within his own party became too much for Nixon, who left office on 9 August.

In 1995, President Clinton began a sexual relationship with White House intern Monica Lewinsky. The White House arranged for Lewinsky to get a job at the Pentagon, where she shared her 'secret' with Pentagon employee Linda Tripp, who began taping their conversations. Tripp gave these tapes in early 1998 to Special Prosecutor Kenneth Starr, who was investigating charges of sexual harassment against Clinton while he was Governor of Arkansas, and various charges of illegal business deals collectively called 'Whitewater'. Starr called the President to testify before a grand jury and Clinton denied a sexual liaison with Lewinsky. Rumours of the affair percolated over several months. The Republicans charged Clinton and Lewinsky with lying to the grand jury and there was much partisan rancour over whether Starr (a strong Republican conservative) and the House Judiciary Committee (controlled by the Republicans) were trying to push Clinton out of office. By late summer, Starr agreed to immunity from prosecution for Lewinsky and Clinton admitted to the affair on national television. Starr pressed for an indictment of the President for lying to the grand jury and Congressional Republicans began impeachment proceedings against Clinton.

The House Judiciary Committee approved four articles of impeachment in early December on party-line votes (though one Republican defected on a single motion). On 19 December, the full House approved two of the four articles with only a handful of Republicans dissenting (five on one vote, twelve on another) and just a few Democrats (five on each vote) joining the Republicans. The Democrats had actually gained five House seats in the 1998 elections, the first time since 1934 and only the second time in the twentieth century that the party controlling the White House had picked up seats (Abramowitz, 2001: 211–12). Clinton's popularity remained high at 75 per cent.[2] House Republicans clearly paid a price for voting to impeach Clinton in November: Speaker Newt Gingrich, who led the charge to force Clinton from office, took the blame for the unexpected seat loss and left office himself, with Clinton still in place. Republican Senators were chastened by this experience, and the Senate trial in February was marked by a united Democratic front and as many as ten Republican defectors on one charge.

These two scandals seem to have little in common. The charges in Watergate were far more serious. Two thirds of all respondents to the 1998

American National Election Study (ANES) said that the charges against Clinton were a private rather than a public affair. There is no similar question in the 1974 survey, most likely because it soon became pretty clear that hardly anyone besides Nixon himself was willing to hold (publicly) that Watergate was a minor crime. The public response to Watergate was severe: Nixon's popularity plummeted to 25 per cent by mid-1974,[3] while Clinton's remained extraordinarily high. The President's party lost 49 House seats (and four Senate seats) in 1974, but gained five in 1998 (with no net change in the Senate). While 71.5 per cent of the public *favoured* impeaching Nixon (after the fact) in 1974, exactly the same share of the public *opposed* impeaching Clinton (before the fact) in 1998.

The single biggest difference between Watergate and the Monica Lewinsky affair, as it came to be known, was the way both members of Congress and the public responded to them. Watergate started out as partisan, but in the end Democrats and Republicans alike forced Nixon from office. Indeed, a group of senior Republicans led by Baker and other party luminaries went to the White House in August 1974 and pressed the President to step down. In November 1974, a majority of Republicans (52 per cent) joined most independents (69 per cent) and Democrats (83 per cent) in favouring impeachment. The Lewinski affair was consistently partisan: in 1998, 56 per cent of Republicans but just 26 per cent of independents and 11 per cent of Democrats favoured impeaching Clinton.

The roots of partisanship

Everything involving Richard M. Nixon smacks of partisanship and meanness. Nixon initially won his House seat in California in 1946 by alleging that his Democratic opponent (Representative Jerry Voorhis) was a Communist party sympathiser. Two years later he defeated Senator Helen Gahagan Douglas by calling her the 'pink lady'. Democrats cheered when Nixon lost the Presidency in 1960 and the Governorship of California two years later – and exulted when he excoriated the press in his farewell speech: 'You won't have Nixon to kick around anymore.' Yet at the end of his career, two Special Prosecutors – a well-connected Republican (Archibald Cox) and a Texas conservative (Leon Jaworski) – played key roles in ending the Nixon Presidency. So did Howard Baker, son-in-law of long-time Senate Minority Leader, Everett Dirksen, and a future Republican leader of the Senate himself. It was Baker who posed the key question: 'How much did the President know and when did he know it?' Baker worked with Sam Ervin, the conservative Southern Democrat, to seek out the truth about Nixon.

In contrast, Gingrich and Starr were strong partisans from the start. Jaworkski was popular with the public, with a 'feeling thermometer' rating of 58 on a 0–100 scale. Starr was unpopular, with a mean score of 35. House Judiciary Committee chair Henry Hyde, who had many friends on both sides of the aisle, became a strong partisan advocate. The debate on impeachment in the House was far from temperate. It was marked by a 'distrust [that] is so deep-seated and enduring that there are only downticks in the steady rise in animosity'. Democratic Representative, Jose Serrano, admonished the Republican majority that voted to impeach the President on an almost strict party-line vote: 'Bullies get theirs and you're going to get yours!' Democratic Representative, Albert Wynn, warned: 'There's raw feelings. It's going to take a long, long time to heal and there's not going to be any love fest.' Democratic Representative, David Skaggs, said: 'Nobody knows whether this place is going to be pulled apart so much that we can't do our business.' And Democratic Representative, David Obey, summed it up: 'We are on the short route to chaos' (Gugliotta and Neal, 1998).

The central reason why the 1998 impeachment was so partisan compared to the 1974 debate has to do with the nature of the charges. For Democrats, the Clinton scandal was about sex. For Republicans, it was about lying to the grand jury. Eighty-four per cent of Democrats, compared to 72 per cent of independents and just 39 per cent of Republicans saw the Clinton scandal as a private (rather than public) affair.

But the partisan conflict in 1998 went well beyond the public–private distinction. Attitudes toward impeachment were shaped by a multiplicity of factors, which I shall consider below. What mattered for Democrats did *not* necessarily matter to Republicans. Different factors shaped the visions of Democrats and Republicans in 1998. In contrast, there was much greater commonality in what shaped impeachment attitudes in 1974.

The conflict between partisans over the public nature of Clinton's misdeeds is important, but it does not tell us why Republicans turned what many saw as trivial misdeeds into a Constitutional crisis.

The Monica Lewinsky case is an example of partisan politics gone wild, or what Ginsberg and Shefter (1999) would call 'politics by other means'. The aim was not to contest the policy agenda of the other party, the 'loyal opposition.' Instead, it was to destroy the opposition (quoting Malcolm X) 'by any means necessary'. Junior Republicans in the House of Representatives under the newly elected Speaker, Gingrich, pressed a series of 'guerrilla' or 'kamikaze' tactics to disrupt House proceedings beginning in 1999. They used the rules of procedure to stop legislation, to embarrass the Democratic leadership, and to bring attention to themselves. 'Regular order' – routine procedure and the norms that make the system work – went out the window because they did not serve partisan advantage. So did working with the majority party (Uslaner, 1993: 52–3).

Extreme partisanship had become the norm when the Republicans took over the Congress in 1995 (Evans and Oleszek, 1997). Strong, ideologically entrenched, parties are not the norm in the United States. But now American parties, at both the elite and mass levels, are more polarised than they have been since around 1900. There is strong evidence that party elites are far apart from each other ideologically. The ideological distance between Democrats and Republicans has increased dramatically since the 1960s and 1970s (Rohde, 1991).

The public is similarly polarised. Democrats are more liberal than ever, and Republicans more conservative than they have been (Hetherington, 2001; Jacobson, 2000; Layman and Carsey, 2002). There are conflicting stories about which came first, but this fight does not matter for my story here. What *is* critical is that there is little incentive for either party to move to the middle, as Downs (1957) recommended many years ago. Strong parties at the elite level cannot persist without powerful partisan divisions at the base (Brady, 1988). These ideological divisions are inflamed by the very small gap between the parties in terms of their levels of support in the country, so that each party fights like the devil for the tiniest share of turf (House or Senate seats). Each seat could determine who has control of a legislative body (as we saw in 2001, when a Republican defector turned control of the Senate over to the Democrats). The only hope for a major party victory, like we saw in 1994, is the complete delegitimisation of the other side and you cannot do this by treating the other party as a 'loyal opposition'.

I shall consider what drives support for impeachment in 1974 and 1998 and how they differ. I expect that: (1) party and ideology will be important in both years, but far more in 1998 than in 1974; (2) support for impeachment in 1974 will more closely reflect general discontent with the political system than will attitudes in 1998; (3) party affiliation will shape attitudes toward specific actors (the Congressional committees, the Special Prosecutors, and the press) more in 1998 than in 1974; and (4) there should be more of a common view between the parties in 1974 than in 1998, so that what shapes pro-impeachment sentiment in 1974 will be more similar for Democrats and Republicans than it was in 1998.

The bases of pro-impeachment sentiments

I shall examine public support for impeachment in 1974 and 1998 using the American National Election Studies. Did public support for the two impeachments rest on similar foundations?

I have tried to make the models as similar as possible. However, there were shifts in questions and question wording between 1974 and 1998 that made complete replications impossible. Also, the 1974 ANES was carried out three months after Nixon resigned, while the 1998 survey was administered a month and a half *before* the House impeachment vote. Nevertheless, the issues were clearly framed in the public's mind so that the timing seems of minor consequence at most.

I will first estimate models for each impeachment for the entire samples. Then I will estimate the same models for Democratic and Republican Party identifiers to determine whether each group of partisans sees the issues in the same way. My expectation is that Democrats and Republicans will see the Nixon impeachment in similar terms more than they will the Clinton impeachment. Each of these estimations is by probit analysis since the dependent variables are dichotomies. For the probits, the measure of impact is what Rosenstone and Hansen (1993) call the 'effect' of an independent variable, the difference in estimated probabilities from the predictor's highest and lowest values, letting the other independent variables take their 'natural' values. The interpretation of an effect is straightforward: it is the change in the probability that a respondent will support impeachment if his/her score moves from the lowest value of a predictor to the highest. The models are presented in Tables 7.1 and 7.2.

For the Nixon impeachment, the biggest impact by far is whether people viewed the hearings of the House Judiciary Committee as fair (see Table 7.1). Someone who thought the hearings were very fair was 44 per cent more

Table 7.1 Probit estimation for Nixon impeachment, 1974

Variable	Coefficient	Std error	MLE/SE	Effect
Party identification	−0.147***	0.045	−3.24	−0.171
Frequency attend religious services	−0.048	0.063	0.76	−0.120
Favour government economic policy	0.168***	0.069	2.41	0.130
Ideology	−0.005	0.070	−0.07	−0.005
Difference between party ideologies	−0.004	0.057	−0.06	−0.004
Employment should be guaranteed by govt	0.085*	0.057	1.48	0.091
Congress job approval	0.075*	0.059	−1.28	0.106
Many in government crooked	0.041	0.073	0.56	0.029
Politics too complicated	−0.064*	0.045	−1.42	−0.046
Politicians don't care about people like me	0.074*	0.046	1.60	0.054
How much tax money government wastes	0.141*	0.088	1.61	0.111
Government run by few big interests	0.045	0.051	0.90	0.034
Watch national television news every night	0.087	0.077	1.14	0.060
Union member in household	−0.039	0.050	−0.79	−0.028
African-American	−0.057	0.478	−0.12	−0.010
Age[a]	−0.002	0.005	−0.03	−0.017
Gender	−0.123	0.175	−0.70	−0.049
House Judiciary Committee hearings fair	0.436****	0.071	6.16	0.440
Press coverage of Watergate fair	0.227***	0.067	3.39	0.181
Special Prosecutor Jaworski thermometer	0.007*	0.004	1.52	0.126
Constant	1.702**	0.938	1.82	

Notes: Estimated $R^2 = 0.727 - 2*$Log likelihood ratio $= 327.37$ $N = 495$.
Per cent predicted correctly: probit: 85.5; Null: 77.2.
**** $p < 0.0001$; *** $p < 0.01$; ** $p < 0.05$; * $p < 0.10$.
[a] Effect for age calculated at 18 and 75 years.

Table 7.2 Probit estimation for Clinton impeachment, 1998

Variable	Coefficient	Std error	MLE/SE	Effect
Party identification	0.204****	0.044	4.60	0.291
Born-again Christian	0.299**	0.169	1.76	−0.061
Frequency attend religious services	0.074	0.071	1.05	0.063
Religion important in life	0.154**	0.071	2.17	0.126
Economy better or worse since Clinton?	0.313****	0.094	3.34	0.286
Which party better handles economy?	0.098**	0.056	1.74	0.126
Ideology	0.086	0.079	1.09	0.110
Important differences between parties?	0.092**	0.041	2.25	0.079
Favour fewer services or more spending	−0.063	0.053	−1.19	−0.081
Feeling thermometer toward blacks	−0.003	0.021	−0.14	0.007
Congress job approval	0.008	0.041	0.19	0.007
Many in government crooked	0.194***	0.060	3.21	0.162
Days watch national television news last week	0.014	0.032	0.44	0.020
Union member in household	−0.394**	0.200	−1.97	−0.082
African-American	−0.773*	0.472	−1.64	−0.153
Age[a]	−0.005	0.005	−1.06	−0.081
Gender	−0.183	0.159	−1.15	−0.039
Approve Congress handling Clinton scandal	−0.008	0.041	−0.19	−0.070
Approve media handling Clinton scandal	−0.031	0.060	0.53	−0.027
Special prosecutor Starr thermometer	0.016****	0.003	4.45	0.381
Constant	−0.623	0.743	−0.84	

Notes: Estimated $R^2 = 0.700 - 2*$Log likelihood ratio = 370.84 $N = 497$.
Per cent predicted correctly: Probit: 84.6; Null: 66.4.
**** $p < 0.0001$; *** $p < 0.01$; ** $p < 0.05$; * $p < 0.10$.
[a] Effect for age calculated at 18 and 75 years.

likely to back impeachment than someone who held the hearings to be very unfair. The next largest impact was for the fairness of press coverage of the Watergate affair, with an effect approaching 20 per cent. Party identification ranks third, with strong Democrats 17 per cent more favourable to impeachment than strong Republicans. Economic performance mattered as well: people who thought the Nixon administration was handling the economy well were 13 per cent less likely to favour impeachment than people who disapproved of government economic policy. In 1998, positive evaluations of the economy helped buoy Clinton's support. But they were of little help during the 1974 recession: barely 6 per cent thought the government was doing a good job managing the economy, compared with 51 per cent who said it was doing a poor job. Indeed, negative evaluations of the economy made people more likely to back impeachment – and, taken together, bad economic times and the Watergate scandal led to major losses for the Republicans in the 1974 Congressional elections (Uslaner and Conway, 1975). Strong approval of Special Prosecutor Leon Jaworski added 13 per cent to support for impeachment, while approval of the (Democrat-controlled) Congress added 11 per cent to public support for impeachment.

However, only four variables are significant at $p < 0.01$ or greater: the fairness of the Judiciary Committee, the fairness of the press, party identification and support for government economic policy. Other variables are significant at the very modest $p < 0.10$ level – including three different measures of political efficacy: if you believe that politicians do not care about people like you, that politics is too complicated, and that the government wastes a lot of tax money, you are more likely to favour impeachment. The impacts individually are modest, but collectively there is a reasonably strong linkage between alienation from government and support for impeachment in 1974. There is also a very modest impact for one policy position: people who believe government should guarantee employment were more likely to favour impeachment. But there is no significant impact for ideology or for perceived differences between the parties.[4] Nor do we see the divide by race and religiosity that has become so important in more recent American politics.

The 1998 models show much greater roles for party and ideology (see Table 7.2). The perceived fairness of Congress and the press in the Clinton impeachment, so important in 1974, were insignificant in 1998. Attitudes toward Special Prosecutor Kenneth Starr had the greatest impact on support for impeachment. Strong support for Starr made people 38 per cent more likely to back impeachment than powerful negative feelings. Not far behind were party identification and the belief that Clinton had made the economy better. Strong Republicans were 29 per cent more likely to back impeachment than strong Democrats – an impact 70 per cent larger than the one I found in 1974. And people who thought the economy was much better since Clinton came to office were 29 per cent less likely to support impeachment. Clinton benefited from a good economy much as Nixon suffered from perceptions of a poor economy. Almost twenty-two times as many Americans thought the economy had got much better (34 per cent) under Clinton than believed it had got much worse (1.6 per cent). Slightly over three quarters of the public gave the administration positive marks for its handling of the economy: 85 per cent of those who thought the economy had got much better since Clinton took office – and 59 per cent of Republicans agreeing with this – opposed impeachment. Perceiving that the Democrats handled the economy better than Republicans also had a significant impact.

Ideology was not significant, nor was support for greater government spending as opposed to fewer government services. Yet, greater party polarisation mattered beyond party identification: people who perceived clear differences between the parties were 8 per cent more likely to *favour* impeachment than people who saw no important differences.

Beyond policy issues, we see far greater impacts for variables reflecting partisan divisions than we did in 1974. African-Americans were 15 per cent less likely to support impeachment than whites, reflecting Clinton's close ties to the African-American community and his standing in it as the (honorary) 'first black President'. Households with union members were 8 per cent less likely to support impeachment. Born-again Christians were 6 per cent *more* likely to back punishing the President, while people who said that religion was very important in their daily lives were 13 per cent more supportive of impeachment. These variables reflect strong divisions in the electorate: African-Americans and union members are strong Democrats. Fundamentalists are strong Republicans.

While these divisions are hardly new in American politics, they were muted in the 1970s. In 1972, 38 per cent of people from union households voted for Nixon and only 47 per cent cast ballots for Hubert Humphrey. In 1974, 41 per cent of people from union households voted for Republican Congressional candidates. In 1974 blacks were considerably more supportive of impeachment than whites, but the racial gap was much larger twenty-four years later. So the impact of race in 1974 was captured by a host of other variables. Religiosity was far less important in American politics in 1974 than in 1998: born-again Christians were not an organised force within the Republican party – indeed Jimmy Carter carried the South as a born-again Christian *and as a Democrat* in 1976. By 1998, fundamentalism had become a far more important force within the Republican Party; religiosity divides the parties as much as economic ideology does (Layman and Carsey, 2002).

As in 1974, perceptions of an unresponsive government mattered in 1998. I did not include the entire battery of efficacy items in the 1998 estimation because most proved insignificant and cluttered the analysis. However, the perception that many in government are crooked boosted support for impeachment by 16 per cent, one of the more powerful effects in the model.

So there are many similarities between 1974 and 1998. If you were upset with the state of the economy in 1974, you were more likely to back impeachment and if you were pleased with economic progress in 1998, you were less likely to favour ousting the President. Support for impeachment was strong among people who distrusted politicians more generally. In neither case did attention to the media matter. However, there are also important differences. And the key differences reflect the growing importance of partisanship in 1998. Party identification, perceptions of differences between the parties, and the social bases of the parties all played a more important role in 1998 than in 1974. Perceptions of fairness by Congress and the media shaped impeachment attitudes in 1974, but concerns for procedure were of little consequence two and a half decades later.

The greater impact of partisanship comes through even more clearly in truncated models that exclude the fairness questions and the feeling thermometers about Special Prosecutors. In these models, we see increments in the effect for party identification in 1974 (from -0.171 to -0.284) and especially in 1998

Table 7.3 Summary of significant effects by party, 1974

Variable	Democratic identifiers	Republican identifiers
Ideology	−0.094*	−0.001
Approve House Judiciary Committee	0.284****	0.582****
Approve press coverage	0.361****	0.060
Government wastes taxes	0.181**	0.196*
Politicians don't care about me	−0.010	0.198***
Favour government economic policy	0.036	0.290***

Notes: Entries are effects from probit analyses and asterisks represent significance levels.
**** $p < 0.0001$; *** $p < 0.01$; ** $p < 0.05$; * $p < 0.10$.
$N = 271$ (Democrats), 182 (Republicans).

(from 0.291 to 0.424). The proportional increment is about the same in both cases (0.60 in 1974 and 0.68 in 1998). However, the effect for partisanship now dominates the model for 1998. Only evaluation of the economy (with an effect at 0.327) comes close. The truncated model for 1974 leads to significant coefficients for attending religious services (effect = −0.120), guaranteed jobs (−0.159) and ideology (−0.169). There are also large increments in effects for all three measures of efficacy. So 1974 represents a reaction against government as much as it does a partisan battle.

I estimated the models separately for Democratic and Republican identifiers. The models were identical except that they necessarily excluded party identification and the Republican models excluded the African-American variable. In Tables 7.3 and 7.4, I report summaries of the significant effects for each party in 1974 and 1998 respectively.

In both years, what matters for one party does not necessarily matter for the other. In 1974, however, perceptions of fairness are important for both sets of party identifiers (see Table 7.3). For Republicans, perceptions of fairness by the House Judiciary Committee was by far the most important factor shaping impeachment attitudes (effect = 0.582). Press coverage mattered most for Democratic identifiers (and not at all for Republicans), but the Judiciary Committee ranked close behind (effect = 0.284). For both Democrats and Republicans, believing that government wastes taxes moves attitudes toward impeachment by 20 per cent. Ideology matters for Democrats and both economic policy and perceptions of political unresponsiveness are significant for Republicans.

This jumbled pattern – some things matter for both, others for just one party – gives way to crystal clarity in 1998. The factors that shape Democratic support for (or opposition to) impeachment are largely irrelevant for Republicans, and vice versa. For Democrats, perceptions of which party can best handle the economy, media fairness and union membership are the key to

Table 7.4 Summary of significant effects by party, 1998

Variable	Democratic identifiers	Republican identifiers
Union member in household	−0.079**	−0.109
Party best to handle economy	0.128*	−0.002
Approve media handling of Clinton scandal	−0.114**	−0.004
Born-again Christian	0.003	0.138**
Religion important in life	0.038	0.217**
Important differences between parties	0.020	0.187***
Economy better since Clinton	0.016	0.395***
Most politicians crooked	0.004	0.220***
Special Prosecutor Starr thermometer	0.049	0.578****

Notes: Entries are effects from probit analyses and asterisks represent significance levels.
**** $p < 0.0001$; *** $p < 0.01$; ** $p < 0.05$; * $p < 0.10$.
$N = 236$ (Democrats), 234 (Republicans).

impeachment attitudes. None of these variables is significant for Republicans. For Republican identifiers, attitudes toward the Special Prosecutor, the state of the economy, the belief that most politicians are crooked, the importance of religion in daily life, seeing important differences between the parties and being a born-again Christian are all important for Republicans. None is significant for Democrats and none has an effect greater than 0.05. What mattered for one party did not matter for the other in 1998. Democrats and Republicans had a very different world-view of the impeachment process. For Democrats, it was all about private behaviour (sex); for Republicans, it was all about public behaviour (lying to the grand jury).

We see this even more clearly in Table 7.5, where I present correlations between the effects of common variables among party identifiers in 1974 and 1998. Here I take the effects estimated from each model by party and compute correlations among the effects for variables common to both parties in each year. For each group of partisans in 1974 and 1998, the Ns in the table represent the number of variables common to each set of estimations. And here is stronger evidence that different partisans see the world differently. In 1974 there is a modest correlation (0.540) between Democratic and Republican identifiers. By 1998, the correlation drops to 0.385. Democrats and Republicans were far more likely to use the same mental heuristic to judge impeachment in 1974 than they were in 1998.

There is more than a partisan disconnect. Democrats in 1998 seemed to use different criteria to the ones used by their fellow partisans in 1974. This is hardly surprising, since the issues in the two impeachments were so very different. However, Republicans were more consistent over time ($r = 0.490$). Indeed,

Table 7.5 Intercorrelations of probit effects

Sample	Republicans 1974	Democrats 1998	Republicans 1998
Democrats 1974	**0.540** (15)*	0.372 (14)	0.169 (13)
Republicans 1974		0.498 (13)	0.490 (13)
Democrats 1998			**0.385** (18)**

Notes: Entries are correlations among probit effects with the number of variables shown in parentheses.
* Correlation increases to 0.688 without press fairness variable.
** Correlation increases to 0.443 without economic approval variable.

Republicans in 1974 used similar heuristics to 1998 Democrats – both groups were defending a President belonging to their own party.

The correlations between parties in 1974 and 1998 are both depressed by outliers. In 1974, the fairness of the press mattered mightily for Democrats but not for Republicans. In 1998 economic evaluations were an outlier for Republicans. When I delete both observations, the 1998 correlation rises modestly to 0.443 but the 1974 correlation increases to 0.688. Different partisans had similar world-views in 1974 but not in 1998.[5]

Whither the differences?

Of course, one might say, the parties saw the world similarly in 1974 but not in 1998. In 1974, there was a clear-cut allegation of criminal wrong-doing. In 1998, the nation went through a wrenching and unresolved debate over what the nature of an impeachable offence was.

Yet, this hardly counts against my argument. In the 1970s, when party lines and ideological conflict were muted, a hotly contested impeachment such as Clinton's would never have emerged from committee. In 1974, 40 per cent of the Republicans on the House Judiciary Committee voted with all Democrats to impeach President Nixon. In 1998, no Democratic member of the Judiciary Committee voted to impeach President Clinton. Impeachment in 1998 was a political tool. Congressional Republicans used legal tools to do what many of them had wanted to do anyway – to get rid of a popular Democratic President. Indeed, one of the House managers, the Republican, Bob Barr, had filed a motion to impeach Bill Clinton a year before anyone had heard of Monica Lewinsky.

Voters in 1974 reacted to Watergate by punishing the Republican Party and giving the Democrats an overwhelming majority in both Houses of Congress. The political response in 1998 was far more muted, largely because the partisan battle was still raging at the time of the election. Two years later the issue had faded, but still voters were so polarised by party and ideology that few entertained any thoughts of crossing party lines to punish *either side* for unethical behaviour.

There is support for this thesis in the data from the 1974 and 1998 election studies. In 1974, the correlation between partisanship and evaluations of the Special Prosecutor Leon Jaworski was meagre (–0.234). In 1998, the correlation between evaluations of the Special Prosecutor and party identification was more than double the value of the 1974 correlation (0.530). In 1974, there was a partisan division over the role of the press (the correlation with party identification was 0.360), but by 1998 there was no conflict over the media ($r = -0.095$ with party identification). The press, supposedly a more neutral force, was critical in 1974. In 1998, it was largely a bystander. The battle came from within.

We see continual conflict in everyday politics. Campaigns have become nastier. Congress is a much less civil place. The Democratic Party leaders in Congress are barely on speaking terms with either the Republican President or the Republican leaders in Congress. Impeachment was supposed to be an extreme remedy for a very troubling problem. Now it has become just one more weapon of the weak.

Notes

1 I am grateful to the Russell Sage Foundation and the Carnegie Foundation for a grant under the Russell Sage programme on The Social Dimensions of Inequality (see www.russellsage.org/programs/proj_reviews/social-inequality.htm) and to the General Research Board of the Graduate School of the University of Maryland, College Park. The data employed here come from the Inter-University Consortium for Political and Social Research, which is not responsible for any of my interpretations.
2 From the 1998 American National Election Study. Highton (2002: 2) reports a lower figure (56 per cent).
3 See http://web.mit.edu/dburbach/www/papers/presaprv/presaprv.xls.
4 The 1974 ANES did not ask voters whether there were significant differences between the parties (as the 1998 ANES did). Instead, I computed a measure of ideological distance from the perceived positions of the parties.
5 It might seem that much of the correlation stems from what does *not* matter for both parties. So I restricted the analysis to effects that had absolute values greater than 0.08. For 1974, the inter-party correlation rose to 0.628 ($N = 8$), while for 1998 it only increased to 0.407 ($N = 14$).

References

Abramowitz, A. I. (2001), 'It's Monica, Stupid: The Impeachment Controversy and the 1998 Midterm Election', *Legislative Studies Quarterly*, 26, 211–26.
Brady, D. W. (1988), *Critical Elections in the US House of Representatives*, Stanford, Stanford University Press.
Downs, A. (1957), *An Economic Theory of Democracy*, New York, Harper and Row.
Evans, C. L. and W. J. Oleszek (1997), *Congress Under Fire*, Boston, Houghton Mifflin.
Ginsberg, B. and M. Shefter (1999), *Politics by Other Means*, 2nd edition, New York, W.W. Norton.

Gugliotta, G. and T. M. Neal (1998), 'Republicans and Democrats Ponder Ever-widening Chasm', *Washington Post*, 20 December, A3.

Hetherington, M. J. (2001), 'Resurgent Mass Partisanship: The Role of Elite Polarization', *American Political Science Review*, 95: 3, 619–31.

Highton, B. (2002), 'Bill Clinton, Newt Gingrich, and the 1998 House Elections', *Public Opinion Quarterly*, 66: 1, 1–17.

Jacobson, G. C. (2000), 'The Electoral Basis of Partisan Polarization in Congress', paper presented at the annual meeting of the American Political Science Association, 31 August–3 September, Washington, DC.

Layman, G. C. and Carsey, T. M. (2002), 'Party polarization and "conflict extension" in the American electorate', *American Journal of Political Science*, 46: 4, 786–802.

Rohde, D. W. (1991), *Parties and Leaders in the Post-reform House*, Chicago, University of Chicago Press.

Rosenstone, S. J. and J. M. Hansen (1993), *Mobilization, Participation, and Democracy in America*, New York, Macmillan.

Uslaner, E. M. (1993), *The Decline of Comity in Congress*, Ann Arbor, University of Michigan Press.

Uslaner, E. M. and M. M. Conway (1975), 'The Responsible Congressional Electorate: Watergate, the Economy, and Vote Choice in 1974', *American Political Science Review*, 79: 3, 788–803.

Part III

Why scandals emerge and what they indicate

8

Political scandals and crisis management in Greece, 1821–2001

Kleomenis S. Koutsoukis

If we wish to understand why scandals emerge and what they indicate, some clues may be furnished by an examination of two of the most devastating political scandals modern Greece has experienced in its two centuries of free political life. The first relates to its War of Independence from the Ottoman Empire during the 1820s, and the second to the transformation of Greek society that was attempted during the penultimate decade of the twentieth century. The former focused on the so-called 'loan of independence', while the latter is known as the 'Koskotas mega-scandal', after the young Greek–American banker who was at its centre. It is obvious that the two scandals occurred under completely different socio-political conditions. In analysing them, I shall describe the strikingly different conditions under which they occurred, the pattern of their unfolding and the overall management of the crises they provoked. Several other scandals in the nineteenth and twentieth centuries will also be briefly described, along with the conditions under which they occurred. My thesis is that scandals are typically associated with rapid social and political change and that behaviour tends to scandalise people if it is perceived as undermining specific collective goals of the society as a whole.

Some theoretical considerations

In this chapter, political scandal is analysed as an exceptional and complex case of corruption. In general, the kinds of acts that are likely to be deemed 'scandalous' if they become public knowledge are determined by the society's values and its ethical sensitivity, as well as by its political dynamics, all of which may affect public opinion to a greater or lesser degree, for or against those involved. Therefore a scandal may be considered as a phenomenon of social pathology, and thus capable of indicating much about the society in which it occurs. Nowadays, serious scientific scandalology can serve this purpose. If it deals with real scandals and does not succumb to the agendas and propaganda of the parties involved, it can provide an index of the values or ethical sensitivity of a society. If it does so succumb, then, by being made to serve the purposes of propaganda, it acts as a tool of social control.

There is a persuasive theory that, even though corruption is an endemic phenomenon in developing countries, the appearance of *scandals* tends to coincide with advances in development (Koutsoukis, 2003). Thus in countries that have not yet achieved considerable levels of social, economic and political development, corruption is so common that it becomes a routine and taken-for-granted aspect of everyday life – to the extent that several economists and developmental theorists have concluded that it is a necessary condition for development (Huntington, 1968). By contrast, in countries characterised as developed – typically liberal or western-type democracies – corruption is usually lower, while at the same time far more likely to create a scandal if and when it comes to light. Thus a developed political culture, together with norms of due process, renders corruption more likely to be regarded as dangerous for the orderly, regular functioning of the political system. Hence, these societies are more liable to be scandalised by it. Indicative of their tendency to produce scandals and not just corruption in the conventional sense is a comparative compilation of about 200 scandals from 1946 to 1990. While 90 per cent took place in western developed countries, such as the UK and the US, only 10 per cent were located in less developed ones (Heidenheimer *et al.*, 1990).

Meanwhile, the extension of those democratic principles that render corruption more likely to be perceived as a threat, at the same time improve the effectiveness of the means available to fight it. Thus, the spread of information brought about by the development of the mass media of communications, and the adoption of transparent procedures in the sphere of public administration, together with their wider acceptance, are all basic factors involved in preventing corrupt practices and improving the functioning of the political system. For, at one and the same time, they reinforce all the elements we commonly take to be the defining characteristics of political development, namely the spread of democracy and the empowerment of ordinary citizens.

Hardly surprisingly, then, a perusal of Transparency International's (TI's) Corruption Perceptions Index reveals that the highly developed liberal democracies achieve the highest scores, while developing countries are located further down the scale.[1] However, it is also noticeable that some of the countries belonging to the category of western liberal democracies – in particular the southern and central European countries like Greece, Italy, Portugal, Spain, Hungary and Poland – are bunched together in the middle of the scale between the lower-placed developing countries on the one hand, and the most highly developed countries on the other. Noticeable too is the fact that this 'middle-ranking' group also includes countries which, though conventionally thought of as 'developing', have achieved higher standards of living than others in that category. One is thinking here of countries such as Peru, South Korea, Malaysia and South Africa.

Greece's TI ranking loses some of its aridness when set against the background of some of the post-war corruption scandals we describe below. We shall also see how, in the period following the War of Independence, there appeared to be a movement away from that taken-for-granted quality of corruption mentioned above, as socio-economic development gradually led to the growth of transparency and the spread of norms embodying principles of due process. We begin, however, with a description of the loans scandal that took place during the revolution.

The Greek Loan scandal

From the very beginning of Greece's emergence as a revolutionary state in 1821, there were strong signs of official sensitivity to matters of moral rectitude and personal propriety. Indicative of this was the fact that one of the first laws passed by the Provisional Assembly – the Code of Laws of 1824 – sought precisely to combat corruption among state functionaries, such as judges, ministers, administrative officials and so forth. The first scandal arising from this sensitivity was connected with the so-called 'Loan for Independence', agreed in London in 1824 and given to assist the Greeks in their struggle for independence against the Ottoman Empire. Like several later scandals, the one associated with the 'Loan for Independence' suggested that behaviour tends to scandalise people when the collective goals of a society are perceived as being undermined rather than promoted. The relevant collective goals at that time were national liberation, rebirth of the nation and the creation of a new Greek state.

In 1821, the Greeks decided to take up arms against the Ottomans but neither side was strong enough for a decisive victory and, during the second year of the revolution, the scarcity of guns and ammunition gave rise to the need for a foreign loan. This idea was favoured by many Greeks of the Diaspora who, on returning to Greece from other parts of Europe, had raised hopes of support from the philhellenic movements in Europe, especially in England where a Philhellenic Committee had been founded in March 1821 soon after the revolution started (Woodhouse, 1978). The Legislature, dominated initially by Peloponnesians under Theodore Kolokotrones, refused to accept the procedure for obtaining a loan proposed by the Executive, which was dominated by the islanders under George Koundouriotes. Their main disagreement was over whom to choose to undertake the negotiations.

Koundouriotes and several other Phanariot politicians (such as the pro-British Alexander Mavrokordatos) managed to send two young 'cosmopolitans' to visit European capitals in pursuit of the loan.[2] One of them was Ioannes Orlandos, Koundouriotes' son in law, the other Andreas Louriotis, confidant to Mavrokordatos. When the two representatives reached London, they were joined by Ioannis Zaimis, a trusted follower of Kolokotrones. There were several disagreements, reflecting preexisting class differences, between members of the Legislature and Executive and by 1823 civil war between the two sides had broken out. Kolokotrones enjoyed the support of the armed peasants and former klephts in the Morea.[3] 'Opposing him were the civilian leaders in the National Assembly . . . which spoke for the wealthy notables, influential primates and rich merchants' (Sowards, 1996).

When the representatives of the provisional revolutionary government arrived in London in the autumn of 1823, they found not only a Philhellenic Committee composed of prominent English personalities inspired by Greek revolutionary ideas, but also a climate amongst City financiers favourable to investments abroad. At this time, the governments of several other European countries – such as Prussia, Spain, Russia, Austria and Portugal – were managing to secure loans through the London money market, as were some of the developing countries of Latin America. The Philhellenic Committee not only welcomed and advertised the Greek loan petition, but many of its members also decided to support it actively by buying shares through the London Stock Exchange (Lignadis, 1970). This made possible the signing of an agreement, with the bankers Loughman and O'Brien, for a loan of £800,000 at 59 per cent (Katsoulis, 1975).

Although the Peloponnesians had managed to send their own representative to the loan negotiations in London, they constantly suspected the two other representatives of acting on behalf of the Anglophile leaders of the Executive, Koundouriotes and Mavrokordatos. They accused them of overspending the loan money in London, of obtaining the loan on unsatisfactory terms and of ordering guns, ammunition and battleships without consulting them beforehand (Howe, 1828; Stamatopoulos, 1964). The opposition asked the Executive to recall to Greece the two loan representatives, Orlandos and Louriotis, while an examining committee was sent to London to investigate how the main part of the loan had actually been spent. It emerged that of the total of £800,000, only £298,000 actually reached Greece. A later report of the Committee of National Accounts, submitted to the Third National Assembly in 1827 (before the end of the War of Independence) noted, 'We nowhere found mentioned the amount of the loan received by the London Committee, nor the quantity of ammunition and other supplies sent to the Administration' (Katsoulis, 1975).

As soon as the first instalments of the loan began arriving in Greece in September 1824, the civil war intensified. Moreover, the concluding of the loan agreement encouraged the search for a second loan. Whereas the first loan seemed to exacerbate domestic conflict, the second worsened the situation to the point where the revolution itself was endangered (Lignadis, 1970). Indeed, a year later, with a second loan, a new civil war began between the Peloponnesian military and the Phanariot politicians who were co-operating with the Islanders. Historians of the Greek Revolution note that only 25 per cent of the second loan of £2,000,000 actually reached Greece, leaving unanswered questions about how much of it, like the first loan, had been spent on the war against the foreign enemy and how much against the domestic opposition in the civil war (Finlay, n.d.; Simopoulos, 1997). As Konstantinos Paparigopoulos puts it: 'news of the arrival of loan instalments increased the passion for power, which in turn led to . . . civil war' (Lignadis, 1970). Battle after battle against the enemy was lost because the loaned money went not towards the war for independence but to those occupying the most significant positions in this war (Finlay, n.d.).

Londos, one of Kolokotrones' allies, asked the Assembly to conduct an enquiry in order to find out what had happened to the money generated by the loans, what had been the exact purpose of the loans and how it had come to be agreed 'to offer our estates to English shareholders' (Londos Archives, vol. B'). In fact, part of the loan agreements had stipulated that repayments would be effected by turning over to the shareholders, and placing under British jurisdiction, Greek lands liberated by the War of Independence. Worse still, all revenues from custom duties, offices, fisheries, mines and so forth would go to them, if the need arose.

Meanwhile, *The Times* editorial of 1825 was very critical of the passion of the British financiers, desperate to invest their money in the most profitable ways possible regardless of any other considerations. In another editorial *The Times* criticised the fact that 'members of the Philhellenic Committee, during the negotiations for the loan, were acting not only on behalf of the English government but of Greece as well . . . and that from the total amount of the loan less than half went to Greece'. As for the attitude to the loan of Philhellenic Committee members themselves, indicative is the statement made by Bowring, one of its leading spokesmen: 'When an issue of economic interest arises, then there is neither philanthropy or patriotism, nor independence' (Lignadis, 1970; *The Times*, 23–28 October 1826). The statement produced an outcry against the exploitative behaviour of the philhellenes, and expressions of indignation in several parts of the country.

Reflecting this, *The Times* heavily criticised leading members of the Philhellenic Committee – such as Bowring, Hume and Ellis, each of whom had received extraordinary commissions as intermediaries – calling them 'swindlers', and concluding: 'Poor Greece! Little cause had she to expect such a treatment from England' (*The Times*, October 1826). William Cobbett devoted several issues of his *Political Register* to criticism of the 'Greek Scandal', which he dubbed 'Greek pie' and which became associated in the public imagination with the name of Bowring. The case was not forgotten in Britain for a long time. Thus when Bowring's son Edgar later stood as a Liberal candidate in Exeter, Conservative papers circulated cartoons showing his father holding a big pie in his hands entitled 'Greek pie' (*Political Register*; *Quarterly Review*, 35; *Knickerborker's Monthly*, II, 1833).

Bowring, overreacting in his *Westminster Review*, was very critical of the Greek loan representatives in London – accusing them of overspending and Greece of not making good use of the money (*Westminster Review*, January–March 1827). These accusations, besides creating panic amongst British investors who formed a committee to investigate the use of the loan money in Greece, also further scandalised the British public, who in 1826 had discovered, through a series of articles and comments published in *The Times*, details of the loan agreement and its extravagant use by the Greek representatives and the British members of the Philhellenic Committee in London. The Greek historian and one-time Ambassador to the UK, Spiro Trikoupis, wrote: 'The English people were astonished at the dreadful use to which the loan was put' (Andreadis, 1904; Trikoupis, vol. 3). After a series of articles and commentaries in its 28 November 1826 edition, *The Times* concluded: 'May the money given in the name of the Greeks turn to anathema on the heads of those who took them!'

Long after Greece's liberation, the loans continued to be the subject of court actions and private negotiations. The Court of Audit, in its decision of 29 October 1834, called Orlandos and Louriotis to account, holding them responsible for the use of the loan money agreed upon in London and ordering them to pay damages of approximately £29,000. Under Otho, the Bavarian King of Greece, the two men compiled, in 1839, a detailed 529-page report outlining the services they had provided. Their views were even criticised by Spiliotakis, who had previously worked with them as the representative who had replaced Zaimis (Kolokotrones' confidant). However, no further action was taken against them (Lignadis, 1970).

Finally, it must be mentioned that, decades later, under the premiership of Charilaos Trikoupis, in 1878, the Greek government sent George Gennadios to London for discussions with the shareholders on repayment of the outstanding debts associated with the loans, thus putting an end to the lengthy mutual recriminations (Gennadios, 1878; Lignadis, 1970).

Corruption, scandal and the modernisation process

After the Greek state was consolidated and began functioning following the end of the War of Independence in 1829, corruption unfolded in wide areas of public policy: from unemployment to the management of crime; from election procedures to policies for dealing with the scarcity of goods and capital. To some degree, corruption could be considered as functional because it served as a safety valve for the problems of lack of mobility and urban unemployment. To that extent it helped integrate ordinary Greeks into the political system. In particular, after 1844, which saw the establishment of a lower chamber of Parliament under wide manhood suffrage, the so-called 'French' party under John Kolettes created 'a mass political machine known as "the System" which delivered votes to the ruling party in return for patronage and favors for the voters: no prefect, tax official, judge or policeman served without an exchange of favors with party leaders. The System was corrupt, but it was also a mass organization which made the Greek people participants in the political system' (Sowards, 1996). Undoubtedly, politicians and men of authority exploited people's needs and delayed the establishment of necessary institutions. However, corrupt practices were consistent with the 'rousfeti' (favour) culture inherited from Ottoman rule, where 'bahchishi' (bribery) had been an everyday practice (Koutsoukis, 1998).

Just fifteen years after Greece's liberation the press and intellectuals began denouncing the widespread dishonesty that was apparent among those in public life. The revolution in Paris in 1848 encouraged intellectuals, from several parts of Greece, to call for a new liberation movement 'to get rid of corruption, "remoula", bankruptcy, poverty, and the high-handedness and dishonesty of governors'. It is indicative that in 1878 Nikolaos Saripolos, professor of Constitutional Law, asked: 'Might not the good citizen despair at the widespread corruption which engulfs all the classes of our society?' (Koutsoukis, 1998).

It was then that Charilaos Trikoupis, son of the well-known historian Spiro Trikoupis, brought to Greece the spirit of parliamentary democracy, having lived in Britain, where he worked at the Greek Embassy, before becoming a politician. Even more, he seemed to have copied practices from such British prime ministers as Disraeli, Gladstone and Palmerstone, whom he admired. He attempted to transfer to Greece those electoral practices and other modern institutions that serve to minimise politicians' opportunities for corruption, including franchise extensions and merit payments for public employees. Despite this, he himself eventually fell victim to scandal. The accusation was based on a law that he himself had introduced into Parliament. Thus, it was that he and several of his ministers were charged with false accounting and improper use of public funds while in power. Thanks to his former political adversary, Deliyannis, he was acquitted and the allegations were not investigated further (Koutsoukis, 1998). The Prime Minister at the time (1891), Deliyannis, had suggested to Parliament that it 'show magnanimity as far as the State's interests are concerned'.

Turning to the twentieth century, Greece experienced two scandals between 1928 and 1932, a period of particularly stable and democratic parliamentary government. The first was the 'quinine scandal', the second the 'Karapanayotis scandal' after the minister accused of violating the standards introduced to Greek public life by such distinguished politicians as Eleftherios Venizelos. The 'quinine scandal' had to do with malaria and its associated high fever, a widespread illness at that time due to poor health conditions and the fact that a cure for it had not yet been fully discovered. It was decided that quinine needed to be made more widely available; for this reason, it was both imported and manufactured in Greece. In the autumn of 1930 the press discovered that, despite being under the supervision of the State General Chemical Laboratory, the pharmaceutical companies producing quinine were not using the proper amounts of the materials necessary to produce the pills. Instead they were holding back most of the materials, using them for other profitable activities later on. The Venizelos cabinet was shaken by the intricacy of the allegations. Although Prime Minister Venizelos strongly defended him, the Director General was considered responsible for what had happened and imprisoned while the matter was investigated. A few months later the Court of Appeal acquitted him in the light of doubts about the soundness of the evidence of his culpability (Dafnis, 1955).

The Karapanayiotis case had to do with influence exercised by the minister in favour of one of his relatives, who had made a bid for a publicly funded project. In this case Prime Minister Venizelos was very clear: 'I find it very disturbing that a minister would use the power provided by his public position to manage a concession in favour of one of his relatives instead of exercising impartial supervision. Therefore, if the accusation is true, I consider [the behaviour] incompatible with the political sensitivity that the public requires of a minister.' The minister was forced to resign (Dafnis, 1955).

It was during this period that the well-known poet Konstantinos Karyotakis, working as a public servant, submitted a memorandum to his superior officer in which he analysed cases of corruption, nepotism and the lack of merito-cracy in the public administration. He concluded his report: 'Time after time public servants indulge in corruption. We need not new sources (he meant of money) but good new administration' (Karyotakis, 1996).

The post war period

The period of constitutional monarchy (1946–66)
The country was liberated from Nazi occupation in 1944 and then, between 1946 and 1949, suffered civil war. The end of the civil war coincided with the onset of the Cold War – which brought with it both the ideological imperative of fighting Communism, under the auspices of NATO, and American financial aid. For these reasons, the political agenda of the period was dominated by post-war reconstruction efforts and the spending decisions associated therewith. This background therefore provided the context for both bureaucratic corrup-tion (Koutsoukis, 1989) and several scandals involving politicians, prominent entrepreneurs and state functionaries who were most closely involved in administering the millions of dollars of American aid. Low levels of transparency and a variety of institutional weaknesses facilitated their corrupt activities. Several of them, however, were brought to justice and punished.

Military dictatorship (1967–74)
Under the military junta, the lack of a free press and thus a relative shortage of relevant information tended to undermine the conditions necessary for the outbreak of scandals. But there is enough evidence to allow us to state that, though it was prevented from giving rise to scandals, bureaucratic corruption of a quite cynical kind proceeded apace (Koutsoukis, 1989). Moreover, the period was not entirely devoid of scandals either. One famous example was the 'Ballosemo scandal', after the minister who found himself at its centre. It broke out after the fall of the dictatorship and was related to the growing imports of meat that were taking place at this time owing to increased levels of domestic demand. The accusation was that intermediaries had for years over-charged for the imports in collusion with the minister, who was sent for trial and eventually died in prison. It produced extensive and scandalised pub-licity, because the military had justified their coming into power on the basis of purifying politics from corruption. Consequently, this case constituted a serious moral accusation against them.

The period of the Republic (1974–2001)
The period since the fall of the junta and the restoration of democracy in 1974 has been dominated by two strong political leaders who, in pursuit of their

political objectives, have had a profound impact on Greek society. By setting himself the goal of bringing Greece into the European Community, Konstantine Karamanlis, founder of the New Democracy party (ND), produced a range of systemic changes necessary to his goal. By setting himself the target of achieving a 'socialist transformation' of Greece, Andreas Papandreou, founder of the Panhellenic Socialist Movement (PASOK), did the same. A prime minister with a strong charismatic appeal, his message was quite simply, 'Allaghe' (Change). Given, then, that they were marked by extensive systemic changes, the 1980s and the 1990s witnessed some of the most serious scandals of the post-war period. Thus, those leading socialist transformation took advantage of their power to benefit themselves. In doing so they undermined the ultimate goal (social transformation) and the collective values and thereby scandalized society. The most famous of them are the following (Koutsoukis, 1995).

1 *The Yugoslav corn scandal.* This arose in 1987 out of the large quantities of corn imported from Yugoslavia that were subsequently exported as 'Greek corn', thus allowing the exporters involved illegally to obtain European Community subsidies. The scandal also involved several public officials whose role had been to supply the documentation needed to allow the corn to be passed off as Greek. Two politicians were also caught up in it – the deputy minister of finance and the head of the State Export Agency, who were eventually tried and convicted.

2 *The procurements scandal.* The first of several scandals in this area, the procurements scandal, exploded in the mid-1990s when retired military officers, state employees and a civilian acting as mediator and claiming to be a friend of Prime Minister Papandreou, were accused of damaging the public interest by violating the provisions governing the public procurement of arms. Senior administrators employed by the Public Electric Agency were also involved. Of these individuals only the civilian, who was later caught up in the Koskotas scandal, was convicted. He was sentenced to five years in prison.

3 *The telephone tapping scandal.* This arose from allegations made by the liberal and leftist opposition parties that the PASOK government was monitoring the telephone conversations of their respective leaders. A few years later, in 1990, PASOK made similar allegations against the liberal cabinet staffed by New Democracy. Eventually, following lengthy debates in Parliament, both cases were dropped.

4 *The public utilities scandal.* This arose from the activities of the chairmen and directors general of a number of public enterprises – such as the State Organisation for Telecommunications, the State Postal Service, the State Water and Sewage Agency and Olympic Airways – who had embezzled public funds by depositing surplus revenues in the Bank of Crete at unusually favourable rates of interest. The bank belonged to Koskotas, later found guilty of corruption. All were accused of violating laws relating to the activities of

the public utilities and of damaging the public interest. Having been sent for trial, some were convicted and sentenced to jail terms, only to be acquitted later by the Court of Appeal. Their activities were directly related to the so-called 'Koskotas Scandal' to which we refer in detail below.

The Koskotas mega scandal

The most devastating scandal was named after a young Greek–American man who became chairman of the Board of the Bank of Crete and who, by doubling the number of its branches, succeeded in extending the bank's coverage to the whole of Greece. However, a scandal exploded when the bank was found to have most of its cash missing.

Later, in court, Koskotas stated that in many of his economic and entrepreneurial activities he had had the support of various high-ranking PASOK officials, in particular the chairman of the party and some of his closest associates with whom he had had close contact. He alleged that, after becoming chairman of the Bank, a small bank at the time, he had the support of the same people in his efforts to enlarge it. Shortly thereafter, he was in a position to buy two of the largest conservative newspapers, *Kathimerini* and *Vradini*. Shortly before this, he had bought the *ENA* magazine, directed by the late Pavlos Bakoyiannis who, in September 1989, was assassinated by the terrorist group, '17 November', as the Koskotas scandal unfolded. Soon afterwards, Koskotas shut down both papers and launched a new daily, *24 hours*, with the intention of using it as a vehicle for the expression of pro-PASOK views and especially the views of its leader, Papandreou. To house his new paper he founded a publishing company called Grammi. To enable this to continue its activities, he had to overcome several bureaucratic obstacles for which purposes he exploited his connections with senior government officials and with ministers. In addition to all of this he bought the famous soccer team, Olympiakos, which had several thousands of fans and which thus enabled him to extend the range of his influence to the area of athletics, as well.

All these activities made Koskotas look suspicious to other publishers who started asking questions about his sources of finance as well as his close relationships with Papandreou who was also Prime Minister at the time. When his illegal transactions finally came to light he tried to hider them by utilising his close ties with the Prime Minister. Later in court, Koskotas claimed that, in exchange for the support he was receiving, he had been giving cash to bodyguards whose job it was to deliver it to the Prime Minister's house, using as an intermediary one of the Prime Minister's close friends.

To avoid further investigation of his banking transactions, Koskotas convinced the Minister of Justice and Deputy Prime Minister to introduce a law that would cover him in future transactions. The bill was passed and, in exchange, he alleged he deposited $2 million in a Swiss bank. When finally the Greek authorities moved to arrest him, he managed to escape from Athens. He went to the US where another 64 charges were waiting for him.

He was arrested and after several months in a US prison he was sent back to Greece to face trial (Bakatselos, 1999).

I do not intend here to fully report this mega-scandal, nor analyse all its affects. Overshadowing all the others occurring the 1980s, it undoubtedly had profound consequences. Greek society went through a traumatic experience during its unfolding. Due to the wide media coverage of the scandal, ordinary citizens witnessed the reprehensible behaviour of large numbers of prominent political personalities, state functionaries, bankers, entrepreneurs, directors of state organisations, lawyers, academics and several other persons who, one way or another, found themselves caught in the web of suspicion surrounding the banker's activities.

First and foremost the scandal illustrates the process of catharsis to which such events typically give rise and which in the present case was of profound significance both for political elites and for ordinary citizens. According to Aristotle's famous definition, catharsis represents a solution to tragic events inasmuch as it enables purification of the souls of the witnesses to the events. In modern Greek the word 'catharsis' means the washing away of dirt or unhealthy materials. Allegorically it is also used to mean someone's return to society free from his dishonest past or unethical behaviour. The latter was the meaning that Greek politicians gave the word in seeking to manage the general sense of public disillusionment with politicians and the widespread belief that all politicians were corrupt. Moreover, 'catharsis' was one of the main slogans used against PASOK, both by ND and the parties of the left, during the subsequent election campaign (Papadopoulos, 1993).

In the light of the reactions of all sides in court, the countless debates taking place on television, radio and in the press and the daily conversations of ordinary people, the trial probably had a cathartic effect for ordinary citizens. In other words, the trial alleviated feelings of collective guilt over destructive acts of wrong-doing, perpetrated within the society's administrative, economic and political structures. For citizens would have been aware of the likely pedagogical effects of the scandal as a deterrent to others contemplating involvement in the practices that gave rise to it. And they will have been able to derive satisfaction from the knowledge of what the trial symbolically (re)affirmed, namely that no one is above the law and that, in the final analysis, the law applies to all without exception. The sense that one was living in a democracy in action may thus have been reinforced by the trial.

During the trials of the former Prime Minister and three of his ministers, the Deputy Prime Minister suffered a fatal heart attack. Thus proceedings, as far as they concerned him, could be taken no further. The former Prime Minister was acquitted by a majority vote, while only one of his ministers was sentenced to prison. It may be relevant in this context to cite the answer given by the then President of the Republic, the late Konstantine Karamanlis, when he was asked to comment on the decision to acquit the Prime Minister: 'In democracies prime ministers do not go to prison. They return home.' In saying this he was, in effect, drawing a line under the matter by both reaffirming the court's decision and acknowledging its positive and negative effects (Koutsoukis, 1998).

It seems that ND's victory in the 1990 election owed at least something to the scandal-mongering it used as a campaign tactic. PASOK's victory in the 1993 election seems likewise to have owed something to scandal-mongering (Koutsoukis, 1995, 2003). This may say something about the circumstances in which scandals typically occur. On the one hand, both the scandals of the 1980s, and those of the 1990s, took place at a time of rapid social and political change. Thus, while the 1980s, under PASOK rule, witnessed the enlargement of the state sector and the socialisation of a large segment of the private sector, the 1990s witnessed a process of desocialisation or the liberalisation and privatisation of the economy. One major scandal during this decade was the one related to selling the biggest Greek State Cement industry 'ΑΓΕΤ' to the Italian consortium 'Callcestrucci' (Koutsoukis, 1995). On the other hand, regardless of their character, the reforms of both the 1980s and the 1990s may have offered, to the politicians and public officials responsible for managing them, fertile ground for the spread of corruption – this by virtue of the confusion and uncertainty that processes of extensive change always give rise to. Corruption in its turn will then have provided fertile ground for scandal-mongering as a powerful tool in the hands of parties and factions anxious to defend the integrity of their preferred reforms against the attacks of rival parties and factions.

Conclusion

While not wishing to downplay the significance of the several other scandals taking place during the same long period, I have chosen to give a short account of the two most important scandals in the two centuries of existence of the modern Greek state: the one associated with the War of Independence at the beginning of the nineteenth century and the one associated with the 'socialist transformation' at the end of the twentieth century.

In both cases the scandals occurred at times when clear-cut systemic goals had been posed: the War of Independence in the first case, 'socialist transforma-tion' in the second. In both cases collective societal goals were undermined by those responsible for taking the lead in achieving them and who therefore had to face social opprobrium. While, in the second case, the revelation of wrong-doing followed the paths laid out for it by the mass media and provided the basis for scandal-mongering as an election tactic, in the first case, patterns of behaviour varied according to the contrasting circumstances in which the wrong-doing came to light. Thus, in England, reactions took the form of indignation on the part of the informed public able to read about what had happened. In Greece, on the other hand, they took the form of a decision by the opposition to react with guns as it realised that the loans could be utilised against them. Thus, it was that two civil wars broke out in the midst of the revolution.

In between the two big scandals there were several other scandals, each of which also revealed the prevailing social and political values of the period in which it took place. Brief mention has been made of scandals that occurred towards the end of the nineteenth century and during the early decades of the twentieth century. During the first of these two periods, under the strong leadership of Charilaos Trikoupis, the country was taking its first steps towards political and socio-economic modernisation; while in the second period, under the charismatic leadership of Eleftherios Venizelos, the modernisation process was being continued and consolidated. The scandals surrounding the production of quinine to combat malaria and the rules for the management of publicly funded projects both appeared to undermine this effort of consolidation. In both cases, however, the damage was limited because government and opposition found a way to reconcile their differences. Such reconciliation was also a feature of the Koskotas mega-scandal when the socialists under Papandreou and the liberal forces under Konstantine Mitsotakis, suspended hostilities following the catharsis of the trial, which offered Greek society a means of finding relief from its collective feelings of guilt.

Notes

1 Transparency International is a Berlin-based international non-governmental organisation 'whose aim is to counter corruption in international business transactions by broadening awareness of the damage caused by the phenomenon and encouraging governments to adopt anti-corruption measures' (Newell and Bull, 2003: 4). Each year, it combines the results of large numbers of surveys among business executives, financial journalists and so forth who are asked to rate countries according to their perceptions of how corrupt they are. In this way it publishes, on an annual basis, an index where large numbers of countries are given a score from zero to ten, where zero represents totally corrupt dealings with government and ten represents totally fair and honest dealings.
2 The term 'Phanariot' came from the 'Phanar' or lighthouse district of Istanbul, which had become 'the center of Ottoman Greek culture after the patriarch took up residence there . . . the well-connected Greeks of the city [thus becoming] known as Phanariots' (Sowards, 1996).
3 The 'klephts' were a type of bandit that flourished in the hills of the Morea (Soward, 1996).

References

Andreadis, A. (1904), *History of National Loans*, Athens.
Bakatselos, K. (1999), *The Ideology of Fraud: The Koskotas Scandal*, Athens, Roes.
Dafnis, G. (1955), *Hellas Between Two Wars*, vol. 2, Athens, Ikaros.
Finlay, G. (nd), *History of the Greek Revolution*, vol. 2 (Greek translation), Athens, Tolides.
Gennadios, G. (1878), *The Greek Loans of 1824 and 1825: How They Were Handled and What the World Thought of It*, London.
Heidenheimer, A., M. Johnston and V. Levine (eds) (1990), *Political Corruption: A Handbook*, London, Transaction.

Howe, S. G. (1828), *Sketch of the Greek Revolution*, New York.

Huntington, S. (1968), *Political Order in Changing Societies*, New Haven, Yale University Press.

Karyotakis, K. (1996), *Need of Honesty*, Athens, Phillippotes.

Katsoulis, G. (1975), *The Establishment in the Neohellenic* History, Athens, Nea Synora.

Knickerborker's Monthly (1833), vol. II, 358.

Koutsoukis, K. (1989), 'Patterns of Corruption and Political Change in Modern Greece: 1946–1987', *Corruption and Reform*, 4, 1–13.

Koutsoukis, K. (1995), 'Sleaze in Contemporary Greek Politics', *Parliamentary Affairs*, 48: 4, 688–96. Also in F. Ridley and A. Doig (eds), *Sleaze: Politicians, Private Interest and Public Reaction*, Oxford, Oxford University Press.

Koutsoukis, K. (1998), *Pathology of Politics: Aspects of Corruption in Modern Greece*, Athens, Papazisis.

Koutsoukis, K. (2003), 'Political Corruption in Greece', in M. J. Bull and J. L. Newell (eds), *Corruption in Contemporary Politics*, Basingstoke, Palgrave Macmillan.

Lignadis A. (1970), 'The First Loan of the Independence', PhD thesis, National and Kapodistrian University, Athens.

Londos Archieves, vol. B, 341–54.

Newell, J. L. and M. J. Bull (2003), 'Introduction', in M. J. Bull and J. L. Newell (eds), *Corruption in Contemporary Politics*, Basingstoke, Palgrave Macmillan.

Papadopoulos, L. (1993), *The Dirty '89: The Scandal, the Coalition Cabinet and the Prosecution*, Athens, Kaktos.

Political Register (L.X.) 366.

Quarterly Review (XXXV) 321 and January–March 1827, 223–30.

Sowards, S. (1996), 'The Greek Revolution and the Greek State', www.lib.msu.edu/sowards/balkan/lecture6.htmlv [accessed 20 March 2004].

Simopoulos, K. (1997), *The Corruption of Power*, Athens, Stahy.

Stamatopoulos, T. (1964), *The Internal War*, vol. I, Athens, Byron.

The Times (1826, 1828) 4, 5, 9, 24, 25, 26 October 1826 and 15, 28 November 1828.

Trikoupis, Spiro, *History of the Greek Revolution*, vol. III, Athens: Yiovanis, p. 172.

Westminster Review (1826), no. VI, 13.

Woodhouse, C. (1978), *The War of Greek Independence* (Greek translation), Athens, Estia.

9

Scandal in a scandalous age: the impeachment and trial of Warren Hastings, 1788–95

Robin Theobald

At noon on 13 February 1788 a diminutive and somewhat emaciated figure in his fifties knelt before his accusers and a vast and fashionable audience in Westminster Hall to hear the charges against him. This was Warren Hastings, until recently Governor General of India. The Hall, draped in scarlet, had been transformed for the occasion into a huge theatrical auditorium. To Hastings' left sat the peers and on his right the Commons. Above them in the galleries were the peeresses and ticket holders. At the far end, the throne and boxes of the royal family were raised upon a dais below which sat the Lord Chancellor and the judges. On the first day the Queen and her daughters seated themselves in the Duke of Newcastle's gallery, whilst the Prince of Wales and Mrs Fitzherbert graced one of the royal boxes. Charles James Fox was sufficiently taken with the solemnity of the occasion to appear in court dress complete with sword. Present were foreign ambassadors and dignitaries, the rich in general and a whole range of celebrities including: companion to the Queen; diarist and novelist, Fanny Burney; the celebrated society beauty, Georgiana, Duchess of Devonshire; actors David Garrick and Sarah Siddons; painters Sir Joshua Reynolds and Thomas Gainsborough; and the historian, Edward Gibbon. Leading for the prosecution in a style which could have provided the model for Andrey Vyshinsky a century and a half later, was Edmund Burke.

On the following day Burke opened the case with what some have described as the greatest oration of his career. The speech, spread over four days and encompassing the whole backdrop of Britain's involvement in India, ended with a final thunderous appeal:

> I impeach therefore Warren Hastings in the name of our Holy Religion, which he has degraded. I impeach him in the name of the English Constitution, which he has violated and broken. I impeach him in the name of the Indian Millions, whom he has sacrificed to Injustice. I impeach him in the name, and by the best rights of Human Nature, which he has stabbed to the heart. And I conjure this High and Sacred Court to let not those pleadings to be heard in vain. (Macaulay, 1909a: 637)

At this point a wave of emotion swept the Hall, many crying out their disgust. Mrs Sheridan, swooning, had to be carried out.

On 22 February, before an assembly even more crowded, Fox moved the Benares charge concerning Hastings' alleged use of undue force against the Raja of Benares, Chait Singh. Fashionable society had risen at 6a.m. to reach Westminster Hall to wait there shivering in the cold until the trial managers appeared at 11a.m. The climax of public interest was reached on 3 June when Richard Brinsley Sheridan opened the Begum charge. Hastings had forcibly withdrawn an allowance previously agreed by an East India Company (EIC) representative, Philip Francis, to the 'begums' (grandmother and mother) of the Nawab of Oudh. Fifty guineas were offered for a seat in the court and many shoes and caps were lost during the stampede when the doors opened at nine (Carnall and Nicholson, 1989: 8–29).

Thereafter, public interest in the Hastings trial dwindled. By the time sittings had resumed in November, Sheridan was expressing himself to be 'heartily tired of the Hastings Trial', wishing that the accused 'would run away and Burke after him'. Other more portentous events began to push the impeachment spectacle into the background: particularly the onset of the King's illness in the autumn of 1788 and the first stirrings of revolution in France.

Nevertheless, the proceedings continued until 23 April 1795 when Hastings was honourably acquitted of all charges.[1] By that time one third of the peers who attended the trial's opening had died. Hastings was awarded a pension of £4,000 a year to run for twenty-eight years from 1785, and a loan of £50,000. But having spent £71,000 on his defence, he was beset with financial problems for the rest of his life. Despite these he was eventually able to realise a childhood dream and re-acquire the family seat at Daylesford. Hastings lived on for twenty-three years surviving Burke, Sheridan, Fox, Dundas and Pitt. In March 1812 he was called to the House at the age of eighty-one to give evidence on the renewal of the EIC's charter. When he left the Chamber after three-and-a-half hours of examination, the members stood as a mark of respect, a gesture normally reserved for kings and princes.

Why was Hastings subjected to this appalling public humiliation when according to most commentators he had devoted the greater part of his adult life not only in dedicated service to the EIC, but to curtailing many of its worst abuses? To answer this question it will be necessary to set Hastings' role in India within the overall context of late eighteenth-century English society and the ruthless political struggle that permeated it.

Background[2]

Hastings belonged to a gentry family, which once had its seat at the manor of Daylesford, Worcestershire. Falling on hard times, mainly due to supporting the wrong side during the Civil Wars, the Hastings of Daylesford were obliged to seek their fortunes in the world. Warren Hastings was born in December 1732 the son of a clergyman. Losing his parents at an early age he was taken under the care first of his grandfather, then an uncle. When both passed on Hastings was assigned to the care of a distant relative who, anxious to relieve himself of the burden, obtained a writer-ship for his ward in the EIC. After briefly studying commerce and arithmetic, Hastings sailed for Bengal in January 1750, soon after his eighteenth birthday. He arrived the following October.

Hastings proceeded to labour behind a desk for two years in the secretary's office at Fort William, Calcutta, which was then a purely commercial settlement. However, in the overall context of a disintegrating Moghul Empire and the subsequent scramble for spoils, Hastings, like Robert Clive before him, found himself transformed from mercantile agent into diplomat and soldier. Displaying tactical and organisational ability in the field after the Battle of Plassey, Hastings was appointed to reside at the court of Bengal's new ruler, Mir Jaffar, as an agent of the EIC. In 1761 he became a member of the EIC's governing Council in Bengal, necessitating his return to Calcutta. Clive's successor, the amiable but considerably less forceful Henry Vansittart, was quite unable to prevent the more ruthless and resourceful English functionaries preying upon a helpless indigenous population. The overriding goal of the typical Company servant was to wring from the hapless peasants and petty traders extremely large sums of money as speedily as possible before heat and disease killed him. He would then hope to 'return home, marry a peer's daughter, buy a rotten Cornish borough, and hold balls in St James' (Macaulay, 1909a: 556). Clive himself picked up a cool £200,000 for replacing Siraj ad Dawlah with his son Mir Jaffar as Nawab of Bengal. He was also granted £25,000 per annum by Mir Jaffar's successor, Mir Kassim. Returning to England much enriched, Clive purchased estates, bought a parliamentary seat and was awarded an Irish baronetcy. In fact few actually achieved such dizzy heights of opulence. But those 'nabobs' who did manage to acquire 'ducal' fortunes, in flaunting their riches provided a role model for the more adventurous not born to wealth and power. They also provoked considerable envy and resentment. As Pitt the elder noted:

> The riches of India have poured in upon us and have brought with them not merely Asiatic luxury but Asiatic principles of government. Without connections, without any national interest in the soil, the importers of Indian gold have forced their way into Parliament by such a torrent of private corruption as no private hereditary fortune can resist. (Riddy, 1989: 31)

As for Hastings' behaviour during this period, the evidence suggests that he did not display the greed and rapacity, which seems to have been the norm. On the contrary, he attempted to persuade fellow members of the Council of the need for greater restraint, but his efforts were always over-ruled by the majority. Growing disenchantment with the state of affairs in Bengal is thought to have been behind Hastings' return to England in 1764. By then he had realised only a moderate fortune, which was soon reduced to nothing through a combination of liberality and mismanagement. Here he remained for four years engaged in study and trying to promote the idea of a university

chair in Persian at Oxford – a project in which he had the support of
Dr Samuel Johnson. But with little to attach him to England – his first wife
and two sons had by now died – and growing pecuniary embarrassment, his
sights once again focused upon India. Soliciting the EIC for re-employment
Hastings was eventually appointed member of the Council at Madras taking
ship in the spring of 1769.

Reaching Madras, Hastings found trade and Company organisation generally in a very poor state. In the face of considerable local opposition he pushed
through a completely new method of procurement as well as other reforms.
So pleased were the Company's Directors with these changes that they placed
him at the head of government in Bengal. Early in 1772, Hastings left Madras
for Calcutta. However, since he had last been in Bengal the disintegration of
the province had gathered speed. The fundamental problem was that with
Company salaries set at such a ludicrously low level – £5 per annum for a writer
– any drive seriously to limit abuse was doomed to fail. In fact by 1772 the
Company was verging on bankruptcy as a result of high administrative costs
as well as the continuing spoliation by its servants and sundry adventurers.

In practical terms the British were the virtual rulers of Bengal, since
authority to collect the revenues was ceded to them by the Mughal emperor
in 1765. But government business was still conducted by Indian officials with
very little European participation. Hastings recognised the system could not
continue in this way: the British had to accept full governmental responsibility. But he embraced no civilising or modernising role in India. He was much
more of a 'traditionaliser'. Fluent in Bengali and with a passable knowledge
of Urdu and Persian, he devoted much time and effort to the study of indigenous institutions and folkways. Hastings' view was that Bengal should be
governed as far as possible in traditional ways, with the people's lives undis-
turbed by (for him) destructive Western intrusions:

> Is it not a contradiction of the common notions of equity and policy that the
> English gentleman of Cumberland and Argyleshire should regulate the policy of
> a nation which they know only by the lacs (lakhs) it has sent to Britain? (Moon,
> 1947: 103)

In what was to be the most constructive period of his administration during
1772–4, Hastings detached the machine of central government from the
nawab's court, bringing the settlement at Calcutta under direct British control. He remodelled the British system of justice throughout Bengal, starting
a series of experiments aimed at bringing tax collection under effective supervision. However, it would be quite inaccurate to claim that his substantial reforms
during this period ended the gallimaufry of abuses so exercising the EIC's
critics back home. On the contrary, Hastings recognised that the stability of
the Company's operations demanded that he largely work *with* rather than
against a very imperfect system. Despite this, during the two-and-a-half years
before the Regulating Act of 1773, there is little doubt Hastings brought considerable order to Bengal's administration.

Hastings' period of undisputed power in Bengal ended in 1774 with changes in Company governance. Under Lord North's India Act of 1773 he acquired the new title of governor general along with increased responsibilities for supervising other settlements in India. However, these powers were now shared with a supreme council, three of whom were new to India. The new representatives were spearheaded by a peppery army officer, Sir John Clavering, and by the ambitious and extremely able former war-office clerk, Philip Francis (now accepted as the author of the 'Junius' letters). It seems certain that these two were sent out on behalf of Lord North's administration under increasing pressure from factions in Parliament and Company headquarters in Leadenhall Street to investigate continuing abuses by Company servants.

Convinced that Hastings was the embodiment of corruption and extortion, Clavering and Francis strained every sinew to make life difficult for him and block every initiative he proposed. Consequently the government of Bengal, indeed of Madras and Bombay, was virtually paralysed for several years. Not until Clavering had died in 1777 and Francis, after fighting a duel with Hastings, had returned to Britain in 1780 was the latter able effectively to assert his authority. Back in England, Francis continued his vendetta against Hastings, a project greatly assisted by his entering Parliament in 1784.

But by 1780 Bengal government energies were increasingly absorbed in war as the Company found itself drawn into the rivalries of powers that had established themselves on the ruins of Empire. Hastings' policy was, where possible, to avoid further conquest and maintain peace with neighbouring states through a series of alliances. But the Company had effectively taken active part in military operations in 1774 by lending or rather renting a brigade to an ally, the Vezier of Oudh, to assist his war against an Afghan tribe known as the Rohillas. In 1778 the Company became involved in an armed struggle against the Marathas, a loose federation of warlike Hindu peoples in western and central India. And after France's entry into the American War of Independence in 1778, Hastings also confronted French expeditionary forces in the Indian Ocean. Finally in 1780 Hyder Ali of Mysore attacked the British settlement in Madras.

War on several fronts presented Hastings with the awesome task of appropriating and organising the financial and military resources needed to meet these threats. The fact that he succeeded – an agreement was reached with the Marathas in 1782, the French were held in check until peace was concluded in Europe in 1783, and hostilities with Mysore were ended in 1784 – is acknowledged by most commentators as a truly remarkable achievement. But there were costs: these engagements stretched Company resources to the limit and disrupted its trade as well as further antagonising opinion back home. Conducting wars on several fronts also seemed to force Hastings into dubious and often highhanded actions to raise funds, particularly the demand for a subsidy from Chait Singh, ruler of Benares, and the requisitioning of the treasures of the begums of Oudh. These formidable pressures, furthermore, took their toll on Hastings personally: having throughout most of his life displayed a relatively tranquil and accommodating disposition, India's first governor general was transformed into an overbearing and unbending autocrat: peevish, rigid and utterly unable to countenance dissent. Unsurprisingly, his health also began deteriorating (as did that of his wife). In 1784, increasingly disenchanted with what he saw as his lack of authority augmented by growing awareness of criticism of his governance back home, Hastings resigned and sailed for England. He arrived in June 1785 to be treated as something of a celebrity, receiving effusive thanks from the EIC directors and the King and Queen going out of their way to be gracious towards him and his wife when presented at court. But just over a week after Hastings had landed at Plymouth, Edmund Burke gave notice in the House of Commons that he would 'at a future date make a motion respecting the conduct of a gentleman just returned from India'. In April the following year Burke laid his charges before the House (Moon, 1947: 308).

Several commentators seem to agree that Hastings laid the secure foundations for Britain's subsequent colonial state in India (Keay, 1991; Macaulay, 1909a; Spear, 1973). He furthermore successfully organised the defence of this emerging state, especially during his last years in India, with hardly any help from home. The significance of Hastings' achievement is enhanced when the enormous odds against which he had to struggle are considered. Not only was he facing aggression from several directions and had to meet it with very slender resources, he also had to deal with personal animosities among his council, major difficulties in asserting his authority over Madras and Bombay and perpetual intrigues at home. Given such achievements it is unsurprising that, on returning to England, Hastings anticipated honours – a peerage perhaps. Instead he met impeachment. Why?

Was Hastings corrupt?

Certainly in the popular view Hastings was portrayed as the epitome of corruption, with both he and his wife being regularly lampooned and libelled by the cartoonists. Hastings' own case was not helped by the stir caused by his wife's fine silks and splendid diamonds – 'the galaxy of jewels torn from Indian begums' as a lampoon insisted – when presented at Court. There was also a whiff of scandal surrounding his second marriage to the wife of a German baron whom Hastings had met during the voyage of his return to India in 1769. The subsequent divorce proceedings were extremely protracted leading to unsavoury rumours that Baron Imhof had to be 'bought off' with enough cash to buy an estate in Saxony (Macaulay, 1909a: 285).

During his service in India, Hastings accepted around £300,000 in presents from rulers, which he turned over to the public service of the Company. Later in 1784 he asked that some of this be credited to him personally. His personal fortune on returning has been estimated at £74,000, a considerable sum but puny compared with those acquired by many others whose position in the Company had been considerably junior to his. Again, his archenemies,

Francis and Clavering, seem to have been more than willing to accept and retain presents. A more serious charge against Hastings is that he only limited and did not stop the private trade of Company officials. His private fortune, furthermore, like those of his subordinates, could have been brought home in diamonds thereby escaping investigation.

However, the case against Hastings was based not simply on corruption in the limited sense of illicit gains from office but on the more general abuse of power displayed in his treatment of Chait Singh and the begums of Oudh. A more dramatic instance of alleged abuse related to Hastings' apparent acquiescence in the execution in 1775 of a moneylender, Nandkumar (Nuncumar). Nandkumar, sensitive to the burgeoning power struggle within the Council, sought favour with the Clavering/Francis faction by claiming to possess evidence of corrupt dealings by the Governor General himself. Hastings responded brusquely by charging Nandkumar with conspiracy. This stern response quickly persuaded the 'bazaar' that the real power still lay with the Governor General, prompting Nandkumar's many enemies to bring forward a pending lawsuit of forgery against him. The moneylender was charged, tried under English law in the Supreme Court, found guilty and executed. Hastings' failure to intervene to save Nandkumar enabled his enemies, particularly Francis, to charge him with the judicial murder of an awkward opponent. Embroidering this theme, Burke subsequently insisted that Hastings' acquiescence was a coded statement of warning to potential opponents and critics: 'Mr Hastings observes that no man in India complains of him. It is generally true. The voice of India is stopped. All complaint is strangled with the same cord that strangled Nuncumar' (O'Brien, 1997: 147). However, Hastings' conduct must be judged not only against the context of prevailing attitudes to public office, but with regard to the character and tone of eighteenth-century social behaviour.

An age of excess

This was a world where, for the wealthy, social and invariably sensual pleasures preceded all else; office was attended to if at all only in the time remaining. Men-about-town, known as 'Bucks' or 'Corinthians', devoted enormous energy to the fashionable pastimes of hunting, drinking and whoring – in 1797 Chief Magistrate of Westminster, Patrick Colquhoun, estimated there were 52,000 prostitutes and bawdy-house keepers in London. The bucks also liked to patronise cockfights, prize-fights and public hangings. Given the range of offences for which one might be executed, there was no shortage of this latter form of entertainment (David, 1998: ch. 5).

Unsurprisingly, gambling was also a craze of the fashionable world. Foreign visitors believed gambling had become a kind of national fever. Ladies filled homes with card parties advertised in newspapers. Men sat up till dawn at Brookes, betting fortunes on the turn of a card. Meaningless wagers were placed about tomorrow's rain, the number of children members of one's circle might have, at what age this or that person would die, or next week's favourite opera singer. Horace Walpole records an incident in which a man fell down in the street, thereby inducing bets from passers-by about whether he was dead or not. When a sympathetic onlooker suggested the unfortunate man be bled, he was immediately shouted down by the gamblers on the grounds that this would affect the fairness of the betting. One wet day Lord Arlington bet £3,000 upon which of two raindrops would first reach the bottom of a windowpane. Charles James Fox and his brother lost £32,000 in a single night. The Duchess of Devonshire, dying of cirrhosis of the liver at the age of 48, left gambling debts of over £200,000. The Earl of Sandwich's addiction to gambling was such that, unwilling to leave the tables for meals, he simply slapped a piece of meat between two slices of bread thereby bequeathing to western civilisation the edible contrivance bearing his name (David, 1998; Hibbert, 1998; Powell, 1989).

In addition to the consumption of prodigious quantities of food, heavy drinking was the norm. A comfortably off gentleman might drink a whole bottle of claret with his dinner, followed by three glasses of port during the remainder of the evening. Fox, no mean toper himself, complained of the entertaining he had to do when canvassing during the Westminster election of 1784: eight guests came in succession, remaining from three to ten o'clock and drank ten bottles of wine and sixteen bowls of punch, each of which would hold four bottles – the equivalent of nine bottles per man. During one of the many parties celebrating Fox's victory, the Prince of Wales collapsed whilst dancing a quadrille. Helped to his feet he was violently sick. Only a month earlier, 'Prinny' with three companions had been arrested for drunkenness and confined overnight in the watchhouse. One of the Prince's circle of louche friends – Richard, Seventh Earl of Barrymore, known as 'Hellgate' – was particularly addicted to pranks. One of his favourites was to drive down Oxford Street in a hackney coach and assume the voice of a screaming woman being ravished. When law-abiding citizens rushed to the rescue, Richard and friends would burst out of the carriage and give them a sound thrashing. The Prince himself was not averse to jolly japes, on one occasion persuading Barrymore to ride his horse up to the top floor of Mrs Fitzherbert's house. At this time London in general was terrorised by aristocratic blades known as Mohocks or Hawkubites who rampaged with impunity through the capital attacking and assaulting innocent passers-by, perpetrating vicious practical jokes against whomever fell in their path (Barker-Benfield, 1992: ch. 2; Varey, 1996: 36–47).

On a more plebeian level, the eighteenth century was also especially riotous in a quite literal sense. Ian Gilmour (1992: 15–16) notes that during the century Englishmen and women rioted against:

> turnpikes, enclosures and high food prices, and Roman Catholics, the Irish and Dissenters, against the naturalisation of the Jews, the impeachment of politicians, press gangs, 'crim' houses, the Militia Act, against theatre prices, foreign actors,

pimps, bawdy houses, surgeons, French footmen and alehouse keepers, against gibbets in the Edgware Road and public whipping . . . against the Excise, against the Cider tax . . . workhouses and industrial employers, against the rumoured destruction of cathedral spires, even . . . a change in the calendar. (Gilmour, 1992: 15–16)

In this context Warren Hastings' conduct, whilst hardly blameless, does not seem excessive, certainly not deserving of the seven years of torment to which he was subjected. With regard to the behaviour during this period of the English in India, Percival Spear concludes that it was simply an exaggerated and vulgarised version of fashionable life in England:

Alongside Hickey's *Memoirs* and descriptions of military dinners must be set the coarseness of the Georges, the drunkenness of the upper classes, and the taste which allowed a relative of Sir Walter Scott to read aloud to fashionable assemblies in her youth books which at the age of eighty she could not read alone without shame. There was never a Medmenham Brotherhood in India. (Spear, 1963: 148)[3]

Patronage and factional politics

Hastings' problem was that, although many thousands of miles from London for most of his adult life, his position in the Company in India and the openings this gave him, placed him at the centre of the political struggle in London. In a world where the appropriation of office was pervasive, where the whole system amounted to a complex web of bargaining, the making and unmaking of alliances, blackmail and deception, any major source of patronage was an obvious target for political contest. So it was with the Company: if one had a son or male relative to provide for, an application to one of the Company's directors might find them places in the service. Although miserably paid, such positions carried the potential for lucrative returns and in some cases considerable fortunes. This situation made it inevitable that directors of the Company should be courted in City circles generally, and that the government in particular should aim to harness as much as possible of EIC patrimony to its enduring quest to control Parliament. In fact, such was the Company's significance in the invariably ruthless game of late eighteenth-century politics that it was widely believed to provide the key to political dominance. Whether accurate or not, such perceptions ensured the centrality of the EIC in the prolonged struggle between the King and the Whigs.

This centrality became particularly apparent during the infighting provoked by the Fox India Bill, introduced into Parliament in November 1783. The Bill ostensibly aimed to reform India's administration by transferring the political responsibilities of the EIC to a commission appointed by Parliament in London. In a sense, such a reform was long overdue and in principle supported by the King who, with many others, was greatly exercised by the vast fortunes made in the sub-continent. But Fox's opponents had little difficulty in representing the Bill not only as a threat to the integrity of all chartered companies, but also as a means whereby the Whigs, in acquiring a controlling interest in the EIC, could enormously bolster their ascendancy over the Commons. The larger-than-life and perennially indebted Fox became an easy target for the cartoonists: a popular example by James Sayers showed Fox fleeing with India House on his shoulders in the process transferring its patrimony from the Company and the Crown to himself and his cronies (Hibbert, 1998: 243–4).

The King, persuaded that the Bill would be used by the Foxites to undermine the royal prerogative, let it be known that he would 'not show favour' to any-one supporting it. Although passed by the Commons, the Bill was defeated by the Lords leading to the collapse of the Fox–North coalition. Ironically, although he played no part in the events leading to the defeat of Fox's Bill, it set Hastings on the road to impeachment. Propelling Hastings down this road was the merciless invective of Edmund Burke.

As principal drafter of Fox's bill, Burke was predictably enraged by its defeat and vented his spleen on the most available target: Hastings. In this project Burke was ably assisted by Philip Francis who, for obvious reasons, sedulously plied Burke with lurid tales of Hastings' alleged infamies in India. Burke was notorious for the intemperance and emotional force, amounting at times to frenzy, with which he presented his arguments. On one occasion during a parliamentary debate, so carried away was he by the passion of his case that colleagues had to seize his coat tails to restrain him. In a debate on the upheavals in France, Burke suddenly produced a dagger from beneath his coat and threw it on to the floor raging, 'This is what you are to gain from an alliance with France. Wherever their principles are introduced their practices will follow' (Powell, 1989: 214). Burke's tirades against Hastings were often ridiculous and embarrassing, even for the latter's enemies. He dwelt at length upon Hastings' background, which was 'low' and 'vulgar'. Hastings began his Indian career as 'a fraudulent bullock contractor'; he was a 'rat' a 'weasel', 'a keeper of a pig sty wallowing in corruption' (Feiling, 1954: 354–5).

More seriously there are those who regard Burke as a somewhat squalid figure, a hack for Whig oligarchs, his invective often fuelled more by disreputable personal animosities than by his much vaunted principles. In Hastings' case it has been alleged that Burke's apparently boundless venom was driven partly by his resentment at losses incurred in India by his cousin, William Burke. Against this view, Conor Cruise O'Brien has defended Burke, finding in his position a genuine sympathy for the peoples of India. This sympathy O'Brien sees as entirely consistent with Burke's reasoned and conciliatory attitude towards the American revolutionaries. More pertinently, it was doubtless underpinned by his resentment at the repression of his fellow Irishmen (O'Brien, 1989: 58–75).

The issue of principle has also been invoked to explain Pitt's apparently perverse behaviour during the Commons debate on the impeachment motion. On the first charge relating to the Rohilla affair, Burke had high hopes the motion would be passed as Hastings' loan of a brigade to the Vezier of Oudh had already been condemned by the Company's directors, by a Parliamentary Committee and by Pitt's lieutenant and spokesman on Indian affairs, Henry Dundas. Nevertheless, on this occasion Dundas, whilst critical of Hastings, maintained his mistakes were mitigated by subsequent dedicated service. Dundas voted against the motion, as did Pitt who did not speak in the debate. The motion was defeated auguring a promising start for Hastings.

In June, Fox brought forward the charge concerning the exactions imposed by Hastings against Chait Singh, Vezier of Benares. Pitt rose to speak amidst general expectation that he would demolish Fox's case. This he proceeded to do, insisting that, in the light of Chait's failure to fulfil certain obligations to the Company, Hastings was amply justified in levying a fine. But then came a sensational twist: since the fine itself 'was utterly disproportionate and shamefully exorbitant' (Moon, 1947: 313), Pitt would vote *in favour* of Fox's motion.

There has been much speculation about Pitt's motives for voting as he did. Sympathisers attribute his action entirely to principle: Pitt found certain aspects of Hastings' behaviour so objectionable that he could not in all conscience support him. Pitt allegedly assured Wilberforce after the debate that he acted from no ulterior motive. Against this view, it is argued that anyone familiar with the facts of the case including the role played by Francis, as Pitt undoubtedly was, could not possibly have taken a position that would guarantee Hastings' impeachment. Accordingly, darker motives have been attributed to Pitt: the principal aim of the Chief Minister was to side-step the moralising onslaughts of the Whigs by detaching himself from Hastings' cause. Pitt, in other words, was far too astute to allow himself to be nailed to the cross being erected for Hastings. Others have detected Henry Dundas' sinister hand in the affair. Dundas, who spent three hours with Pitt before the crucial debate, had been a prominent opponent of Hastings for some time. Dundas was already a member of the Company's Board of Control and keen to appropriate what he could of its patrimony for his Scottish kinsmen. Were he to be cleared, Hastings would doubtless also be appointed to the Board, making him, with his vastly superior knowledge of Indian affairs, a serious rival to Dundas (Moon, 1947: 316; Reilly, 1979: xiii; Watson, 1976: 321). However, the key point is that, whatever his motives, Pitt's stance on the Benares charge made Hastings' impeachment a certainty. Fox's motion was carried 119 to 79. A motion on the spoliation of the begums of Oudh was passed by a larger majority, to be followed by numerous other charges relating to the acceptance of presents, fraudulent dealings and commissions. Finally on 21 May 1787 Hastings was arrested and brought before the bar of the House of Lords where he was formally impeached.

Lastly, it should be noted that Hastings was his own worst enemy: in the subtle and dangerous world of eighteenth-century politics, a world calling for exceptional rhetorical skills as well as influential friends, he acquitted himself with ineptitude. It is interesting to contrast his performance with that of his famed predecessor, Sir Robert Clive, who also found himself arraigned before a committee of the House in 1772. When accused of illicit self-enrichment,

Clive defended himself with all the elan and audacity that had coloured his military operations in India:

> Am I not rather deserving of praise for the moderation which marked my proceedings? Consider the situation in which the victory at Plassey had placed me. A great prince was dependent upon my pleasure. An opulent city lay at my mercy, its richest bankers bid against each other for my smiles. I walked through vaults which were thrown open to me alone, piled on either hand with gold and jewels. Mr. Chairman, at this moment, I stand astonished at my own moderation. (Macaulay, 1909b: 544)

Contrasted with this impressive piece of theatre, Hastings' performance at the bar of the House during the impeachment debate fifteen years later was lamentable. Instead of the eloquent, concise and spirited defence of his actions the situation required, Hastings delivered an oration of such length that his secretary and two clerks had to be called upon to assist with its reading. Beginning at four in the afternoon the delivery had not reached its end by ten by which time the House had emptied. Some indication of Hastings' startlingly unrealistic appraisal of his position is conveyed by the fact that he none the less considered the occasion to have been a great success: 'My credit now stands higher than ever it did' (Moon, 1947: 312).

Conclusion

Although he may have saved India for the Empire, Hastings was hardly the typical imperialist. Apart from his deep interest in indigenous cultures and languages, Hastings viewed what he realised would be the likely expansion of British power throughout the sub-continent, without enthusiasm: 'an event I do not wish to see' (Keay, 1991: 398). Yet he came to personify for many of his contemporaries, not least a burgeoning public opinion, the worst excesses of abuse of unrestrained imperial authority. How do we explain his treatment, particularly the appalling show trial to which he was subjected?

First, and with regard to the trial itself, significant economic expansion together with accompanying urbanisation during the eighteenth century created an urban public eager for news, gossip, entertainment, scandal – in short, for spectacle. Whether this spectacle took the form of plays, operas, balls, prize-fights, horseracing, cockfights and other forms of animal torment, or public hangings, a large and enthusiastic audience could be guaranteed. But spectacle is of itself evanescent; and so, after the first flush of enthusiasm at the exposure of Hastings' alleged villainies, general interest soon evaporated. The ridiculous trial continued for a further seven years only because of the complexity of the business and the limited time that could be given to it, aggravated by Burke's obsession with prolonging the proceedings to secure a guilty verdict.

Second, Hastings was something of an outsider, not only in the sense of having spent most of his adult life in India, but, more pertinently, very much outside the ranks of the rich and powerful aristocracy presiding over political and social life. But from relatively humble beginnings Hastings rose to a position of power and authority, which was commonly believed to have brought him the fabled riches of a detested nabob. In a system pervaded by the frenzied competition for place and fortune, those believed to have acquired wealth and, particularly to have achieved this by what was perceived to be an illegitimate route, were certain to find themselves transformed into objects of envy and resentment.

Third, in the ensuing political struggle, Hastings acquitted himself with considerable ineptitude. His experience of the cut and thrust of politics in the Council, particularly during his battles with Clavering and Francis, nurtured a confrontational style ill suited to the subtle manoeuvres of Westminster. After Francis had left India in 1780, Hastings' word was virtually law. He came to assume an Olympian indifference to criticism and opposition, accustomed to being forever in the right. Unfortunately, this was guaranteed to induce excessive confidence in one's own judgement, leading Hastings radically to over-estimate the strength of his position, particularly his standing with Pitt and his party. He also seriously under-estimated the degree of Burke's enmity and more especially the destructive potential of his rhetoric.

Lastly, we could expatiate at length on Burke's role in the whole affair and the nature of the forces fuelling what amounted to a moral crusade. Clearly the character of his onslaughts against Hastings at times displayed such intemperance as to raise questions about his state of mind. But these excesses apart, there is a significant sense in which Burke's drive for justice as he saw it embodied a reforming ethos, an evangelical zeal for fairness, order and the rule of law, which was emerging out of and contrasted sharply with the turbulence and amorality of eighteenth-century social and political life. This reforming thrust is particularly evident in the rise of Methodism, the devotion of whose adherents was admired by the pious King himself (Hibbert, 1998: 56). It is also manifest in the work of William Wilberforce, friend of Pitt, and an increasingly powerful independent force in the House of Commons. But, in addition to the purely religious impulse, the drive for order and discipline was massively boosted by the loss of the American colonies. We note the nice historical irony that Hastings' successor as Governor General, the agent sent by Pitt to purge the Indian administration of its contagion, was the same Lord Cornwallis who had presided over the decisive surrender of British forces at Yorktown (Briggs, 1978: 70).[4]

Hastings, then, was ultimately a victim of this evolving sea-change in social and political mores. This was not of course because Hastings himself was especially prone to excess. Indeed, compared with most of his peers, particularly a substantial section of the ruling class, he lived a life of relative abstinence. Nevertheless, Hastings represented an earlier inchoate phase of imperialism, an era of easygoing tolerance of local customs and mores, of fratern-isation, even intermarriage. In the interests of imperial governance this stage was beginning to be replaced by one more ordered, efficient, punctilious and, in a narrow sense, undoubtedly less corrupt. But it was also an era which eventually manifested towards its Indian subjects the attitudes of exclusivity, intolerance and contempt, which, in the long run, undermined the very project those values were intended to preserve.

Notes

1 Although actual sittings were extremely intermittent occupying only 235 days over the whole seven year period. See K. Feiling (1954: 252).
2 For biographical details see Feiling (1954), and Moon (1947).
3 'Medmenham' refers to the ruined abbey where Sir Francis Dashwood's 'Hellfire Club' held its debauches.
4 It is also notable that Cornwallis' deputy and eventual successor as Governor General (1793–8), John Shore, was a member of the evangelical Clapham Sect.

References

Barker-Benfield, C. J. (1992), *The Culture of Sensibility*, Chicago, University of Chicago Press.

Briggs, A. (1978), *The Age of Improvement 1783–1867*, London, Longman.

Carnall G. and C. Nicholson (1989), 'Introduction', in G. Carnell and C. Nicholson (eds), *The Impeachment of Warren Hastings*, Edinburgh, Edinburgh University Press.

David, S. (1998), *Prince of Pleasure: The Prince of Wales and the Making of the Regency*, London, Little, Brown & Company.

Feiling, K. (1954), *Warren Hastings*, London, Macmillan.

Gilmour, I. (1992), *Riots, Risings and Revolution: Governance and Violence in Eighteenth-Century England*, London, Hutchinson.

Hibbert, C. (1998), *George III: A Personal History*, London, Penguin Books.

Keay, J. (1991), *The Honourable Company: A History of the East India Company*, London, Harper Collins.

Macaulay, T. B. (1909a), 'Warren Hastings', *Critical and Historical Essays*, vol. I, London, J. M. Dent.

Macaulay, T. B. (1909b), 'Robert Clive', *Critical and Historical Essays*, vol. I, London, J. M. Dent.

Moon, P. (1947), *Warren Hastings and British India*, London, Hodder and Stoughton.

O'Brien, C. C. (1989), 'Warren Hastings in Burke's Great Melody', in G. Carnell and C. Nicholson (eds), *The Impeachment of Warren Hastings*, Edinburgh, Edinburgh University Press.

O'Brien, C. C. (1997), *Edmund Burke*, London, Vintage Books.

Powell, D. (1989), *Charles James Fox: Man of the People*, London, Hutchinson.

Riddy, J. (1989), 'Warren Hastings: Scotland's Benefactor?', in G. Carnell and C. Nicholson (eds), *The Impeachment of Warren Hastings*, Edinburgh, Edinburgh University Press.

Reilly, R. (1979), *William Pitt the Younger: A Biography*, New York, G.P. Putnam's.

Spear, P. (1963), *The Nabobs. A Study of the Social Life of the English in Eighteenth-Century India*, London, Oxford University Press.

Spear, P. (1973), *A History of India*, vol. II, London, Penguin Books.

Varey, S. (1996), 'The Pleasures of the Table', in R. Porter and M. M. Roberts (eds), *Pleasure in the Eighteenth Century*, London, Macmillan.

Watson, J. S. (1976), *The Reign of George III (1760–1815)*, London, Oxford University Press.

10

Diamonds and videotape: political scandals and the presidents of the Fifth French Republic

Hélène Bilger-Street and *Marion Demoissier*

Described by Philip Williams (1970) as 'the classic land of political scandal', France has recently witnessed a major case of political corruption involving the current President, Jacques Chirac. When the affair came to light it threatened not only the President's re-election in 2002 but also the presidency itself. It became public knowledge in the wake of publication of the posthumous memoirs of Jean-Claude Méry in the newspaper, *Le Monde*, on 21 and 22 September 2000. The memoirs, which were the transcription of a video recorded in 1996 by a journalist, Arnaud Hamelin, in the presence of his lawyer, directly accused Jacques Chirac of having accepted, when mayor of Paris (1977–95) and president (1976–94) of *Rassemblement Pour la République* (RPR), illegal payments in return for public works contracts. It was the second time in the history of the Fifth Republic that a president had become personally embroiled in such a long and tormented saga. Like the earlier one – the Bokassa affair involving Valéry Giscard d'Estaing, President from 1974 to 1981 – it was a saga that revealed 'hidden patterns and peculiarities in the nation's political institutions, processes and culture' (Bornstein, 1990: 271).

The only other major scandal implicating a French president dates back to the beginning of the Third Republic: Jules Grévy was forced to resign his post in 1887 when his son-in-law, Daniel Wilson, was accused of selling honours in the gift of the President to the highest bidder. However, presidents during the Third Republic did not wield the same amount of power as their successors in the Fifth Republic and were not directly elected. They were effectively confined to ceremonial and formal roles. This meant that, even though the presidency was in 1887 in its infancy, its place within the institutional framework was not severely threatened by the aforementioned scandal. The Méry and Bokassa affairs had a much deeper impact on the political system.

The Bokassa affair in particular marked the beginning of two decades in which there were an ever-increasing number of scandals involving politicians. The first two presidents of the Fifth Republic, De Gaulle (1958–69) and Pompidou (1969–74) were never directly implicated in any political scandals (Jenkins and Morris, 1993). Valéry Giscard d'Estaing was the first to be attacked on such terrain. His successor, François Mitterrand, is a more ambiguous figure, but, while during the course of his long career many scandals surrounded him, none managed to tarnish his reputation during his presidency.[1] The latter can thus be seen as a transitional phase leading to the current situation in which the repercussions of the Méry affair have undermined the consensus that once existed regarding the role of the President in the French political system.

By examining the political scandals surrounding the presidency in the Fifth Republic, and in particular by comparing the Bokassa and Méry affairs, this chapter will thus explore what the two scandals reveal about the deeper changes affecting the French political system and the values embodied in its institutions. In this way we might hope to contribute to filling an important gap in the literature. For among French political scientists there seems to be a reluctance to see political scandals as worthy of study.[2] To the extent they study them at all, they at most do so 'indirectly' – either via the tradition of corruption studies within political science or through study of the measures adopted to try to stem corruption's spread. For example, Yves Mény, the most prominent representative of corruption studies in France, focuses on specific practices within the administrative system that might lead to corruption.[3] Another strand of studies has been concerned, following a series of illegal party-financing scandals, with the funding of political parties.[4] A third field of study has been provided by the issue of political responsibility following the 1992 blood transfusion scandal.[5] This affair demonstrated the lack of political accountability at the heart of the French political system and spawned a new genre of literature analysing the distinctions between political and legal responsibility (Beaud, 1999; Soulez Larivière, 2000). This debate has been further stimulated by the Méry affair.

What none of this literature has been concerned with, however, is *scandals* – as opposed the underlying conduct that gives rise to them, or the issues surrounding or emanating from them. Among French academics Véronique Pujas – who has written extensively about the growth of scandals relating to party funding in France, Italy and Spain (Pujas, 2000; Pujas and Rhodes, 1999) – is almost alone[6] in a field that has largely been left to journalists[7] and foreign scholars working in the area of French studies. Most of these scholars, however, adopt a historical perspective.[8] The main objective of this chapter is to challenge the way political scandals have been studied and to demonstrate that they have to be conceptualised not only historically and institutionally but also sociologically.

Contexts, processes, actors: how the scandals emerged

The birth of a scandal can often be traced to the publication of a single newspaper article.[9] In the case of the Bokassa diamonds, two articles can actually be deemed to have 'launched the scandal' into the public arena. On 10 October 1979, the *Canard Enchaîné*, a French weekly satirical paper, alleged that President Giscard d'Estaing and several of his relatives had received substantial gifts of diamonds (valued at £110,000 in 1979) from Emperor Bokassa of the Central African Republic. This, as Giscard d'Estaing (1991: 327–8) recalls in his memoirs, did not initially trouble him. But the fact that *Le Monde*, which was seen as a much more serious newspaper, immediately took up the story on its front-page lent further weight to the allegations (*Le Monde*, 1979a). The President reacted the next day by issuing a press statement, which was seen as not answering directly the accusations made by the newspapers. Six weeks later, he appeared on television to make a 'categorical and even scornful denial' concerning the value of the gift he had received.[10] Such words did not endear him to the journalists who had been investigating the case, or to the public. The scandal might then have died down but it was given added fuel in September 1980, when the *Canard Enchaîné* published a telephone conversation with Bokassa himself confirming the value of the gifts received by Giscard. At that point, another protagonist emerged. This was Roger Delpey, an ex-soldier and writer, who had been working with Bokassa on his memoirs. According to Bokassa, Delpey knew everything about the diamonds (*Le Canard Enchaîné*, 1979). As it happened, Delpey was being held in prison at the time for a breach of national security concerning his relations with suspected Lybian spies. The newspapers were prompt to infer that he was actually being held for what he knew about the Bokassa affair, and this inference ensured that the diamonds stayed in the news right up to the 1981 presidential elections. In fact, French newspapers even managed to publish an article on the topic the day before the second round of the election (*Le Monde*, 1981).

Similarly, the Méry affair first became public in September 2000 after the publication in *Le Monde* of the posthumous memoirs of Jean-Claude Méry, who was a property developer, unofficial banker to the ruling RPR and a businessman. Before his death in 1999, Jean-Claude Méry was implicated in an affair involving illegal invoices for public housing maintenance in Paris, which was investigated by the judge, Eric Halphen, who during that period was unable to implicate the RPR. During the 1980s, Méry was in charge of managing the public works contracts of the Public Housing Office in Paris. In his published memoirs, Méry stated that, in the late 1980s, companies angling for housing, water and power-installation projects parted with 35 or 40 million francs. This was cash that reached the coffers of the dominant RPR, and sometimes those of the Socialist and Communist Parties as well, by the most discreet and circuitous of routes. Méry's work was mainly to collect illegal funds for the RPR and for Jacques Chirac through the management of public works contracts. Chirac claimed to be outraged and insulted after *Le Monde*'s publication of the transcript of the video, but Judge Halphen pursued his investigation by summoning Chirac as a witness. However, the French President has been able to shelter behind the landmark constitutional decision by France's highest court on 10 October 2001 that 'for the duration of his mandate, the President of the Republic cannot be questioned as a witness, placed under formal investigation, cited or charged with any infraction by a court of common law'

(Henley, 2001) – a decision that has been challenged in the course of the public debate.[11]

What do these affairs suggest about the conditions that give rise to scandals? As Pujas and Rhodes (1999) point out, the emergence and expansion of corrupt forms of political finance are linked to particular political opportunity structures. From the two case studies reviewed here, it is possible to point out a number of such opportunity structures. Moreover, the scandals' emergence can be examined using an analytic framework consisting of three elements: contexts, actors and processes. As far as the first of these is concerned, it is worth noting that both affairs, which could be classified as pre-electoral scandals, started eighteen months before the presidential elections of 1981 and of 2002. Both developed around the person of the president (actors). Both involved a contest over the distribution of power between the judiciary, the presidency and the press (processes). What is striking in both affairs is the growing number of attacks on the political leadership of the President. The Méry affair has echoes of the earlier Bokassa scandal in the sense that it could be analysed as the result of a long and contested evolution of the semi-presidential character of French government.

The role of the media and the judiciary are often cited as crucial in understanding contemporary scandals in France. According to Pujas and Rhodes, 'at the core of these developments, lay the competitive mobilisation of actors with a new agenda' (Pujas and Rhodes, 1999). Beyond this, however, there is little consensus among authors. Some stress the action of individual judicial investigators as crucial; others contend that the judiciary is still shackled by its links with the power structure[12] and that an increasingly investigative press has played the major role in recent scandals (Pujas and Rhodes, 1999; Wright, 2000: 110–11). The Bokassa and Méry affairs allow us to explore this uncertainty and to chart the shifts that have taken place in the balance of power between these two actors.

Both the press and the judiciary played a considerable role in the two scandals, but their roles and the interaction between them were very different. In the Bokassa scandal, investigation was very much in the hands of the press and especially the newspaper, *Le Monde*. It is often said that *Le Monde* only started to play a major role in the investigation of scandals in the 1980s (Bornstein, 1990). In fact, even though the newspaper did not actively uncover facts relating to the scandal, it increased the impact of the facts uncovered by other papers, mainly the *Canard Enchaîné* (but also *Le Point* or *Le Matin*) by lending respectability to their discoveries. It is clear that, without the first article published by *Le Monde*, there would certainly not have been a scandal. In the Méry affair, *Le Monde* was always to the fore, publishing the first account of the videotape and fuelling the scandal through both its editorials and its opinion pages. Interestingly, no cartoons appeared in *Le Monde* in 1979, while the *Canard Enchaîné* is littered with them. Twenty years later, *Le Monde* had a much more satirical bent as seen in the cartoons by Plantu on the Méry affair. In effect, it has assumed the satirical and investigative functions that were reserved to *Le Canard Enchaîné* in the 1970s. Scandals have now become a mainstream subject for French journalists. This is best exemplified by the fact that Edwy Plenel, who started his career at the *Canard Enchaîné* in the 1970s is currently editor-in-chief at *Le Monde*. The perceived proliferation of scandals during the 1990s has therefore been fuelled by this new investigative role taken on by the press.

The evolution of the judicial system between 1979 and 2001 was, however, even more pronounced. In the diamonds affair, judges played no investigative role; indeed, rather the reverse. This was partly due to Giscard d'Estaing himself. At the start of his term of office in 1974, he had announced that, unlike his predecessors (De Gaulle in particular), he would not sue media organisations for libel (*Le Monde*, 1982).[13] He kept his promise even though it cost him dearly. However, his cousins, who had been implicated in the scandal by the *Canard Enchaîné* as private individuals, were not restrained from suing the paper and they won on appeal in December 1980. The protection of the libel laws is often cited as a reason for the slight impact of scandals in France but, in this instance, the protective role of the judges went further. The papers made much of the fact that Delpey was being unjustly detained by the state. Proceedings were actually taken against *Le Monde* by the Minister of Justice for daring to question the validity of the judgements made in the Delpey case. The judiciary was seen then as lending official respectability to the President's alleged manoeuvres against Delpey (*Le Monde*, 1980a). The media and the judicial system were clearly at loggerheads in the Bokassa affair.

Today, the balance between the two has altered. Some believe that the two have forged a 'dubious alliance', with individual judges acting hand-in-hand with the press. In the Méry scandal, for example, coverage by *Le Monde* was closely linked to the progress of judge Halphen's enquiries culminating in his indictment of Chirac in April 2001 (*Le Monde*, 2001). Meanwhile, the series of cartoons published by the newspaper throughout the affair illustrates well the nature of the interplay between the two actors: the judge is depicted as besieging Chirac ensconced at the Elysée under the watchful eye of the press. In fact, it has been abundantly demonstrated in recent years that both the judiciary and the media have become the principal actors in the making of political scandals in France. The names of individual investigative judges have become widely known, with their every move in political or business scandals being covered by the newspapers. Judges use the media as much as the media use them. It is the alliance between the two that has made recent scandals more potent than their predecessors. The Bokassa affair was mainly fanned by the press. When Valéry Giscard d'Estaing failed to get re-elected in 1981, the scandal died a natural death. The Méry affair was uncovered first by the press but actively investigated by the judiciary. While media interest in scandals is short-lived and largely dictated by the political calendar – the Bokassa scandal was kept in the press because of the pre-electoral context – the intervention of the judiciary follows a different timescale. Judge-led investigations have a different, much slower pace than those of journalists, taking several years to reach a conclusion. This explains the enduring presence of political scandals in France during the 1990s as judges rather than the press dictated when a scandal was definitively closed. The media are, of course, indispensable in the making of political scandals, however; for they provide the necessary channels through which legal cases are transmuted into political scandals and political scandals become legal cases, as happened in the Méry affair. This alliance between judges and the press goes a long way towards explaining why the presidency has been much more seriously threatened by the Méry affair than by than the Bokassa affair.

What do these scandals indicate?

Both affairs demonstrate that political scandals offer a fruitful perspective from which to investigate the profound changes affecting French politics. The case studies spanning twenty years show how political scandals are increasingly prompting questions about the nature of the French political system. According to Sighard Neckel (1989), scandals raise basic questions of power and legitimacy, and can play a role in clarifying the normative bases of mass-elite interaction and the political rules that govern a society. Political scandals, in order to exist at all require certain *actions* by publicly accountable officials or representatives of the state in relation to certain *general norms*, and a *public audience* that is made aware of such actions. In this context, Neckel argues that political scandals emerge when political norms are violated by actors in the political system itself and when the revelation of such violations leads to a conflict between different power groups within society (Neckel, 1989: 149). Scandals can thereby function as indicators of the ongoing tensions associated with changes in the political sphere.

In this light, the Bokassa affair can be analysed as one of the first serious attempts to downgrade the presidency even though it affected Valéry Giscard d'Estaing personally more than it affected his role. The video-cassette affair then struck at the heart of the French presidency. For the first time, a French president in office was directly implicated in a financial scandal. Prior to this, while parties and party officials had not infrequently been prosecuted in court and by the media, the presidency had been considered unassailable. Even though, on 10 October 2001, the *Cour de Cassation*, the highest court of justice, finally decided that Jacques Chirac could not indeed be tried, or even called as a witness, in an ordinary court of law by virtue of the fact that 'he is directly elected by the people to ensure the continuity of the state',[14] the President has nevertheless faced a constant barrage of accusations in the press and among political circles. True, the second round of the presidential elections in June 2002 confirmed the 'sacrosanct' nature of the office of President and the attachment of the public to the political institution, thereby also confirming the semi-presidential character of French government. However, politically, if not legally, presidents are no longer 'untouchable' in the way they once were and a growing number of people are now calling for a reform of the presidential prerogative to allow presidents to be tried for actions committed prior to their assumption of office.

The declining force of the President's 'untouchable' status can be clearly seen in the contrast in the way the two scandals were reported and discussed in the media. In the case of the Bokassa affair, Giscard was presented as a monarch facing public criticism and attempting to impose a distant and authoritarian interpretation of his role. Cartoons in the *Canard Enchaîné* portrayed him either as an absolute monarch standing on his own, a crown on his head and a sceptre in his hand, or as a very aloof, intellectual president who speaks the language of the upper class. In the Méry affair, the image that has been conveyed of Chirac has been quite different. In *Le Monde* published on 30 January 2001, Plantu shows Chirac at the top of the Elysée, behind the French flag, protecting himself from the judges. As the scandal unfolded, the presidency was subject to increasingly insistent questioning by the judiciary and the press, and finally by the political class. Several articles published recently in the French press have argued for a 'more democratic and less sacrosanct dimension'[15] to the presidency. It is interesting to note that, in both cases, the spectre of De Gaulle – a political 'reference point' that is often invoked in definitions of the President's role – was raised in an attempt to defend the presidency. But, contrary to Giscard d'Estaing who was attacked very much on a personal level, Chirac's *public role* was under scrutiny in the Méry affair: the institution itself was being targeted through Chirac. In their criticisms of Jacques Chirac, the press and the judicial system have challenged the Gaullist idea of the presidency as the keystone and embodiment of the nation and state (Gaillard and Cluzel, 2000).

In doing so, they have called into question the features of the French system of government identified by Stephen Bornstein (1990: 273) when he points to the 'extraordinary concentration of power and initiative in the Executive and especially in the presidency' as the most important source of the Fifth Republic's propensity for scandal. According to him, the hegemonic role of the President – that is the existence of broad areas of policy that have come to be regarded as the 'special preserve' of the presidency, the subordinate role assigned by the Constitution and constitutional conventions to the Prime Minister and, finally, the absence in France of any well-established tradition of Cabinet government and collective responsibility – has allowed considerable scope for the presidents and their close circles of advisers and ministers to do as they wish and to abuse their powers.

In this context, the presidencies of De Gaulle and Mitterrand could be seen as periods in which the authority deriving from the personal charisma of the presidential incumbents served to reinforce the authority of the office – while, in Giscard's and Chirac's cases, the opposite has been true. In Giscard's case, hindsight suggests that this was largely due to various aspects of the President's character. He was seen and portrayed as a stiff-necked aristocrat and techno-crat who lacked the common touch and natural authority of his predecessors. He was, for instance, very much derided when he invited road-sweepers to the traditional Christmas party at the Elysée. In Chirac's case, structural changes and changes in underlying cultural and societal values have been more important. The main sources of contestation of the role of the presidency have, however, been the new and younger professional politicians demanding more inclusive processes of political decision making. Among the most prominent of these has been the Socialist MP, Arnaud Montebourg, who has been at the forefront of efforts to overcome the constitutional obstacles impeding invest-igation of Chirac's role in the Méry affair:

> To break up France's 'electoral cronyism and duty-sapping careerism,' Monte-bourg wants to reform the legal structures of French democracy and government. First, he argues, legally binding term limits should be introduced to enhance 'the turnover and circulation of the elected élite' and give younger politicians a chance. Second, new mechanisms must be found to ensure that politicians are held to the same laws as other citizens. 'Without this, politicians enjoy a higher degree of impunity that encourages irresponsible behavior', Montebourg says. (Crumley, 2003)

Nor should the role of 'cohabitation' in mediating the impact of scandal on demands for institutional and constitutional change be overlooked. 'Cohab-itation' is the term that is used to refer to periods of government in which the Prime Minister and President are drawn from opposing parties. In the Fifth Republic, there have been three such periods: Mitterrand/Chirac 1986–88; Mitterrand/Balladur 1993–95; Chirac/Jospin 1997–2001. Their significance lies in what they suggest about increasing competition between political part-ies and the delicate negotiations between President and Prime Minister that are necessary if both are to be able to perform their roles with any effective-ness. The fact that the Méry affair came to light during the most recent period of 'cohabitation' served to heighten the passion of the debate it generated, in the newspapers and on French television, concerning what the functions of the President and the Prime Minister ought to be. And it meant, too, that demands for change found echoes right across the political spectrum, from the far left to the far right. At the time of the Bokassa affair, when, by contrast, there was no cohabitation, things were very different. Then it was only the opposition parties that found themselves at the forefront of demands of change, the Socialist Party, for example, twice devoting their party political broadcasts to the diamonds affair (*Le Monde*, 1979b, 1980b).

If, then, the level of authority attaching to the office of President has declined in recent years, the concomitant has been a growing requirement that pre-sidents periodically test their legitimacy through elections and referendums. The most recent of the latter – the 2000 referendum on a proposal to reduce the presidential term of office from seven years to five – confirmed just how far presidential authority had sunk. In July 1999, Chirac had declared him-self opposed to moves to cut the term, but then when it became clear that Prime Minister Jospin would be his chief rival in the 2002 presidential election and would back a move to cut the term, Chirac was forced to reverse his position.

A bill embodying the necessary constitutional change was thus introduced in the National Assembly in June 2000 and the confirmatory referendum required by the Constitution was fixed for 23 September. On a 30 per cent turnout – itself arguably an indication of the extent to which the public was prepared to spurn the political class – 73 per cent voted in favour of the change. Whether this outcome was to be interpreted as a victory or a defeat for Chirac, there was no doubting that it bore witness to the depth of the processes of change that French politics were undergoing and of the role of scandal in fuelling such changes (the Méry affair had come to light just two days before the referendum).

Despite institutional changes such as this one, the office of President retains an important symbolic dimension. That is, political anthropologists such as Marc Abélès 1997: 267) have shown how, in order to ensure continuity of the political system, the Fifth Republic presidents have had to portray themselves both as uncontested political leaders and as absolute monarchs. In his work on medieval politics, Kantorowicz (1957) argues that the monarch is endowed with a double nature: he is a corporeal individual rooted in contingency, a fallible and mortal human being, but he is also the living incarnation of the continuity and the transcendence of political institutions. According to Revel (1992), the pomposity of French presidential rituals under the Fifth Republic is explained by the need to bridge the symbolic gap between the continuity of the office of President and the earthly nature of its incumbent. In the cases of De Gaulle and Mitterrand, the 'symbolic construction' of their leaderships was embedded in the performance of a large number of complex political acts and rituals. Since then, there have been growing tensions between the presidential role and the personalities of its incumbents, the two scandals we have considered demonstrating clearly how political changes and changes in societal values have contributed to a growing debate over the major contours of the office.

Yet the results of the 2002 presidential elections seem to confirm the unassailability of the presidency. During the campaign, the question of Chirac's involvement in political scandals was carefully avoided by the entire political class except Jean-Marie Le Pen. Le Pen's success in the first round of the elections ironically enabled Jacques Chirac to achieve, in the second round of voting, a wide base of support cutting across the usual political cleavages, apparently in order to save a republic and a semi-presidential system whose authority he had allegedly helped to undermine. The President's apparent violation of moral standards had created a 'legitimisation deficit' that needed to be addressed. The peculiar circumstances of the 2002 elections – when in the second ballot a vote for the incumbent could be portrayed as a vote to save the Republic from fascism – provided an opportunity for this to happen, for they helped to reinforce the authority of the presidential role as the guarantor of institutional continuity. According to Pierre Bourdieu: 'by assuming public dignity, political representatives mystify their own persons' (Bourdieu, 1984). The violation of moral standards by power figures and especially by the president has created a 'deficit in legitimisation' that needed to be addressed by the judiciary, the press and the political class in order to ensure the continuity of the political system. By referring to the function and the structural context in which the presidential function is defined, Jacques Chirac has reintroduced a legitimacy attached to his personal character enabling the institution – the presidential function – to prevail to the detriment of his moral being which was called into question. By so doing, Chirac following in the footsteps of Giscard did not respond as expected to the formal and numerous requests from the press, the judiciary or the political class. The electoral context and the 2002 presidential elections gave him the long-awaited opportunity to re-establish his political leadership. This electoral victory has offered him a second chance. However, the fragile nature of the elected candidate remains at stake. Political scandals have contributed greatly to this fragility, both by revealing the inner workings of the semi-presidential system and by shifting the goal posts of acceptability within the system. Political scandals have proved a powerful tool for the press and the judiciary to expose the lack of accountability at the core of French politics and they are unlikely to relinquish it for long.

Notes

1 During the Fourth Republic, he was implicated in various scandals. For example, while he was Minister of the Interior in 1954, he was accused of leaking confidential defence documents to the Communist Party about the Indochina war, in what became known as the *affaire des fuites* (the leakages affair). He managed to exonerate himself entirely by defending himself vigorously in Parliament and directing an administrative investigation that led to the trial of the real culprits. Three decades later, he used very similar tactics during his fourteen years as President to avoid being directly implicated in the numerous scandals affecting his party and his friends. Mitterrand's handling of the ambiguous aspects of his life and career was masterful. He repeatedly defused the impact of potentially damaging secrets, such as his Vichy collaboration or the existence of his illegitimate daughter, by himself divulging details of his past.

2 Historians, of course, have long been interested in scandals. One need only mention the 'affaire Dreyfus' which has been the object of numerous studies both in France and abroad.

3 Such practices include multiple office-holding (*cumul des mandats*) and *pantouflage* – the practice that allows senior civil servants to obtain lucrative jobs in the private sector, while retaining their civil service status (Mény, 1992).

4 This issue pre-occupied lawyers and political scientists when, from 1988, a number of laws were passed, which, following a series of illegal party financing scandals, aimed to regulate party funding.

5 The blood transfusion scandal started in April 1991 with the publication of a report in 'L'évènement du Jeudi' revealing that the national blood transfusion centre was knowingly distributing in 1985 contaminated blood. The ex-Prime Minister, Laurent Fabius, and the ex-ministers, Georgina Dufoix and Edmond Hervé, were all summoned before the 'Cour de Justice de la République' (CJR) for manslaughter.

Laurent Fabius and Georgina Dufoix were both released without charges, while Edmond Hervé was found guilty of 'atteinte involontaire à l'intégrite physique de personnes'.

6 One exception would be Daniel's (1992) article, which compares the Irangate with the Flick scandals in Germany and with the *Carrefour du Développement* case (yet another case of illegal party financing) in France.

7 These are often actively involved in the discovery or investigation of misconduct, and tend to be more interested in finding the 'truth' and denouncing the wrongdoings of politicians than with reflecting on the nature of French political scandals themselves. Jean Montaldo's various books on the scandals surrounding Mitterrand are a good example of this type of literature. See for instance, his bestseller on *Mitterrand et les 40 voleurs* [Mitterrand and the forty thieves] (1994).

8 Philip Williams' (1970) study of Fourth and early Fifth republic scandals is the classic starting point. See also Bornstein (1990) and Jenkins and Morris (1993).

9 See, for example, the chapter by Moncrieff in this volume.

10 'Une heure avec le président de la République', Antenne 2, quoted in *Le Monde* (6 December 1979).

11 See the special issue of *Pouvoirs*, 92, on 'La responsabilité des gouvernants'.

12 Judges in France are civil servants and as such are subordinate to the Executive. There are safeguards to ensure their independence but political allegiance and political pressures are undoubtedly brought to bear on French judges' careers and actions. In fact, according to the Constitution, the President himself, ironically is the guarantor of the independence of the judiciary against interference from the government.

13 However, when Bokassa tried to publish his memoirs in May 1985, Giscard d'Estaing did not hesitate to sue him and obtained a court order that all copies of his book be pulped as they contained, according to his lawyer, 'inadmissible attacks on the intimacy of the private life, and offences of exceptional gravity against the personality of the elderly President of the French Republic'. See *Le Monde* (1985a and 1985b).

14 See Cour de cassation, Assemblée plénière, arrêt 481, 10 October 2001.

15 *Le Monde*, 13 June 2001.

References

Abélès, M. (1997), 'La mise en représentation du politique', in M. Abélès and P. Jeudy, *Anthropologie du politique*, Paris, Armand Colin.

Beaud, O. (1999), *Le sang contaminé: essai critique sur la criminalisation de la responsabilité des gouvernants*, Paris, Presses Universitaires de France.

Bornstein, S. (1990), 'The Politics of Scandal', in P. Hall, J. Hayward and H. Machin (eds), *Developments in French Politics*, London, Macmillan.

Bourdieu, P. (1984), 'La délégation et le fétichisme politique', *Actes de la recherche en sciences sociales*, 52/53, 49–56.

Crumley, B. (2003), 'A Reasoned Revolution', www.time.com/time/europe/generatione/profiles/montebourg.html [accessed, 24 April 2004].

Daniel, J. (1992), 'Les démocraties pluralistes face aux scandales politiques', *Revue française de science politique*, 42: 6, 981–1007.

d'Estaing, V. G. (1991), *Le pouvoir et la vie: L'affrontement*, Paris, Hachette.

Gaillard, M. and B. Cluzel (2000), 'Les nouveaux impératifs de la fonction présiden-tielle', *Revue politique et parlementaire*, 102: 1008, 2–8.

Henley, J. (2001), 'Waiting for the Fall', www.guardian.co.uk/elsewhere/journalist/story/0,7792,567972,00.html [accessed, 23 April 2004].

Jenkins, B. and P. Morris (1993), 'Political Scandal in France', *Modern and Contemporary France*, 2: 127–37.

Kantorowicz, E. H. (1957), *The King's Two Bodies: A Study in Medieval Politics*, Princeton, NJ, Princeton University Press.

Le Canard Enchaîné (1979), 'Bokassa: quand je parle, je parle . . .', 17 September.

Le Monde (1979a), 'Le Canard enchaîné met en cause M. Valéry Giscard d'Estaing à propos de cadeaux de M. Bokassa', 11 October.

Le Monde (1979b), 'TF1: le PS et les diamants de Bokassa', 20 December.

Le Monde (1980a), 'Les poursuites contre Le Monde suscitent de vives réactions du P.S. et du R.P.R.', 11 November.

Le Monde (1980b), 'Au cours de l'émission du Parti socialiste, TF1 a diffusé des décla-rations de Bokassa sur l'affaire des diamants', 4 October.

Le Monde (1981), 'Dans une interview au "*Washington Post*", l'ancien empereur Bokassa affirme avoir offert au président Giscard d'Estaing des diamants de 10 à 20 carats', 9 May.

Le Monde (1982), 'L'affaire des diamants', 18 September.

Le Monde (1985a), 'L'ex-empereur Bokassa censuré', 16 May.

Le Monde (1985b), 'Le livre de l'ex-empereur Bokassa est détruit', 29 June.

Le Monde (2001), 'Le juge Halphen accuse Jacques Chirac', 27 April.

Mény, Y. (1992), *La corruption de la République*, Paris, Fayard.

Montaldo, J. (1994), *Mitterrand et les 40 voleurs*, Paris, Albin Michel.

Neckel, S. (1989), 'Power and Legitimacy in Political Scandal: Comments on a Theoretical Framework for the Study of Political Scandals', *Corruption and Reform*, 4, 147–58.

Pujas, V. (2000), 'Carences et nouvelles dimensions de la responsabilité politique: Eléments de politiques comparées', *Pouvoirs*, 92, 165–80.

Pujas, V. and M. Rhodes (1999), 'Party Finance and Political Scandal in Italy, Spain and France', *West European Politics*, 22: 3, 41–63.

Revel, J. (1992), 'La Cour', in P. Nora (ed.), *Les lieux de mémoire, III, Les France*, vol. II, Paris, Gallimard.

Soulez Larivière, D. (2000), 'La Cour de justice de la République et l'affaire du sang contaminé', *Pouvoirs*, 92, 91–101.

Williams, P. M. (1970), *Wars, Plots and Scandals in Post-War France*, Cambridge, Cambridge University Press.

Wright, V. (2000), 'The Fifth Republic: From the droit de l'Etat to the Etat de droit', in R. Elgie (ed.), *The Changing French Political System*, London, Frank Cass.

11

Contaminated blood and political scandal in Ireland

Anne-Maree Farrell

Introduction

The Hepatitis C/Anti-D blood contamination episode that became a political scandal in Ireland in the mid-1990s, has been described as 'the greatest health scandal in the history of the state' (Cowen, 1997: 7). As a result of the contamination episode, over a thousand Irish women were infected with the Hepatitis C virus due to the administration of a blood product, known as Anti-D, between 1976 and 1994. In early 1994, when the government announced that the contamination episode had taken place, it was an issue that was narrowly defined, by both the government and the media, in medical and scientific terms. As more information about the extent of the contamination became public, however, it developed into a major political scandal. Growing political, media and public pressure led the government to convene an independent Tribunal of Inquiry into the matter. The Tribunal's report was damning of institutional practices and individuals involved in the contamination episode. By mid-1997, a newly installed government had accepted full political responsibility for what had come to be known as the 'Hepatitis C/Anti-D scandal'.

This chapter will examine how and why the episode developed into a political scandal. For our purposes, 'political scandal' refers to behaviour that transgresses accepted societal norms or standards and which, once revealed, results in public disapproval (Moodie, 1988; Thompson, 2000; Williams, 1998). We accept the argument advanced by Markovits and Silverstein (1988: 2–4) that political scandal is 'inherent in the very structure of politics' of liberal democracies (such as Ireland) given the presence of 'open competitive elections, a free press and constant tension between the accumulation and curtailment of the exercise of political power'. In examining the circumstances surrounding the emergence of political scandal and its consequences in liberal democracies, writers like Lowi (1988) and Barker (1994) have expressed concern about the difficulties involved in drawing any overarching conclusions about how and why a transgression or 'episode' becomes a full-blown political scandal. They have argued that, more often than not, one must examine the specifics of national political culture and historical traditions for such an explanation.

Other writers, while acknowledging such concerns, have nevertheless attempted to identify, mainly through comparative research into corruption scandals (Markovits and Silverstein, 1988; Mény and Rhodes, 1997; Pujas and Rhodes, 1999), common characteristics in the development of political scandals. This chapter draws upon some of the findings of this research to suggest that the following factors were influential in the development of political scandal in the Hepatitis C/Anti-D blood contamination episode: (1) a society in the process of socio-cultural and economic transition; (2) the 'entrepreneurial' role played by organised interest groups; (3) the media's role in generating and sustaining interest in the political scandal; (4) the development of public mistrust caused by the public revelation of previously concealed information and activities; and (5) the absence of effective institutional arrangements to facilitate political accountability. We will first review the circumstances leading to the blood contamination episode and its political consequences before examining how the factors outlined above influenced the development of political scandal in this instance.

The Hepatitis C/Anti-D blood contamination scandal

In February 1994, the Irish government announced that a number of women were likely to have contracted Hepatitis C due to the administration of a blood product known as Anti-D. The product had been administered to women with a specific blood type (Rhesus negative) in order to prevent foetal abnormalities and death in second and subsequent pregnancies (known colloquially as 'blue baby' syndrome). The product had been manufactured and supplied by the Blood Transfusion Service Board (BTSB) since the early 1970s. The BTSB had been created as an executive agency (known as a 'state-sponsored body' in Ireland) in 1961. It was a separate legal entity with a board of management reporting regularly to the Minister for Health, who was politically accountable to the Irish Parliament (the *Dáil*) for the BTSB's activities. The BTSB's main functions were to manage the national blood transfusion service and ensure a safe and adequate supply of blood to meet the needs of Irish citizens, based on a system of voluntary blood donation. In practice, the BTSB operated with little ministerial or political oversight. Decision making remained predominantly in the hands of the medical and scientific professionals responsible for managing its day-to-day activities (Report of the Expert Group on the BTSB, 1995).

In 1976, it first came to the attention of the BTSB that one of the donors whose blood had contributed to a batch of Anti-D had been diagnosed with 'infective hepatitis'. Notwithstanding their knowledge of the episode, senior staff continued using the donor's blood in the manufacture of subsequent batches of Anti-D. In 1977, the BTSB were notified that a number of women who had received Anti-D had developed hepatitis. Senior staff at the BTSB attributed such diagnoses to 'environmental factors' and took no further action. A blood test to establish the presence of Hepatitis C became commercially available by the early 1990s. In 1991, senior staff at the BTSB were informed that blood samples retained from the 1977 Anti-D incident were positive for Hepatitis C. Again, they elected to take no further action to investigate the matter. In a separate incident in the early 1990s, another donor's blood, which had tested positive for Hepatitis C but was believed by staff to be a 'false positive result', was used in the manufacture of multiple batches of Anti-D. In January 1994, a member of staff at a regional blood bank reported on a study she had conducted, which showed a high incidence of women donors testing positive for Hepatitis C. The one thing they had in common was that they had been administered Anti-D (Report of the Expert Group on the BTSB, 1995; Report of the Tribunal of Inquiry into the BTSB, 1997).

The Minister for Health was informed of the findings of the regional study in February 1994. The government decided that it was necessary to inform the wider public of the contamination episode and take decisive action on the matter. When it announced that contamination had taken place, however, it was clear that it viewed this as a narrowly defined medical and scientific issue. The Minister for Health stated there would be a screening programme and a recall of available stocks of Anti-D, and generally reassured the public that the matter was now under control (*Dáil* Debates, 439: 2, 299–314). In March 1994, the Minister for Health announced that an Expert Group had been appointed to inquire into the circumstances that had led to the contamination episode.

The findings of the Expert Group were published in April 1995. They reported that clear mistakes had been made by staff at the BTSB, resulting in the Hepatitis C contamination of Anti-D. Based on evidence provided by the BTSB, the Expert Group found there had been no definite diagnosis of infective hepatitis in the case of the 1977 donor. However, it concluded there had been significant departures from good medical and scientific practices in relation to the manufacture of Anti-D on the part of the BTSB. In the wake of these findings, the government announced a financial compensation and medical treatment package for the growing numbers of women being diagnosed with Hepatitis C due to Anti-D. The government emphasised its lack of 'political culpability' in the matter, given that it was not legally responsible for the activities of the BTSB. By adopting this approach, the government sought to contain the financial, legal and political fall-out (*Dáil* Debates, 451: 7, 1555–71; Cowen, 1997).

Following the initial flurry of media interest in the episode in the wake of the announcement of the Minister for Health in early 1994, and the subsequent publication of the findings of the Expert Group in April 1995, the issue remained a matter of periodic reports in the media. Although the issue was clearly not going away, the contamination episode was predominantly reported in the media as a medical and scientific issue, with an element of human interest as Positive Action (the group representing the infected women) battled with the government for a better deal for the victims (Hegarty, 1995; Hennessy, 1995; *Irish Times*, 1995). However, there were individual journalists who consistently followed the story during this period. They were already describing the contamination episode as a 'scandal', with one journalist observing in September 1995: 'the information emanating from the Blood Bank has been poor [with the public having to] rely on media leaks for information . . . the Hepatitis C scandal has not as yet run its course. Handled badly, it has the capacity to severely damage the government' (Bowers, 1995).[1]

Positive Action was founded in 1994. Although initially formed as a support group to lobby for financial support and better treatment for its members, it had subsequently acquired legal representation. Positive Action had an able and presentable media spokesperson in Jane O'Brien, an experienced journalist, and chairperson of the group. It was unified with clear and coherent objectives: first, it wanted the full truth told about the circumstances leading to the Hepatitis C contamination of Anti-D; second, it wanted the government compensation tribunal to be put on a statutory basis; finally, it wanted the government formally to accept political and legal responsibility for what had happened. From 1995 onwards, Positive Action formed strategic relationships with several female parliamentarians from the political opposition and their concerns began being voiced in the *Dáil* on a regular basis. The group's lobbying efforts also yielded some success in late 1995 when the *Seanad* (Upper House) of the Irish Parliament forced the government to back down over legislation, which did not address the concerns of Positive Action.[2]

In 1996, debate surrounding the Hepatitis C/Anti-D blood contamination shifted significantly as the episode gave rise to a full-blown political scandal. In early 1996, Brigid McCole, a mother of eleven children, who had been infected with Hepatitis C through Anti-D administered in 1977, had her case against the BTSB listed for trial. This was due to take place in October 1996, and would be a 'test case'. Positive Action saw it as an opportunity to discover from key witnesses exactly what had led to the contamination episode. Unlike Positive Action, the government feared the revelations that seemed likely to emerge from the case. It had little control over either the terms of any award of financial compensation or the escalating legal costs. In April 1996, McCole's legal representatives accused the BTSB of withholding documents that showed that the batch of Anti-D given to her in 1977 had come from a donor previously diagnosed with 'infective hepatitis'. Positive Action and the political opposition began to cry 'cover-up', and, in face of contradictory comments by different Ministers and the BTSB over the origin of both the documents and the diagnosis of the donor, the media began uniformly to describe the matter as a 'scandal' (Haughey, 1996; O'Regan, 1996).

In early October 1996, shortly before her case was due to be heard Brigid McCole died from Hepatitis C. Her death gave a 'human face' to the contamination episode. Her family called for a judicial inquiry into the circumstances leading to it so that the full truth could be told.[3] Her death brought about a fundamental shift in public perceptions of the episode, and how it was dealt with at a political level. It was now described as 'the worst crisis of its kind in public administration . . . in the history of the state' (*Cork Examiner*, 1996a).

The scandal was linked by the media to wider political and institutional issues, with constant references in articles and editorials to 'morality', 'accountability', 'trust' and the need to know the 'truth'. Comments included the following from Irish newspapers:

> It wouldn't matter if this was just another political cock-up with which the politicians, placemen and timeservers were playing Pass the Parcel. This is about people's health, about living and dying and telling the truth. (Kerrigan, 1996)
>
> Government in this country is not just about managing the finances of the nation. Government confers moral responsibilities upon the holders of office to do what is right. An awful wrong has been done to thousands of Irish women and it has to be rectified . . . the nature of Irish life, in both public and private sectors, is to pay people to go away . . . those who are in positions of power are not required to explain their actions publicly . . . that's another matter that has to be addressed. But first the government should do the honourable thing: admit it is responsible for the BTSB and say sorry. (*Sunday Tribune*, 1996)

Governmental attempts to distance itself from political responsibility for the matter, as well as to advocate caution against the potential for escalating legal costs associated with a tribunal of inquiry, were described in the media as being secondary to discovering the truth and to the victims obtaining justice for the wrongs committed against them by the state institutions in which they had placed their trust (*Cork Examiner*, 1996a).[4] Calls were made by both the political opposition and the media for the criminal prosecution of those staff at the BTSB involved in the blood contamination (Tynan, 1996a). Within two weeks of McCole's death, and following mounting criticism of his handling of the matter (*Cork Examiner*, 1996b; Cunningham, 1996; *Irish Independent*, 1996; MacCormaic, 1996; Tynan, 1996b) the Minister for Health agreed to establish a tribunal of inquiry with full judicial powers to inquire into the circumstances leading to the Hepatitis C contamination of Anti-D. In a speech to the *Dáil*, moving legislation for the creation of the Tribunal of Inquiry, the Minister acknowledged that it was of 'considerable importance to the well-being of the democratic system that we can be seen to address the critical issues of accountability and responsibility through the systems available to us' (Dáil Debates, 470: 3: 518).

The Tribunal heard evidence between December 1996 and February 1997, with witnesses being called from the victims' groups, the BTSB, the Department of Health, former Ministers for Health and medical and scientific experts. Daily media coverage of the evidence detailed a catalogue of misdeeds, negligent action and incompetence by civil servants and political representatives exposing, at its core, the lack of institutional arrangements to ensure political accountability in the public interest. More tellingly, it exposed a seemingly callous disregard for women who had placed their trust in a state institution charged with providing them and their children with the 'gift of life' through Anti-D – an institution that had instead handed them a potential death sentence in the form of Hepatitis C. The Tribunal's findings were highly critical of the BTSB and its staff. It recommended wide-ranging reform of all state institutions involved in the supervision, regulation and operation of the national blood supply (Report of the Tribunal of Inquiry into the BTSB, 1997). Following release of the findings, the Minister for Health acceded to most of the demands of Positive Action but refused a formal admission of legal and political responsibility. The scandal became an election issue with the political opposition agreeing to release details of the legal strategy that the state had adopted in the McCole case. The political opposition, a coalition of Fianna Fáil and the Progressive Democrats, was elected to government in May 1997. In August 1997, the new government published a report revealing the former government's legal and political strategies in the McCole case. Here, the new Minister for Health formally admitted political responsibility on behalf of the government for the episode (Cowen, 1997).

Factors in the emergence of political scandal

Having reviewed the circumstances leading to the Hepatitis C/Anti-D episode as well its political consequences, we will now examine the factors influential in the development of this particular political scandal.

A society in the process of socio-cultural and economic transition

The evolution of the episode from a narrowly defined medical and scientific issue to a full-blown political scandal occurred during a period of significant social and economic change in Ireland. Such change brought with it a clash between traditional and modern values (Breen *et al.*, 1990; Hardiman and Whelan, 1994). There had been a breakdown in the social and religious consensus, with the influence of the once all-powerful Catholic Church declining in the face of growing secularisation (Coakley, 1999). In addition, Ireland's entry into the EU had led to growing Europeanisation, the effects of which were felt most keenly by citizens in the 1990s (Keatinge and Laffan, 1999). These changes were underlined by rapid economic success in the face of Ireland's successful integration into the European, and indeed, global economy (Crotty, 1998).

The clash between traditional and modern values in the context of a society undergoing socio-economic change has been identified as an important factor in the emergence of political scandal (Mény and Rhodes, 1997; Pujas and Rhodes, 1999). Ireland had traditionally been a society deeply rooted in communal values, with a strong trend towards personalism reflected in close-knit social and political relationships, translating into a tendency towards 'brokerage politics' (Garvin, 1991). This approach to politics had created a fertile breeding ground for the development of political corruption, the extent of which was revealed in a series of scandals also emerging in the 1990s (Murphy, 2000). Unlike the corruption scandals, however, the scandal arising out of the Hepatitis C/Anti-D episode exposed serious maladministration by a public institution responsible for performing an important social function, namely collecting and supplying the 'gift of life': blood. This particular scandal highlighted not only the clash between the old and the new, but also public concern and uncertainty over the way Irish society was changing. The collection and supply of blood emphasised the importance of traditional communal values, which were now being undermined by the episode. The latter also violated the traditional social and religious role accorded in Irish society to women as mothers, now infected with a deadly disease by a state institution to which they had entrusted their well-being. The Hepatitis C/Anti-D scandal would highlight clearly the impact of change in a country that was happy to embrace the benefits brought about by economic success, but that was also uncertain about the consequences of such change for the underlying social fabric.

The 'entrepreneurial' role played by organised interest groups
As we have seen in the previous section, Positive Action played a crucial role in the emergence of political scandal in this instance. Members of the group did this in several ways: first, they forged links with the media; second, they developed strategic relationships with a number of parliamentary representatives; and, finally, they pursued legal action. The 'entrepreneurial'[5] approach taken by Positive Action highlights a trend in interest group action that has been observed by Marmor *et al.* (1999) in relation to blood contamination scandals generally. One of the hallmarks of these interest groups is their ability to utilise the media as well as other methods outside the established political process to ensure their concerns reach not only a political, but also a wider public audience. Positive Action soon recognised the importance of making use of a range of methods (whether political, media or legal) by which information about what had happened to their members could be made available to the wider public. The methods were outside the direct control of the government.

Thompson (2000: 13–15) has pointed out that the essence of political scandal is the public revelation of the contravention of certain values, norms or moral codes governing the exercise of political power. Public revelations of previously concealed information about the extent of Hepatitis C/Anti-D contamination were important in the development of political scandal in this instance. The revelations pointed to serious maladministration by a state institution, and a government more intent on limiting its financial liability than addressing the needs of the victims. The failure to reveal the extent of such maladministration undermined public trust not only in those in government, but also in the BTSB, a state institution responsible for the performance of an important public service for the community. Through its links with the media, Positive Action was crucial in ensuring that key information reached the wider public. The ability of an 'entrepreneurial' interest group to build strategic relationships with other actors, which were independent of government control, would prove crucial to the emergence of political scandal.

The role of the media in generating and sustaining interest in the political scandal
Initial media reporting viewed the episode in narrow medico-scientific terms. This would change for two reasons: first, journalists gained access to further

information about the reasons for the contamination; second, strategic relationships were formed between individual journalists and Positive Action and
its members, facilitating the flow of further information about the issue.
When the government first announced the contamination episode, little independent information was available to the media about the matter. It would
only be with a series of 'leaks' plus the publication of the findings of the Expert
Group and the Tribunal of Inquiry, that the media would be able to publish
previously concealed information about the extent of the episode. At the same
time, the media were able to give the contamination tragedy a 'human face'
through reporting the life-stories of members of Positive Action, particularly
Brigid McCole. The combination of increased access to information, and being
able to portray the human tragedy involved, was crucial to continuing media
interest and ensured that the issue would remain in the public domain. The
media would prove to be crucial actors in structuring the way the contamination episode evolved into a political scandal.

One of the key roles the media play in political scandals is quickly and
widely to disseminate information about the transgressions involved. As
actors independent of the established political process in a liberal democracy,
the media can serve as important links between the political and public
spheres. In this sense, they play a strategic role in cases of political scandal,
particularly where actors and institutions within the established political
process are endeavouring to conceal or withhold information relevant to
the public interest. In terms of mobilising public opinion, those in charge of
the communications media have a range of options. They can report on the
episode in question on a regular or infrequent basis. They can devote greater
or lesser financial and personnel resources (perhaps in the form of an investigative journalist) to reporting the issue. They can decide whether or not to
run a 'campaign' by devoting editorial time and resources to bringing the episode
to public attention over an extended period. In making use of such options,
the media operate to 'mobilise' public opinion and to structure the way in which
a particular 'episode' or transgression becomes transformed into a political
scandal.

The media can also structure the way actors involved in the political
scandal are perceived, as well as the public response to such actors. In an
era in which personality politics have replaced ideological politics, those in
political power have become much more reliant on the media and upon 'spin-
doctoring', as a way to ensure they pass the 'credibility test' with the public
(Smith, 1995). This has been combined with an increasingly competitive media
market, a proliferation of outlets and the ability to disseminate information
rapidly. The combination of the two has transformed what Thompson (2000:
6) has called the nature of 'visibility' in the modern world and altered the
relations between public and private life. Politicians and those institutions
over which they have control have become much more vulnerable when the
'media gaze' has been turned upon them as a result of investigations into transgressions contrary to the public interest. The net effect has been to increase

the power of the media as a key actor in structuring the emergence of polit-ical scandal.

The role in the development of political scandal of public mistrust

As more and more information was forthcoming about the extent of Hepatitis C/Anti-D contamination and the reasons for its occurrence, Irish public opinion was mobilised against both the government and the BTSB over their failure to take appropriate action on the matter. There was clearly a disjunc-ture between what those in political power had told the public about the episode and what was revealed through the Expert Group and the Tribunal of Inquiry. In the eyes of the public, both the experts and the Tribunal had greater legitimacy and credibility, being independent of the established polit-ical process. As more independent and credible sources of information became available, there was further mobilisation of public opinion, because of the way the government sought to deal with Brigid McCole. These two elements combined together not only to mobilise public opinion but also to generate public mistrust of the BTSB and the government.

Public mistrust of those in political office and/or of state institutions is an important factor in the emergence of political scandal. Thompson (2000: 250) has argued that political scandals have become a credibility test for the 'politics of trust' in the modern era, and that they have the capacity to act as 'reputation depleters' for both public officials and institutions. Garment (1992: 2) has also recognised the significance of this factor in the growth of political scandals in the US, noting the creation of a 'culture of mistrust', where the focus is now on individual behaviour rather than on the failure of political institutions or the failure of political will. In the modern political era, the focus is now on the credibility of those in political power, over and above their commitment to a particular ideology or policy orientation. It is therefore unsurprising that one of the key factors to emerge in modern political scan-dals is a culture of public mistrust, where the credibility of those in political office and/or individual state institutions is called into question.

Public mistrust may also be a particular issue in the case of a political scan-dal arising from contravention of deeply rooted social or moral norms in a given society. The giving and receiving of blood is viewed as a valued and altruistic act on behalf of the community in many liberal democracies (Titmuss, 1971). The failure of the BTSB to ensure a safe blood supply by exposing Irish women to a deadly virus contravened communal values and engendered a culture of mistrust both of the institution and of those in political power accountable for its operations. The symbolic significance of blood still resonated strongly in Irish society and the public revelation of its contamination resulted in the BTSB losing not only a significant degree of public trust, but also much of its reputation as a respected national institution. In the case of the Hepatitis C/Anti-D episode the breach of public trust caused by the contravention of deeply rooted social values would play a particularly influential role in the transformation of the episode into a full-blown political scandal.

The absence of effective institutional arrangements to facilitate political accountability

A central problem in the development of the Irish state and its institutions has been one of legitimacy, with a significant militant minority opposed to the state and a continuing dispute over territory. The legacy of the imposition of British rule remained in the organisation of political institutions, the state bureaucracy and its legal system. These particular problems made for the development of a weak, centralised state and a lack of feelings of allegiance to it on the part of citizens (Coakley, 1999). For many decades following the founding of the state, these issues dominated the national political agenda. As a result, successive Irish governments failed to focus in a clear and coherent way on state institutional development. This lack of focus also meant that public policy making was driven by the need to maintain continuity over change. If political crises arose, reactive, short-term opportunism was favoured at the expense of a long-term approach (Hardiman, 1998; O'Halpin, 1993).

The historical legacy of such an approach to state institutional development and public policy making was exemplified in the creation of the BTSB and in the supervisory arrangements made for it. In the 1960s, the then Irish government decided to create a series of executive agencies, known as state-sponsored bodies, as a convenient administrative solution to its ever-expanding executive functions. Little or no thought was given to how government was to supervise these bodies (Breen *et al.*, 1990; Dooney and O'Toole, 1992). The BTSB was created as a state-sponsored body at this time to perform the important role of managing the Irish blood supply. This task was considered, by those in government, as one best left to those with medical and scientific expertise in blood-banking. The scientific personnel in charge of the BTSB therefore ran the organisation with little or no supervision from the Department of Health. Although the Minister for Health was responsible to the *Dáil* for the activities of the BTSB, the absence of any proper supervision meant that ministerial accountability was more apparent than real.

The lack of proper institutional arrangements to facilitate political accountability has been identified as an important factor in the occurrence of political scandal, particularly in cases involving political or financial corruption (Doig and Wilson, 1995; Jiménez, 1998; Logue, 1988). Mény and Rhodes (1997), and Pujas and Rhodes (1999) have argued that particular institutional settings breed relationships and social practices that can create 'political opportunity structures' in which corrupt behaviour can occur. These authors' arguments are equally applicable to blood contamination episodes such as the one analysed here. There were no suitable structural arrangements for ensuring the political accountability of state-sponsored bodies, such as the BTSB, a legacy of a long-standing failure by successive Irish governments to develop a coherent strategy for managing and supervising its ever-expanding executive functions. The failure to create appropriate mechanisms for ensuring the political accountability of bodies, such as the BTSB, meant those in charge of the organisation could conceal the contamination episode over an extended period of time. It would be left to actors outside the established political institutions to reveal the full extent of what had happened and demand that the BTSB, as well as its political masters, be held accountable for the episode and its tragic consequences.

Summary and conclusion

In this chapter, we have examined factors influencing the emergence of a political scandal in Ireland. First, we suggested the episode occurred at a time when Irish society was undergoing significant socio-economic change. Such change had brought with it a clash between traditional and modern values, and the Hepatitis C/Anti-D episode brought such a clash into sharp focus, violating thereby traditional communal values typified by the act of giving and receiving blood. The transformation of the episode into a political scandal highlighted the impact of such change in a country happy to embrace the benefits of economic success but simultaneously uncertain about the consequences of such success for traditional social and cultural values.

Second, we examined the role played by an organised interest group representing the victims of this episode. Positive Action pursued strategic relationships with other key actors, both within and outside the established political process, to obtain justice for what their members had suffered as a result of being infected with Hepatitis C. The group's 'entrepreneurial' approach to representing their members' interests would prove a crucial factor in the episode becoming a political scandal.

Third, we examined the media's role in transforming the episode into a political scandal. The media published previously concealed information about the extent of contamination. They also gave a 'human face' to the suffering of those infected. The combination of these factors meant that the media were able not only to mobilise public opinion on the issue, but also to structure the way the public perceived key actors involved in blood contamination. This in turn influenced the nature and intensity of the public response to the consequences of the contamination episode. The media proved to be crucial to mediating the transformation of the episode into a political scandal.

Fourth, the development of public mistrust of those in political power also proved important. Public opinion was mobilised not only because of public revelations of previously concealed information about the contamination episode, but also because it contravened important communal values, typified by the giving and receiving of blood. The combination of the two resulted in the development of public mistrust of those in political power. The loss of public trust caused by the contravention of important social values proved an important factor in the development of political scandal in this instance.

Finally, we examined whether institutional arrangements within the Irish polity facilitated the development of the scandal. The way the Irish state had developed meant there had been no clear or coherent strategy concerning the development of institutional arrangements facilitating political accountability.

This was particularly so in relation to executive agencies, like the national blood transfusion service. Those in charge of the service were thereby allowed to manage the blood supply with little ministerial or parliamentary oversight, with the net result that senior medical staff could cover-up the extent of contamination for a considerable time. It was left to other actors outside the established political process, like the organised interest group Positive Action and the media, to demand that those responsible be held to account for what had happened. Without effective arrangements to facilitate accountability within established political institutions, the government was forced to rely upon independent 'experts' and a tribunal of inquiry to uncover both the extent of the contamination episode, as well as restore its credibility on the issue. In resorting to such independent sources to hold those responsible to account, the government lost the ability to influence the way the public responded to the contamination episode. Eventually, the lack of effective institutional arrangements to facilitate political accountability contributed to the development of the scandal.

This examination of the Hepatitis C/Anti-D blood contamination episode reveals that a combination of different factors, rather than one single factor, determined how and why it developed into a political scandal. Of all the factors we have examined, however, the development of public mistrust of those in political power was particularly influential. Such mistrust originated not only in the attempted cover-up of previously concealed information, but more importantly in the perceived contravention of a valued social norm of community life, namely the giving and receiving of blood. This suggests that where an 'episode' involving the contravention of important social norms is publicly revealed, the 'politics of trust' may prove highly influential in transforming such episode into a political scandal in liberal democracies.

Notes

1 Feargal Bowers was Chief Reporter with the *Irish Medical News* at this time. The other journalists who consistently followed the Hepatitis C/Anti-D story during this period were Sam Smyth, then at the *Irish Independent*, and Fintan O'Toole at the *Irish Times*.

2 Interview by author with Jane O'Brien, Chair of Positive Action, 20 November 1997.

3 A copy of the letter sent by the McCole family to the Minister for Health demanding an inquiry into the circumstances which led to the Hepatitis C/Anti-D contamination was published in the *Irish Times* on 9 October 1996.

4 The Irish government was wary of establishing tribunals of inquiry because of what had happened with one such tribunal (known as the 'Beef Tribunal') in the early 1990s, which had given rise to enormous legal costs and resulted in inconclusive findings.

5 By using the term 'entrepreneurial role' in relation to organised interests in blood contamination scandals, I am drawing on Kingdon's (1995: 195) analysis of the way in which an issue comes to be placed on the political agenda and to result in government policy making. He argues that 'policy entrepreneurs' take advantage of the opening of a 'policy window' to link a problem to their preferred proposal in conditions of political receptivity.

References

Barker, A. (1994), 'The Upturned Stone: Political Scandals and Their Investigation Processes in Twenty Democracies', *Crime Law and Social Change*, 21, 337–73.

Bowers, F. (1995), 'Many Questions Unanswered in Blood Debacle', *Irish Independent*, 26 July.

Breen, R., D. Hannan, D. Rottmann and C. Whelan (1990), *Understanding Contemporary Ireland: State, Class and Development in the Republic of Ireland*, Dublin, Gill and Macmillan.

Coakley, J. (1999), 'Society and Political Culture', in J. Coakley and M. Gallagher (eds), *Politics in the Republic of Ireland*, 3rd edition, London, Routledge & PSAI Press.

Cork Examiner (1996a), 'Taxpayers' Fears Should not Deter Pursuit of Justice', 9 October.

Cork Examiner (1996b), 'Hepatitis C Scandal Inquiry is Welcome', 18 October.

Cowen, B. (1997), 'Report on behalf of the Government by Brian Cowen TD, Minister for Health and Children on the Legal Strategy adopted by the Defence in the case of the late Mrs Bridget McCole', Dublin, Department of Health.

Crotty, W. (1998), 'Democratisation and Political Development in Ireland', in W. Crotty and D. Schmitt (eds), *Ireland and the Politics of Change*, London, Longman.

Cunningham, G. (1996), 'Cool-hand Noonan Light a Fire under the Hepatitis C Fiasco', *Cork Examiner*, 18 October.

Dáil Debates, vol. 439: 2, 299–314; vol. 451: 7, 1555–71; vol. 470: 3, 518.

Doig, A. and J. Wilson (1995), 'Untangling the Threads', in F. F. Ridley and A. Doig (eds), *Sleaze: Politicians, Private Interests and Public Reaction*, Oxford, Oxford University Press.

Dooney, S. and J. O'Toole (1992), *Irish Government Today*, Dublin, Gill and Macmillan.

Garment, S. (1992), *Scandal: The Culture of Mistrust in American Politics*, New York, Archer Books.

Garvin, T. (1991), 'Democracy in Ireland: Collective Somnambulance and Public Policy', *Administration*, 39: 1, 42–54.

Hardiman, N. and C. T. Whelan (1994), 'Political and Democratic Values', in C. T. Whelan (ed.), *Values and Social Change in Ireland*, Dublin, Gill and Macmillan.

Hardiman, N. (1998), 'Inequality and the Representation of Interests', in W. Crotty and D. Schmitt (eds), *Ireland and the Politics of Change*, London, Longman.

Haughey, N. (1996), 'Group Claims Hepatitis C Was Not the Result of Mistake', *Irish Times*, 18 April.

Hegarty, T. (1995), 'Nooan Accused on Hepatitis C Payments', *Irish Times*, 21 June.

Hennessy, M. (1995), 'Hepatitis C: "No Further Concessions",' *Cork Examiner*, 8 December.

Irish Independent (1996), 'Blood Inquiry', 18 October.

Irish Times (1995), 'A Political Imperative', 13 September.

Jiménez, F. (1998), 'Political Scandals and Political Responsibility in Democratic Spain', *West European Politics*, 21: 4, 80–93.

Keatinge, P. and B. Laffan (1999), 'Ireland: A Small Open Polity', in J. Coakley and M. Gallagher (eds), *Politics in the Republic of Ireland*, 3rd edition, London, Routledge & PSAI Press.

Kerrigan, G. (1996), 'The State Has Disgraced Itself', *Sunday Independent*, 6 October.

Kingdon, J. W. (1995), *Agendas, Alternatives and Public Policies*, 2nd edition, New York, Harper Collins.

Logue, J. (1988), 'Conclusion: Appreciating Scandal as a Political Art Form or Making an Intellectual Virtue of a Political Vice', in A. Markovits and M. Silverstein (eds),

The Politics of Scandal: Power and Process in Liberal Democracies, New York, Holmes & Meier.

Lowi, T. (1988), 'Foreword', in A. Markovits and M. Silverstein (eds), *The Politics of Scandal: Power and Process in Liberal Democracies*, New York, Holmes & Meier.

MacCormaic, M. (1996), 'Minister has shown "lack of compassion",' *Irish Independent*, 18 October.

Markovits, A. and M. Silverstein (eds) (1988), *The Politics of Scandal: Power and Process in Liberal Democracies*, New York, Holmes & Meier.

Marmor, T., P. Dillon and S. Scher (1999), 'The Comparative Politics of Contaminated Blood: From Hesitancy to Scandal', in R. Bayer and E. Feldman (eds), *Blood Feuds: AIDS, Blood and the Politics of Medical Disaster*, New York, Oxford University Press.

Mény, Y. and M. Rhodes (1997), 'Illicit Governance: Corruption, Scandal and Fraud', in M. Rhodes, P. Heywood and V. Wright (eds), *Developments in West European Politics*, Houndmills, Macmillan Press.

Moodie, G. (1988), 'Studying Political Scandal', *Corruption and Reform*, 3, 243–6.

Murphy, G. (2000), 'A Culture of Sleaze: Political Corruption and the Irish Body Politic 1997–2000', *Irish Political Studies*, 15, 193–200.

O'Halpin, E. (1993), 'Policy-making', in J. Coakley and M. Gallagher (eds), *Politics in the Republic of Ireland*, 2nd edition, Dublin, Folens and PSAI Press.

O'Regan, E. (1996), 'Anti-D Group in Call for Probe at Cover-up', *Irish Independent*, 18 April.

Pujas, V. and M. Rhodes (1999), 'Party Finance and Political Scandal in Italy, Spain and France', *West European Politics*, 22: 3, 41–63.

Report of the Expert Group on the Blood Transfusion Service Board (1995), Pn. 1538, January, Government Publications, Dublin.

Report of the Tribunal of Inquiry into the Blood Transfusion Service Board (1997), Pn. 3695, March, Government Publications, Dublin.

Smith, T. (1995), 'Causes Concerns and Cures', in F. F. Ridley and A. Doig (eds), *Sleaze: Politicians, Private Interests and Public Reaction*, Oxford, Oxford University Press.

Sunday Tribune (1996), 'Never Saying Sorry', 6 October.

Titmuss, R. (1971), *The Gift Relationship: From Human Blood to Social Policy*, 1st American edition, New York, Pantheon Books.

Thompson, J. B. (2000), *Political Scandal: Power and Visibility in the Media Age*, Cambridge, Polity Press.

Tynan, M. M. (1996a), 'Infected Woman Makes Complaint against BTSB', *Irish Times*, 5 October.

Tynan, M. M. (1996b), 'Noonan's Gaffe is Set to Haunt Him', *Irish Times*, 19 October.

Williams, R. (1998), *Political Scandals in the USA*, Edinburgh, Keele University Press.

Part IV

The results and functions of scandals

12

The role of scandals in post-Communist Russia

Julia Wishnevsky

During the twentieth century in Russia, political scandals have tended to serve as signals of forthcoming revolutions – both violent and relatively non-violent, as was the case with the events bringing about the end of Communism and the collapse of the Soviet Union in 1991. The abundance of scandals in the late 1990s, however, seems to have produced a kind of 'crisis of genre': today's public – not unreasonably – no longer seems to care about the reputations of the country's public figures. How and why this has happened is the theme of this chapter. After discussing what can be termed 'scandal' in the Russian context, the chapter adopts a chronological approach, evaluating in turn the types of scandals occurring in Gorbachev's, Yeltsin's and finally President Putin's periods in power.

On the use of terminology

A modern Russian dictionary defines the term 'scandal' as 'an event or occurrence, which receives publicity and discredits those involved'.[1] In essence, this does not seem different from that offered by the *Oxford Illustrated Dictionary*, which views scandal as a 'thing that occasions general feelings of outrage and indignation'.[2] Yet there is a difference of emphasis. And there is a reason for such difference. As far as Russia is concerned it is important to distinguish genuine cases of public indignation from government-orchestrated propaganda campaigns, aimed at smearing one's political opponents. The Soviet propaganda machine, particularly under Stalin, gained worldwide notoriety for its ability to create the false impression that there was public wrath about events that, for some political reason, irritated the authorities. The means used, though hardly the themes, would be very similar to those involved in genuine, spontaneously erupting political scandals in democracies, and included the organisation of mass rallies, media articles and letters to newspaper editors, whereby loyal Soviet citizens would condemn various 'outcasts', such as the poet Boris Pasternak, who dared in 1958 to be awarded the Nobel prize for his novel, *Doctor Zhivago*, which had been banned in his home country. Although some of the ordinary people involved in such campaigns might have quite sincerely shared the government's disapproval of their victims' deeds, it is clear that government-orchestrated witch-hunts cannot in any sense be termed 'political scandals'. Scandals belong to the public, not the governmental, domain and therefore require the existence of at least a modicum of independent public opinion.

Scandal frequently leads to a loss of, or damage to, reputation (though, as we shall see, may sometimes actually enhance it) caused by some actual or apparent violation of morality or propriety – an element of disgrace. It is well known that the kinds of activities that can disgrace a public figure vary from country to country. For example, philandering is more likely to damage a British leader's reputation than that of a French, German or, for that matter, Russian one.[3] In liberal democracies, corruption and other forms of financial misconduct are generally believed to be the most common causes of public indignation. But media exposure of corruption may leave the public feeling rather indifferent if the phenomenon is believed so widespread in the society in question that it is perceived as 'normal'. In Russia, for instance, the first media report of bribery among highly placed Soviet government and party officials in the late 1980s did indeed create a scandal. In the years since then, however, almost everybody who is anybody in Russian politics has at one time or another been publicly accused of involvement in financial irregularities – but few have been found guilty of wrongdoing in court. No wonder, then, that the public in today's Russia has become tired of such fruitless revelations.

Historical background

It is only a slight exaggeration to say Russia has never witnessed a non-political scandal like the British scandal involving the private affairs of the writer Oscar Wilde. Unlike the British, Russians simply do not regard the private lives of public figures as sufficiently important to fuss about. So much so that the famous Russian staging of Richard Sheridan's *The School for Scandal* at the Moscow Arts Theatre in 1954 did not include the scenes on the Academy of Scandals itself, thereby turning it into a play about hypocrisy rather than scandal. In contrast, state power is all-important in Russia. Thus, whilst the most famous British scandal is arguably that involving Oscar Wilde, the most famous Russian one involves Grigorii Rasputin.

Rasputin was an illiterate Siberian mystic and influential favourite at the court of Tsar Nicholas II and his wife Alexandra. Rasputin's licentiousness, along with his undue interference in affairs of state, such as the appointment of government ministers, became an ongoing scandal in imperial Russia. The timing of the Rasputin scandal seems to have been particularly important, and this is what makes it similar to Russian political scandals in the late twentieth century. The Rasputin scandal occurred between two Russian revolutions: that of 1905 – which resulted in the abolition of media censorship and brought into existence an elected legislative body, the State Duma – and the revolution of February 1917 – which ended the monarchy and paved the way for the ensuing Bolshevik takeover. Similarly, Gorbachev's reforms of the late 1980s also produced a relatively free media, as well as more or less democratically elected bodies of government. Similarly, the Gorbachev era opened the way for the collapse of the then-existing regime (and thence, in this case, the dissolution of the Soviet Union).

The Rasputin affair, like scandals in contemporary Russia, followed a long period of dictatorship, when censorship was very strict, and 'whistle-blowers' were effectively silenced by the police. Thus, on both occasions, Russian political scandals differed from those in liberal democracies in various ways. The first and the most obvious is the relative novelty of scandals from the public's point of view. Moreover, both in the 1910s and in the 1980s, the Russian public perceived the luxury of being scandalised by events of political significance not just as a new phenomenon, but a newly acquired right or privilege, in line with their newly acquired access to information and the right to vote as they wished in national and local elections. The result has been that political scandals have been both abundant and intense in these periods of transition, even while many of the most scandalous accusations have lacked any substance. For example, many Russians in 1911 were far too willing to believe that the Empress, as well as her four daughters, had sexual relations with Rasputin. Furthermore, although Rasputin opposed Russia's involvement in the 1914–18 war, there was no evidence of either his or the Empress's espionage for Germany, as was commonly rumoured at the time. Many Russians of the late 1980s and the early 1990s demonstrated a similar partisanship about the content of political scandals in the Gorbachev era – being too willing to accept negative revelations about 'reactionary' politicians, while rather too mistrustful of criticism of the latter's 'democratic' opponents.

Scandals during *glasnost* and *perestroika*

The first sensational events of the Gorbachev era were the trials, in 1985–8, of top Soviet officials, including the son-in-law of the late Soviet leader Leonid Brezhnev, for corruption. Stories about these actual and alleged cases of misconduct by Russia's ruling elite enjoyed broad media coverage, which in itself was unusual for the USSR. No wonder such stories enjoyed virtually universal public interest and generated genuine public wrath. At this stage, however, the Gorbachev leadership still enjoyed strict control over the media. The authorities, represented by a rather narrow circle of policy makers, decided that the high-placed bribe-takers should be punished; and they mobilised the country's propaganda machine to ensure public support for their decision. For this reason, the events of 1985–8 could hardly be regarded as a genuinely spontaneous public phenomenon, and they therefore fail to conform to the definition of scandal offered above.

In the next few years, the situation changed. As a result of Gorbachev's policy of *glasnost* (openness), the Soviet media steadily gained freedom from government control and censorship, and ordinary citizens acquired the right to organise independent rallies and form non-governmental organisations. As happened between 1905 and 1917, the new freedoms were accompanied by a series of scandals.

One of the most notorious scandals of the Gorbachev era involved a stream of allegations of corruption by high-placed officials and of cover-up attempts by the government. During the scandal, some key members of the Soviet ruling elite, including Gorbachev's conservative first deputy, Egor Ligachev, were reported to have been involved in bribery. The accusers, former detectives Telman Gdlyan and Nikolai Ivanov, claimed they had been prevented from proceeding with their investigations, thus accusing almost the entire Gorbachev leadership of obstructing justice. Gdlyans' and Ivanov's allegations provoked one of the greatest public outcries in Russian history.

In the late 1980s, hundreds of thousands of admirers rallied to Gdlyan's and Ivanov's support in Moscow, Leningrad and elsewhere. In March and April 1989, both Gdlyan and Ivanov were elected by large majorities as deputies in the relatively democratic elections – the first in the USSR – for the new parliament, the USSR Congress of People's Deputies. In May, workers in Zelenograd near Moscow declared a political strike in support of Gdlyan and Ivanov – the first officially permitted political strike of Russian workers since the 1920s. During the scandal, various journalists, including many popular and well-known representatives of the Soviet media, as well as legal and law-enforcement agencies, repeatedly accused Gdlyan and Ivanov of using torture and detaining relatives of the accused in order to obtain false confessions and force the accused falsely to incriminate others. All such pronouncements were rejected as libellous by supporters of the two detectives (Wishnevsky, 1989). Yet, the latter failed to provide any evidence to support their charges either at the time or after the collapse of the Communist regime. As a result, their activities proved counterproductive as means of rooting out corruption. On the contrary: the scandal frightened the authorities, so the campaign against corruption stopped and most officials charged with various forms of the offence from 1985 onwards were released. Furthermore, it proved the first in a series of similar events eventually producing the phenomenon already noted: the current public indifference to media exposure of corruption.

It seems worth mentioning that the scandals of the Gorbachev era differed from the one involving Rasputin in one important respect. The stories about Rasputin – whether true or false – drew attention to political problems that were important at the time: for example, the Tsar's right to appoint government ministers without the consent of Parliament. In contrast, the scandals of the Gorbachev era mostly distracted public attention from issues of political importance. The reason appeared to be the lack of political experience on the part of most Soviet citizens – who were suddenly being invited to participate in the country's policy making, but who were mostly ill equipped to do so. In response, many people tended to focus on personalities rather than policies. One such personality was the first Russian President, Boris Yeltsin, who owed much of his public popularity and his consequent rise to power to a series of scandals starting in 1987 and continuing until his resignation in December 1999.

From the time when, in October 1987, he complained at the Communist Party Central Committee that he was being obstructed in his work as head of the Moscow City Party organisation and urged 'revolutionary' rather than gradual reform, he acquired a reputation as a kind of Soviet Robin Hood. In this context, potentially scandalous allegations – including reports of his drinking problem and of a mysterious fall into the Moscow river – only fuelled the Yeltsin myth. Thus Yeltsin's career demonstrates the peculiar nature of Russian political culture in the period of transition. Politicians did not try to avoid scandals, but rather found they could capitalise on them – a point we shall take up again, below.

At first glance, political scandals in transition periods can be viewed as the writing on the wall for *ancien regimes*, since they demonstrate the public no longer trusts or respects the existing governmental institutions or rulers. In this way it becomes clear that the regime's days are numbered. At the same time, the events involved in such scandals tend to bear the imprints of the *ancien regime* itself. For example, Rasputin's murder in December 1916 by members of two aristocratic families and an extremist right-wing politician could only bring to mind a famous saying one hundred years earlier about the Russian 'constitution' being merely 'absolutism moderated by assassination' (Herbert and Münster, 1868: 19). The cult in Gorbachev's days of the two unscrupulous detectives revived memories of a notorious feature of the Soviet regime: Stalinist methods of forcing prisoners to incriminate themselves and other innocent people. In addition, one can argue that Gdlyan and Ivanov's phenomenal success may at least partially be ascribed to a feature seldom mentioned in writing on political scandal, namely popular culture. Indeed, the honest policeman who single-handedly fights the almighty mafia is not an unknown hero of Western movies and TV serials. The influence of such films was particularly strong in Gorbachev's USSR, if only because they had been banned under his predecessors. They were consequently new and exiting for many Soviet citizens. Overall, the specific characteristics of political scandals in a given period reflect the nature of that period's political processes.

Boris Yeltsin: the fruits of political scandal

Following the attempted coup against Gorbachev and the USSR's subsequent collapse in 1991, Boris Yeltsin became President of Russia. Yeltsin's term in office lasted eight years, and, from the perspective of scandal, it may be divided into three periods. The first dates from December 1991 until October 1993 when Yeltsin sent troops to suppress a rebellion organised by the national parliament, the Congress of People's Deputies, against the President's attempt to disband it; the second from October 1993 until June 1996 when Yeltsin was re-elected for a second term; the third from June 1996 until the President's resignation in December 1999. The first period was one in which scandal-mongering became a weapon used by the President and the representatives of other institutions in a struggle over the distribution of power between them.

In the initial period Yeltsin's power was constrained by the Congress and by various other institutions including the Russian Constitutional Court, the Prosecutor General's Office and the Vice-presidency, at the time staffed by Alexandr Rutskoi. A power struggle between the two men was not long delayed. During the struggle, Rutskoi presented Parliament with allegations that dozens of important members of Yeltsin's immediate entourage had abused their positions for monetary gain through the process of privatisation of public property.[4] Rutskoi spoke in his capacity as chairman of the Joint Commission for Combating Crime and Corruption, which had been established by Yeltsin himself. Immediately after Rutskoi's address, Russian Prosecutor General, Valentin Stepankov, suggested establishing a special commission under his own Office to examine the allegations, and Parliament voted in favour. In response, Yeltsin hired a lawyer, Andrei Makarov, who presented Russian TV viewers with a Xerox, purportedly showing that Rutskoi had a Swiss bank account, and was therefore himself guilty of corruption.[5] Later, it became known that at least some of Rutskoi's diatribes were justified, whereas the Xerox was forged.[6]

The second period – which saw the introduction of a new Russian constitution severely limiting Parliament's powers and expanding the President's – differed from the first in several important ways. First, if during the first period public opinion – a social phenomenon not visible in Russia since the 1920s – mattered considerably in the actions of politicians, in the second period it was increasingly ignored. This was clearly visible in relation to the scandalised reactions provoked by allegations of electoral fraud. Contrary to official statements concerning the referendum on the new constitution held on 12 December 1993, various reports, including those by Western observers, claimed the turnout was below the 50 per cent required for the results to be valid. Others maintained that less than half those who did participate voted for the constitution (Tolz and Wishnevsky, 1993). Doubts were from then on regularly expressed about the reliability of official results for national and local elections held in Russia, including the 1996 presidential elections. Sceptics argued, for example, that Yeltsin would not have won the 1996 elections had they been genuinely free and fair.[7] Several minor electoral officials in remote provinces were tried and punished for their part in the fraud.[8] The federal authorities, however, opted to ignore public outrage about these and other allegations, and, indeed, never even tried denying them.

Second, the period was marked by a series of scandals arising from Yeltsin's personal conduct. His drinking problem had been an open secret from the beginning of his political career. Until 1994, the public tended to view it as something that made Yeltsin 'one of us'. After 1994, it began being viewed as a cause of international embarrassment. For example, in August 1994, during a state visit to Berlin to celebrate the final withdrawal of Russian troops from Germany, Yeltsin stumbled after a champagne lunch, seized a conductor's baton to direct an oomph band, grabbed a microphone and began singing a Russian folk song. This episode was followed by a similarly embarrassing incident on 30 October, when he suddenly cancelled an appointment with the Irish Prime Minister. On his way back from a visit to the US, Yeltsin was supposed to attend a state dinner with Albert Reynolds, who had cut short a visit to Australia and New Zealand to meet the Russian President. Yeltsin, however, failed to get off the plane, leaving the Irish premier, his wife, a military band, a guard of honour and a group of children with flowers all standing on the tarmac for about thirty minutes.[9] Not surprisingly, then, a major development dominating the Russian political scene in the second period was Yeltsin's collapsing public popularity. Thus, whereas he had enjoyed approval ratings ranging from over 90 per cent in autumn 1991 to over 50 per cent in autumn 1993,[10] by October 1994, according to one survey, 61 per cent of respondents said they did not trust their president, while only 13 per cent said they trusted him, of which only 3 per cent said they trusted him absolutely (Interfax, 1994).

Third, growing public cynicism and apathy concerning the conduct of public figures was fuelled by the fact that routine media revelations frequently failed to have any real consequences. For example, by the second Russian presidential race in 1996, Western observers had begun defining the regime as one of 'crony capitalism' (Reddaway and Glinski, 2001), with contract killings of businessmen, politicians and journalists shattering public trust on a regular basis. Yet, more often than not, no one was arrested and sentenced. On at least one such occasion – the murder of the Russian TV star Vladislav List'ev – the suspect was named in the media; some time later both the detective in charge of the case and the Prosecutor General said they knew the murderer's identity, but allegedly Yeltsin personally forbade an arrest (Skvortsova, 1998). The media further claimed the organiser of the assassination played a major role in fund-raising for Yeltsin's 1996 presidential campaign.

One of the most notorious scandals occurred between the two rounds of this election. In the event, the chief of Yeltsin's bodyguards, KGB General Alexander Korzhakov, detained two of Yeltsin's campaigners for attempting to smuggle from his electoral headquarters a box containing $500,000 in cash. They appealed to Yeltsin and were immediately released. Korzhakov was accused of attempting a *coup-d'état* and fired along with all his subordinates (Korzhakov, 1997).

This 'Xerox box scandal' opened the third period of Yeltsin's era, one marked by a series of events giving the impression of almost amounting to one gigantic scandal, as virtually all officials of any importance were continually accused of gross financial violations. Overall, the scandals of the Yeltsin era left the public with the impression that virtually everyone in positions of power in their country, including journalists, were corrupt,[11] and that anyone could be accused of anything without any way of establishing the accuracy of the charges, because the judicial system was also corrupt and under official control. This impression – though unsurprising in a country where the absence of a libel law meant there were few means of forcing journalists to take responsibility for the accuracy of their reports – was not, of course, absolutely accurate.

Some officials exposed in the media were punished. In February 1999, for example, former Russian Minister of Justice, Valentin Kovalev, was arrested and charged with misappropriating $50,000 in the form of state subsidies to a human rights foundation that he had chaired, and with illegally possessing firearms.[12] Kovalev was pressured out of office in June 1997, following publication in a monthly Russian tabloid of a steamy sauna video, purportedly of him and some female companions (Kislinskaya, 1997). The article alleged Kovalev had ties with organised crime – an allegation that apparently had little in common with the crime for which he was eventually arrested and sentenced. In autumn 1997, Yeltsin fired Alfred Koch, the deputy Prime Minister in charge of public property, along with three other economics ministers: Petr Mostovoi, Aleksandr Kazakov and Maksim Boiko. The move followed a large-scale scandal, unleashed in the media by journalist Aleksandr Minkin.[13] According to Minkin, the four officials, together with the former head of the privatisation programme, Anatolii Chubais, had each received bribes amounting to $90,000 from a Swiss company in the form of royalties for a book as yet unwritten. In the wake of the scandal, Chubais resigned as first deputy Prime Minister and was appointed chairman of the state-owned electricity monopoly. Koch and the others gained employment in private businesses. The outcomes of these two affairs were rare exceptions to the general rule that those 'punished' were the accusers rather than the cronies accused of all sorts of outrageous behaviour.

The scandals arising from Russian corruption sometimes became international in scale (Wedel, 1996). One minor scandal even touched American Vice-president, Al Gore. In his capacity as co-chairman, alongside Russian Prime Minister, Victor Chernomyrdin, of a commission on US–Russian co-operation, Gore allegedly ignored CIA warnings about Russian corruption, and was criticised in the American Congress and the media (House of Representatives, 2000). The last scandals of the Yeltsin era did not even originate in Russia but the West, particularly the USA and Switzerland. Members of Yeltsin's family, including his two daughters and their husbands, were accused of gross financial violations amounting to billions of dollars. During the scandal, Yeltsin's financial manager, Pavel Borodin, was prosecuted by the Swiss authorities for the alleged misappropriation of $30,000,000 in the form of bribes from foreign contractors.[14]

The Borodin case culminated in probably the dirtiest modern Russian scandal. The Russian Prosecutor General, Yurii Skuratov, agreed to co-operate with the Swiss Federal Prosecutor, Carla del Ponte, whereupon Yeltsin urged Skuratov to resign. When the latter refused, state-controlled Russian television broadcast a secretly filmed videotape of Skuratov naked with two prostitutes.[15] A Moscow deputy prosecutor was reportedly taken, at two in the morning, to Chubais's office, where he was forced to fill in a form charging Skuratov with taking bribes from Borodin. Yeltsin allegedly used this 'evidence' to justify sacking Skuratov.[16] As soon as a new Russian Prosecutor General was appointed, all charges against Skuratov were dropped. It may be added that the first decree issued by Yeltsin's successor, Vladimir Putin, in his capacity as acting Russian President, provided that the former President and all members of his family would be immune from prosecution for any crime committed while in the office.[17] Some cynical observers would doubtlessly view Putin's move as an indirect admission of the family's guilt.

Vladimir Zhirinovsky: Russian 'scandal man'

Like most phenomena, political scandals are relative matters: some are more significant than others. For this reason, no chapter on contemporary Russian political scandal would be complete without a section on the politician who has acquired world-wide notoriety as the nation's 'Mr Scandal', namely, Deputy Speaker of the Russian Parliament, Vladimir Zhirinovsky. A profile of this politician is indicative of the way behaviour otherwise deemed scandalous may sometimes actually enhance an individual's reputation – and of the characteristics of Russian culture that may be responsible for this phenomenon.

Zhirinovsky is founder and leader of the far-right Russian Liberal Democratic Party (LDPR). His ultra-nationalist pronouncements, his friendship with international political outsiders, like Iraq's Saddam Hussein, Libya's Muammar al-Qaddafi and France's Jean-Marie Le Pen, have turned Zhirinovsky into an internationally egregious figure. He has been the object of several critiques by prominent Western academics (Laqueur, 1993, 1997; Solovyov and Klepikova, 1995; Kartsev and Bludeau, 1995). Political extravaganza has been the instrument whereby Zhirinovsky has gained and retained his status as a constant generator of news abroad. In the domestic arena, he has never hesitated to use scandalous behaviour for essentially the same end. Thus Russian TV archives are full of footage of Zhirinovsky doing things like: throwing a glass of orange juice at a political opponent during a live television discussion; tearing hair from the head of a female deputy during a session of the Russian Parliament; forcing a female journalist into his Mercedes car on a Moscow street in broad daylight.

These film-clips are rebroadcast each time Zhirinovsky succeeds in shocking public opinion by means of some statement or interview. And Zhirinovsky is careful to do this often. In February 2003, for example, he scandalised Russian lawmakers with a clandestine videotape, containing an interview by two Arab journalists during his recent visit to Iraq. The video, according to Russian television producers, had appeared on an unidentified Internet site. In it, a highly intoxicated Zhirinovsky uses obscene language in an angry outburst about US President George Bush. The speech was little more than an obscene depiction of the sexual activities of Bush's predecessor in the White House and a suggestion that the US should bomb the capitals of Georgia and Azerbaijan instead of Iraq.[18] Incidents like these have turned Zhirinovsky into probably the most well-known Russian politician, aside from the President himself. Indeed, it is difficult to turn on Russian television without finding Zhirinovsky being interviewed on one channel or another. Sometimes he appears on more than one channel simultaneously. Zhirinovsky clearly prefers notoriety to oblivion.

It is of course true that it is not unheard of for voters, in Russia or elsewhere, to support a politician whose personal behaviour fails, to put it mildly, to conform to the highest standards of respectability. But the point is that Zhirinovsky has made his political career not *in spite* of his outrageous behaviour, but arguably at least in part *because* of it. In December 1993, in the first parliamentary elections in modern Russia, Zhirinovsky's LDPR won the largest proportion of the vote among the eight blocs that cleared the 5 per cent electoral threshold. None of its members, Zhirinovsky apart, was known to Russian voters. True, in the next parliamentary elections four years later, the party lost almost half its supporters, gaining only 11.8 per cent of the vote – but it was still the second largest of four parties (Oleshchuk and Pavlenko, 1997: 30–3). And, although the LDPR's fortunes have declined since 1993, it is by no means finished. Zhirinovsky's electorate might be smaller than Yeltsin's was in the late-Gorbachev era, but it is still, at the time of writing (2002), larger than those of the two genuinely liberal and democratic parties, namely the Union of Right-wing Forces and Yabloko, put together.

What explains the apparent benefits to Zhirinovsky of his scandalous personal conduct? We know from other scandals that Russians tend to view outrageous behaviour by political outsiders in the manner of the good Christian: 'He that is without sin among you, let him first cast a stone at her' (John, 8: 7). There was an interesting illustration of this response in September 1988, when Yeltsin's opponents amongst the Communist leadership of the Gorbachev era lambasted the future Russian president for the scandalous drinking episodes marking his first visit to the US earlier that year.[19] According to eyewitnesses, Yeltsin's critics at the session were genuinely scandalised, yet attacked him, not without some outward embarrassment, because they too were heavy drinkers. Eleven years later, the already unpopular Russian President repeatedly asked the parliamentary upper house, the Federation Council, to approve his decision to replace the Prosecutor General, Yurii Skuratov. Yeltsin supported his request with a videotape of a naked and tipsy Skuratov sharing a bed with two equally naked prostitutes. Yet the Council three times overwhelmingly refused to endorse Yeltsin's request. Moreover, they stated openly on national television that the pornographic video had been counter-productive, arousing feelings of 'male solidarity' with Skuratov in the Chamber.[20]

True, Zhirinovsky's behaviour has so far met with very little tolerance among the kinds of well-to-do citizens from whom the bulk of television interviewees are generally drawn. However, Zhirinovsky's followers consist of very different people – those who were already relatively poor during the Communist era and then suffered additional hardships as a result of ill-thought-through market-oriented reforms (Specter, 1995). They live, or have only recently vacated, communal apartments where ugly scandals over shared facilities have been every-day occurrences. In general, they drink heavily, sometimes beat up their wives and girl friends. They tend to formulate their political ideas in extreme terms. They naturally tend to feel the same sense of solidarity with Zhirinovsky as their more well-to-do fellow-countrymen once felt for Yeltsin and Skuratov.

All this seems to suggest that Russians of all classes expect public figures to behave no more properly than private citizens. Power in Russia has traditionally been viewed as a source of privilege and abuse rather than responsibility and obligation. This last point may appear to be contradicted by the nation's deep-rooted cultural traditions. Russians, after all, are almost universally literate, and indeed relatively well read. Yet strangely enough, the country's cultural heritage might be a factor contributing to citizens' responses to their leaders' personal conduct. National expectations of political leaders may be traceable to stereotypes derived from history, and particularly from the images of those leading the country at the best-remembered points in its history. We have already argued that the British would seem to have higher expectations of their politicians than the citizens of many if not most other countries. If this is so, then it may be because the pinnacle of the nation's power – and, for many, its 'splendour' – coincided with the rule of the austere Victoria and Albert. By contrast, Russia's first Tsar was known as 'Ivan the Terrible', while the Russian Empire's founder was Peter the Great. Apart from their unbelievable cruelty, they both distinguished themselves for their frequent orgies and all kinds of other abuse. It would indeed be a sad irony if what was happening was that the Zhirinovskys of today were capitalising on national nostalgia for Ivan and Peter.

Vladimir Putin: a period of stagnation

In sharp contrast with that of his predecessor, the rule of President Putin has so far been relatively short of scandals. A colonel in the KGB, Putin served in the mid-1990s as a middle-ranking municipal official in St Petersburg, Russia's second largest city. Later, he became head of the KGB's successor, the Federal Security Service (FSB). In his search for a successor, Yeltsin replaced as many as five Prime Ministers in the course of a year (1998–9). Putin was the sixth. He had served in this capacity for several months when Yeltsin announced that he would resign before the end of his presidential term, and urged Russians to support Putin in the ensuing elections. In March 2000, Putin was elected. According to some Russian experts, while there was fraudulent counting, it was not decisive: even with total electoral honesty, Putin would still have won, albeit on the second rather than the first ballot.[21]

As a member of Yeltsin's team, Putin played an active part in events that gave rise to several scandals, including the Skuratov controversy.[22] As President, Putin has so far managed to scandalise the public only twice, most famously when he failed to interrupt his holiday on the Black Sea during the Kursk submarine disaster.[23]

The second occasion was when he tried to destroy Russia's largest private media empire, Media-most, as part of his on-going efforts to establish control over the independent media organisations critical of his policies in the break-away Russian republic of Chechnya. The State Prosecutor's office, the FSB, the police, the tax authorities and the courts were all mobilised by the government in a campaign against Media-most. By April 2001, the authorities had suc-ceeded in seizing control of the group's major television company, NTV, and in closing its daily newspaper and weekly magazine. During Putin's crusade against Media-most, its principal shareholder – the multi-millionaire Vladimir Gusinsky – was arrested.[24] After agreeing to sell his shares in Media-most to the state-controlled gas monopoly, Gazprom, he was released and all charges of financial misconduct against him were dropped. Gusinsky flew to Spain, announced he had agreed to part with his shares under duress, and said he would not honour the agreement. Almost immediately, the criminal charges against him were revived, and the Russian Prosecutor General's office appealed to its Spanish counterpart requesting Gusinsky's extradition, which was refused.

The purge of NTV provoked mass public protests in the form of street demonstrations, as well as widespread criticism in the media. No other controversial policies under Putin, including restrictions on the number of electable national and local offices, have so far provoked anything that could be described as a 'political scandal'. Perhaps one reason has been a loss of faith in elections, or more particularly in their utility as a means of changing things for the better. Increased government control over the media has no doubt also contributed.

Given Putin's position as Yeltsin's chosen successor, it may sound paradoxical to suggest that both his personal popularity and the sparseness of scandals in today's Russia are traceable to the general disappointment with his pre-decessor. Why, for instance, does manifest election fraud not really scandalise Russians, at least at present? Perhaps people prefer to ignore developments they cannot change. However, perhaps also, Yeltsin and his associates, as self-proclaimed democrats, have given democracy a bad name.

Conclusion

As is evident from the examples above, scandal in Russia frequently gives questionable public figures and politicians, like Gdlyan or Zhirinovsky, the publicity they need to enable them to further their careers. Much more rarely does it lead to the downfall of unpopular politicians, something normally only possible if the authorities have no vested interest in keeping the politicians in question on board. Contemporary Russian scandal is unlikely to produce legal, institutional or structural reform due to the country's deep-rooted authoritarian traditions. Most Russian officials take little notice of scandalised public opinion and, indeed, where not subject to elections, they take no notice of it at all.

The Russian media today enjoy more freedom than in the Soviet era. But precisely because of this freedom, their effectiveness as channels for the communication of conduct that scandalises, and thus as vehicles for holding the authorities to account, has, paradoxically, been vitiated. When, as mentioned, the absence of effective libel laws undermines the pressures on journalists to check the accuracy of their stories and when, therefore, media allegations of misconduct become a routine part of the everyday struggle for power between this or that political grouping, it is unsurprising that public apathy rapidly sets in and genuine cases of misconduct go unpunished – with the consequence, of course, of that public cynicism is heightened still further. Besides, when economic and administrative difficulties lead thousands of teachers, doctors and other groups of workers being denied back pay for months at a time, and when society as a whole seems powerless to change the situation – what impact, against this background, can allegations of personal misconduct against this or that politician really be expected to have?

Notes

I am very grateful to Vera Tolz for her helpful comments and suggestions on an earlier draft of this chapter.

1 *Bolshoi tolkovyi slovar' Russkogo yazyka*, published under the auspices of the Institute of Linguistic Research of the Russian Academy of Sciences, St Petersburg, 'Noring' Publishing House, 2001, p. 1192.

2 *The Oxford Illustrated Dictionary*, 2nd edition, London, Book Club Associates, 1976, p. 759.

3 This topic has been repeatedly discussed in the British media. See, for example, Glover (2003).

4 Rutskoi's address was broadcast live on Russian television on 16 April 1993.

5 Ostankino Television, 24 August 1993. The document was published, along with Makarov's comments, in the Russian daily, *Izvestiya*, on 26 August 1993.

6 See *Novaya ezhednevnaya gazeta*, 14 May 1994; *Novaya gazeta*, no. 8, 29 February 1996, p. 1; *Nezavisimaya gazeta*, 1 March 1996; *Literaturnaya gazeta*, no. 13, 2 April 1997, p. 7.

7 See, for instance, the detailed account by Guiseppe Chiesa, the veteran Moscow correspondent of the Italian daily *La Stampa*, in *Svobodnaya Mysl*, no. 5, 1997. For more on electoral fraud in 1996, see: *Obshchaya gazeta*, no. 26, 1996, p. 8; no. 27, 1996, p. 8; and no. 39, 1996, p. 7; *Pravda*, 16 July 1996; *Sovetskaya Rossiya*, 18 and 23 July 1996.

8 See *Izvestiya*, 28 February 1998; Interfax, 21 February 1997; *Sovetskaya Rossiya*, 27 February and 27 September 1997; *Argumenty i fakty*, no. 39, 29 September 1999.

9 For a list of Yeltsin's gaffes see www.ABCNEWS.com.

10 *Pravda*, 12 September 1991, p. 2; *Los Angeles Times*, 17 September 1991; *Guardian*, 20 April 1993. The monthly reports on Yeltsin's rating for January–October 1993, were also published as an appendix to the book: *Eltsin-Khasbulatov: Edinstvo, kompromiss, bor'ba*, Moscow, Terra Publishing House, 1994, pp. 601–2.

11 See, for example, *Moskovskie novosti*, no. 38, 21 September 1997.
12 In 2001, Kovalev was tried, found guilty and received a nine-year suspended prison sentence. See *Nezavisimaya gazeta*, 4 October 2001.
13 See *Novaya gazeta*, nos. 31–48, 4 August–1 December 1997.
14 See, for example, *Izvestiya*, 9 February 1999 and 23 March 1999; *Argumenty i fakty*, no. 6, 10 February 1999, p. 2, no. 12, 24 March 1999, p. 2, and no. 39, 29 September 1999; *Moskovskie novosti*, no. 10, 16 March 1999, pp. 1–3; *Novaya gazeta*, no. 10, 22 March 1999, p. 1; *Kommersant-Daily*, 24 March 1999; *Sovetskaya Rossiya*, 25 March 1999, p. 2.
15 The tape was shown during the state-owned *RTV* television's newscast on 17 March 1999.
16 See *Novaya gazeta*, 3 April; *Tribuna Vremya MN*, 6 April 1999.
17 The decree – no. 1763, dated 31 December 1999, i.e., the day of Yeltsin's resignation – was published in *Rossiiskaya gazeta* on 4 January 2000.
18 For the text see *Novaya gazeta*, no. 7, 30 January 2003.
19 A collection of recollections of the relevant session of the CPSU Central Committee plenary session was published in a series entitled, 'Scandals of the Past', in the Moscow newspaper, *Vechernii klub*. The collection was reprinted in the Israeli Russian-language weekly, *Globus*, no. 363, 27 September 1999, pp. 6–7.
20 Russian television newscasts, 17 March and 24 April 1999. See also, *Novaya gazeta*, no. 10, 22 March 1999, p. 7; *Moskovskie novosti*, no. 11, 23 March 1999, p. 2; *Obshchaya gazeta*, no. 12, 25 March 1999, p. 7; *Argumenty i fakty*, no. 12, 24 March 1999, p. 2. It is worth noting that the similar footage relating to the former Justice Minister, Kovalev, did not win him any sympathy in Russia. Kovalev was reputed to be a time-server, while Skuratov was believed to have been this way avenged for his part in unmasking corruption of Yeltsin's immediate entourage.
21 See the detailed analyses by Vladimir Pribylovsky in *Deadline.Ru*, 19 December 2000. See also the article by Boris Kagarlitsky in *Novaya gazeta*, no. 12, 30 March 2000.
22 ITAR – TASS, Interfax, 19 March 1999.
23 *Financial Times*, 17 August 2000; *The Times*, 27 October 2000; *Time Magazine*, 27 October 2000.
24 *Izvestiya*, 19 and 24 June 2000.

References

Glover, S. (2003), 'British Hacks May be Disgusting but We Keep the Politicians on Their Toes', *Spectator*, 25 January, p. 29.
Herbert, G. and C. Münster (1868), *Political Sketches of the States of Europe, 1814– 1867*, London, 1868.
House of Representatives (2000), 'Russia's Road To Corruption: How the Clinton Administration Exported Government Instead of Free Enterprise and Failed the Russian People', Washington, DC, US House of Representatives, 20515, September.
Interfax (1994), *Presidential Bulletin*, no. 202 (702), 1 November.
Kartsev, V. and T. Bludeau (1995), *Zhirinovsky*, New York, Columbia University Press.
Kislinskaya, L. (1997), 'A ministr-to golyi', *Sovershenno secretno*, no. 6, June.
Korzhakov, A. (1997), *Boris Eltsin: Ot rassveta do zakata*, Moscow, Interbuk Publishing House.
Laqueur, W. (1993), *Black Hundred: The Rise of the Extreme Right in Russia*, New York, Harper Collins.

Laqueur, W. (1997), *Fascism: Past, Present, Future*, Oxford, Oxford University Press.

Oleshchuk, V. A. and V. B. Pavlenko (1997), *Politicheskaya Rossiya: Partii, bloki, lidery: God 1997: Spravochnik*, Moscow, Ves' mir Publishing House.

Reddaway, P. and D. Glinski (2001), *The Tragedy of Russia's Reforms: Market Bolshevism against Democracy*. Washington, DC, US Institute of Peace Press.

Skvortsova, E. (1998), 'Ubiistvo List'eva: Godovboi otchet' [The Assassination of List'ev: Annual Report], *Obshchaya gazeta*, no. 9.

Solovyov, V. and E. Klepikova (1995), *Zhirinovsky: Russian Fascism and the Making of a Dictator*, New York, Addison-Wesley.

Specter, M. (1995), 'Russia's Most Angry Man', *New York Times*, 13 August.

Tolz, V. and J. Wishnevsky (1993), 'Election Queries Make Russians Doubt Democratic Process', *The RFE/RL Research Report*, no. 13, 1 April.

Wedel, J. R. (1996), 'Clique-Run Organizations and US Economic Aid: An Institutional Analysis', *Democratizatsiya: The Journal of Post-Soviet Democratization*, 4: 4, 571–602.

Wishnevsky, J. (1989), 'The Gdlyan-Ivanov Commission Starts Its Work', *Radio Liberty Report of the USSR*, 30 June, pp. 1–7.

13

How far and why do corruption scandals cost votes?[1]

Fernando Jiménez and *Miguel Caínzos*

This chapter starts from our perplexity concerning the widespread idea amongst observers of Spanish politics that scandals have devastating political effects. After the ruling Socialist party's heavy losses in the 1994 European and the 1995 local and regional elections, most political pundits expected a clear Socialist defeat in the 1996 general election. This expectation was based on 'the corruption syndrome', that is, the persistent wave of scandals that monopolised public debate in the early 1990s. Since the Socialists lost the election by a very slight margin (1.3 per cent of the vote), some regarded it as an anomaly showing a lack of civic virtue among many Spanish voters.

The assumption is shared by observers of politics in many other countries, even though it is contradicted by large numbers of empirical studies that have been done from the 1970s onwards and that are presented in Box 13.1. On the basis of a review of these studies, the aim of this chapter is to challenge the assumption. In its place, we suggest that there are six conditions that need to be fulfilled if a scandal is to affect voter choice.

Two main findings have consistently emerged from previous research: first, the impact of a scandal on voting choice depends on a complex process and is mediated by several different factors; second, although scandals usually do have appreciable effects on the vote, their influence is usually quite modest because voters have many other concerns besides corruption or other forms of inappropriate behaviour when they make their choices. As Dobratz and Whitfield (1992: 178) put it, 'although some may suggest that ideally scandals alone result in toppled governments, the voters are likely to have more than one consideration in their minds when they actually vote'.

If we acknowledge that electoral choice is complex, we should ask two questions: First, what conditions are necessary for a scandal to undermine public trust in a political agent – an individual candidate or a whole party – that is, to produce widespread changes of attitude towards this agent? Second, what makes it possible for such changes of attitude to translate themselves into actual voting decisions aimed at punishing that agent?[2]

Box 13.1 Empirical literature on the electoral effects of scandals

1 Effects on US elections
- Presidential elections 1896–1992: Fackler and Lin, 1995
- Congressional elections in the 1970s and 1980s (Kiewiet and Zeng, 1993; Peters and Welch, 1980; Welch and Hibbing, 1997)
- Watergate and the 1974 Congressional election (Conway and Wyckoff, 1980; Jacobson and Kernell, 1983; Jacobson *et al.*, 1986; McLeod *et al.*, 1977; Uslaner and Conway, 1985)
- The House Bank scandal and the 1992 election (Ahuja *et al.*, 1994; Alford *et al.*, 1994; Banducci and Karp, 1994; Dimock and Jacobson, 1995; Groseclose and Krehbiel, 1994; Jacobson and Dimock, 1994; Shea, 1999; Stewart, 1994)
- The Lewinsky scandal and the 1998 congressional and the 2000 presidential elections (Fiorina *et al.*, 2003; Jacobson, 1999)

2 Effects on US public opinion
- Gary Hart scandal (Stoker, 1993)
- Iran-Contra scandal (Krosnick and Kinder, 1990)
- Lewinsky scandal (Ladd, 1998; Miller, 1999; Newman, 2002; Renshon, 2002; Shah *et al.*, 2002; Sonner and Wilcox, 1999; Zaller, 1998)

3 Experimental studies
Chanley *et al.*, 1994; Funk, 1996; Gonzales *et al.*, 1995; Rundquist *et al.*, 1977; Schwartz and Bless, 1992.

4 Effects on elections outside the US
- June 1989 Greek elections: Dobratz and Whitfield, 1992
- Japanese elections 1947–1993: Anderson and Ishii, 1997; Bouissou, 1994; Reed, 1999
- Support for British Labour party 1992–1997: Clarke *et al.*, 1998
- British 1997 general election: Farrell *et al.*, 1998
- Mexican presidential elections 1988 and 1994: McCann and Domínguez, 1998
- French 1995 local elections: Lafay and Servais, 2000
- Spanish 1996 general election: Barreiro and Sánchez-Cuenca, 2000; Caínzos and Jiménez, 2000; Criado, 2003; Fraile, 2001.

We think that for a scandal to have an electoral impact at the individual level six conditions must be met: (1) *awareness*: the voter must have information about the scandal; (2) *evaluation*: knowledge of the affair or affairs must, for either normative or utilitarian reasons, provoke discontent or rejection on the part of the voter; (3) *responsibility*: the voter must perceive some of the competing parties or candidates in the election as being directly or indirectly responsible, through action or inaction, for the states of affairs she finds reprehensible; (4) *saliency*: voter must place corruption in a high position in her hierarchy of public concerns; (5) *alternative*: the voter must be willing to vote for an opposition party or candidate or, at least, she must not be unduly worried by the prospect of victory on the part of opposition parties or candidates; (6) *consistency*: when at the polling station, the voter must actually cast a ballot that is consistent with these orientations. In this paper, we will discuss the first five of these conditions.

Each condition is affected by two main sets of factors: on the one hand, the external inputs voters receive from both specific actors (such as political elites, journalists, courts, etc.) and the broader circumstances in which the scandal in question takes place (the economic or political situation, for instance, but also the prevailing cultural patterns); on the other hand, the prior predispositions, filters and frames through which individuals process these external inputs.

Awareness

For voters to be aware of a scandal, they must be exposed to information about it. In its turn, the degree of exposure depends on two other factors: the extent to which the new information is broadcast and how much attention the individual pays to it. The extent of broadcasting usually depends on media coverage of the affair and on the different social networks within which the individual is embedded and thus processes political information. However, the media's role is neither a sufficient nor a necessary condition for bringing about attitude change in the individual voter. For, on the one hand, there is no direct relationship between the extent of media coverage, and the degree of the impact of scandals on the actor(s) involved in them.[3] On the other hand, as various examples from authoritarian regimes show, the conventional media are not the only channel through which information can be broadcast although they are the most usual one in democratic mass societies.

A second requirement is that the broadcast information attracts the attention of the recipients for whom it is intended. The degree of attention depends partly on external inputs and partly on individuals' priorities. For instance, the particular moment at which a scandal takes place will mean that it attracts a higher or lower level of attention depending on what other issues of public concern happen to be competing with it at the time. The same charge against a politician can find a considerable echo (as is likely when, for example, competing news items are relatively scarce) or can be quickly forgotten about (as is likely in a context in which, for example, the country is about to go to war). The degree of attention also depends on the role of the agent involved (Jackson and Smith, 1996; Peters and Welch, 1978). It is obvious, for example, that wrong-doing by a town councillor will not attract the same level of attention as an analogous act of wrong-doing by a prime minister.

Previous research has also pointed to individuals' levels of political information (a factor highly correlated with degree of political interest) as one of the key factors accounting for differences in the way they react to scandals (Chanley *et al.*, 1994; Funk, 1996; Gonzales *et al.*, 1995; Krosnick and Kinder, 1990; Stoker, 1993).

Finally, a crucial factor affecting the degree of attention an individual pays to information relating to scandals is the credibility of the accusers. This factor is a composite of both external inputs and individual priorities. Electors' proneness to believe charges depends both on the accusers' credibility and on the state of public opinion when the charges are made. In its turn, the credibility of accusers depends on voters' perceptions of the incentives accusers have to tell the truth or otherwise. It is obvious that such perceptions will vary from one individual to another according to their political stances. Much research insists on the relevance of party identification: the individuals most ready to believe accusations are those who identify with the same party as the accusers – while the individuals most resistant to accusations are those who identify with the party of the agent whose conduct is in question (Chanley *et al.*, 1994; Dimock and Jacobson, 1995; Funk, 1996; Gonzales *et al.*, 1995; Krosnick and Kinder, 1990; Rundquist *et al.*, 1977; Stoker, 1993).

However, as shown by Lupia and McCubbins (1998), although party identification is very important and people usually resort to it in making political judgments, it is not the only heuristic shortcut they use to decide whether or not to believe a particular statement. According to these authors, if there is a particularly favourable institutional framework (that is, one that either makes it possible easily to verify charges and/or that ensures that false charges are heavily punished), informers with whom we do not share common interests may make us believe them. Such a situation might be said to exist when, in the case of some particular scandal, there exist formal, automatically applied procedures of investigation concerning the deeds in question. However, the few pieces of research taking into account this factor have not yet found conclusive evidence supporting its relevance (Peters and Welch, 1980 and Welch and Hibbing, 1997).[4]

The 'public mood' at the time of the scandal's outbreak also has some influence on the credibility of charges and accusers. Citizens' proneness to believe charges is usually mediated by their satisfaction or dissatisfaction with the state of the economy or with the political situation generally. The coincidence of a scandal with a political or economic crisis is usually an explosive mix for the affected agent. Many citizens who in a different situation would be more sceptical are now prone to judge harshly an agent who can be held responsible for the unsatisfactory state of affairs. For instance, it is doubtful that an affair like Watergate would have brought about the same deep political crisis had it happened in a different moment not marked by the profound economic crisis caused by the first oil shock and by the huge wound opened by the Vietnam war. It is highly likely that Bill Clinton's fortunes would have been very different had the Lewinsky scandal not coincided with a particularly buoyant economic situation (Jacobson, 1999; Ladd, 1998).[5] In fact, as Brian Newman (2002) has shown, the Lewinsky affair did have an important negative effect on Clinton's presidential approval ratings, but it was outweighed by the higher positive effect of respondents' satisfaction with the economic situation.

Evaluation

Both external inputs and individual priorities affect this condition too. The external inputs affecting voters' evaluations have to do first with the types of misbehaviour that are alleged to have taken place and thus with the severity of the wrongdoing in question. It is obvious that not every instance of wrong-doing causes the same level of discontent, rejection or anger. However, it is impossible abstractly to determine which types of conduct provoke what levels of reaction, because this is something that depends on cultural factors which change from one age to another, from one society to another and probably also from one social group to another. In the context of US politics, Peters and Welch (1980) and Welch and Hibbing (1997) found major differences in levels of electoral punishment associated with different types of corruption charges. According to their analysis, what they termed 'morals charges' were those most heavily punished.[6] On the other hand, it seems reasonable to expect that for a given type of misbehaviour, our evaluation of it will be harsher the more severe or serious the specific offence that is involved.

But voters' individual priorities affect their evaluations as well. As with the credibility of accusers, change-inducing information is filtered through the different criteria of judgment individuals use to oppose different levels of resistance to it. These criteria are in turn affected by a complex set of factors composed of both external inputs and individual predispositions, such as: the individual's own political stances; whether the politician whose conduct is in question is an incumbent or a challenger; the political environment, which leads the voter to use either particularistic or universalistic patterns of judg-ment; different ways of incorporating the negative information associated with the scandal – where these have to do both with voters' levels of political information and with the kinds of exchange relationship they establish with their political representatives.

As Samuel Popkin (1991: 65–7, 1993: 32–3) has suggested, the criteria we use to estimate a particular politician's competence in office differ according to whether the actor in question is an incumbent or a challenger. Only in the latter case, and owing to the impossibility of knowing his or her actual per-formance in office, should the rational voter take into account the challenger candidate's private morality – this as an indirect indicator of likely future competence in office.[7]

From a different point of view but still assuming that voters behave ration-ally, Fackler and Lin (1995) analysed US presidential elections from 1896 to 1992 and found a greater proneness of voters to punish political corruption from the 1932 election onwards. They explained this finding as the result of a change in the evaluative frameworks used by voters to assess corruption. According to these authors' not very convincing argument,[8] the important transformations undergone by American society during the 1930s – with the transition from a type of social organisation based on small isolated rural communities where political machines exerted great influence, to a mass society where national and impersonal forms of social life predominated – brought about a substantial change in how political corruption was regarded. As long as the community-oriented forms of political life prevailed, information about corruption reached voters through local channels and was accompanied by certain material benefits, so that it would have been irrational for them to punish these types of behaviour. However, once the impersonal forms of social life predominated, indulgent attitudes towards corruption were no longer rational. Now, information came through the modern mass media and 'voters [had] few community-oriented reasons to ignore, discount or tolerate negative political information' (Fackler and Lin, 1995: 975). That is, the social transformations described brought about a change from particularistic to universalistic patterns of judgment.

Although Fackler and Lin (1995) make this contrast to distinguish two different historical contexts, the idea that different groups of citizens resort to different evaluative criteria when they judge their political representatives appears frequently in reflection upon these topics. Miller *et al.* (1986) and Wilson and Banfield (1964 and 1971) found associations between correlates of the degree of political information (such as level of education or degree of political interest) and the likelihood that competence and civic norms would be used to evaluate politicians. A similar view is expressed by Víctor Pérez-Díaz (1996: ch. 3) in his interpretation of the 1993 and 1996 Spanish general elections. He argues that the different social composition of the electorates of the Socialist Party and the conservative People's Party in these elections (with a prevalence of young, educated and urban individuals among PP voters) can serve as an indicator of different degrees of moral sensitivity to scandals of the parties' supporters. In particular, according to Pérez-Díaz, among PP voters there appear to predominate civic patterns that make these citizens more concerned about public issues and more demanding of their representatives; while among PSOE voters (who are older, less well educated and more rurally based) more deferential patterns appear to predominate.

Other studies however invite us to discard the idea that different groups of citizens use different evaluative criteria. On the one hand, the few studies that analyse the criteria citizens use to judge different acts of corruption (Jackson and Smith, 1996; Johnston, 1986) find few important differences among various social groups.[9] On the other hand, Pierce (1994) and Glass (1985) show that the determinants and criteria voters use globally to evaluate candidates in an election (and, in particular, the role in that evaluation of candidates' personal traits) are barely associated with voters' degrees of political sophistication or their educational levels (see Funk, 1996). In their account of the 1996 Spanish election, Caínzos and Jiménez (2000) tried to test Pérez Díaz's hypothesis of the existence of different degrees of moral sensitivity to scandals among different socio-demographic groups, but their results were negative. There is a different way to explain why people with different levels of political information make different judgments about their representatives without recourse to the view that these different groups have unequal degrees of moral sensitivity.

As the work by Stoker (1993) and Funk (1996) interestingly suggests, the different judgments of those with different levels of political information could be due, not to inherently distinctive moral and civic sensitivities, but to differences in the way they incorporate the negative information generated by scandals into their general evaluations of the candidates in question. Funk's research uses an experimental design with fictitious situations to support this idea. Stoker analyses American National Elections Study panel data[10] that was generated just before and after the sex scandal that ended Senator Gary Hart's political career when he was competing for the Democratic Party nomination for the 1988 presidential election. Stoker found in the second wave of the survey that one of the groups that showed most hostility to Hart (second only to the most politically aware and morally conservative Republicans) was composed of those Democrats who had previously based their support for Hart on their positive evaluation of his personal character traits. This latter group reacted more negatively to Hart than the Democrats who had not previously identified with this candidate. The group that was least affected by the scandal was composed of those Democrats who had previously identified with Hart but on the basis of partisan and programmatic criteria and not on character, to the extent that this group valued Hart more positively after the scandal than before it. Thus, Stoker's analysis of the Gary Hart case provides an excellent example of how the different priorities of groups of voters affect the way they incorporate the negative information conveyed by a scandal.

Since our more or less subtle judgments of politicians affected by scandals are finally expressed in our hard electoral choices, we find it more interesting to work with the idea that voters differ in terms of the way they process the negative information associated with scandals than to postulate that some social groups have more exquisite moral sensitivities than others. Following this line of thinking, the analyses of Fackler and Lin (1995), Funk (1996) and Stoker (1993) all suggest that voters' evaluations of their representatives are affected by the kind of exchange relationships they establish with their political representatives.

Since the seminal laboratory research carried out by Rundquist *et al.* (1977), most of the available research has suggested that, although the negative information conveyed by a scandal can change voters' attitudes towards the affected agent(s), many citizens discount the information or their changed attitudes when they come to vote.[11] Rundquist *et al.* (1977) suggest two possible mechanisms underlying this tendency to discount negative information in voting choices, both of which are based on the exchange relationship between voters and politicians. They call the first one 'the material inducement explanation' – defining a situation in which voters exchange their votes for material benefits that are usually of an economic nature. This situation coincides with the typical political landscape of the US up to the 1930s described by Fackler and Lin (1995). But this explanation requires the existence of huge political machines that can control both the information conveyed to voters and their actual electoral behaviour. In our current post-industrial advanced societies at least, the existence of such huge and powerful political machines is in most places doubtful.[12] For this reason, Rundquist *et al.* advance an alternative hypothesis, one which their experimental analysis corroborates: the 'implicit trading' explanation. According to this second account, a rational voter will knowingly support a corrupt candidate if he decides that this candidate 'is closer to his own preferences on other issues' than is a 'clean' candidate (Rundquist *et al.*, 1977: 956).[13] Thus, the material benefits and huge political machines indispensable to the viability of the first explanation are unnecessary.

This idea of implicit trading – suggesting tolerance of certain inappropriate practices in exchange for the defence of policy positions that are important to the voter – has received strong empirical support. We have just seen that the group least affected by the Gary Hart scandal was the one that had previously formed a positive view of this candidate upon the basis of the programmatic issues defended by his candidacy (Stoker, 1993). The same idea underlies the explanation that Dimock and Jacobson (1995) offered to account for the scarce impact that the House Bank overdraft had at the time of the 1992 House of Representatives election. According to these authors, voters' opinions of the severity of this scandal depended on two aspects: first, how much malfeasance they believed their district representative to be involved in; and, second, their opinions of the representative's previous performance in office. In general, the respondents who regarded the scandal as less important were those who were more satisfied with their representative's work and, vice versa, the voters who judged the case most harshly were those with the lowest opinions of their representative. But still more interesting, the respondents who attributed the least importance to the scandal were not just those who were most satisfied with their representative but, among these, those who believed that their representative was actually involved in the scandal. As Dimock and Jacobson argue (1995: 1154), their data seem to suggest that 'for some voters, opinions on check-kiting served more to rationalize [in line with the theory of cognitive dissonance] than to shape the vote choice'.

The most suggestive explanations about the Lewinsky scandal's lack of effect on public opinion (Miller, 1999; Sonner and Wilcox, 1999; Zaller, 1998) and on the 1998 mid-term election (Jacobson, 1999) are based on a similar idea. According to Zaller (1998), for example, the fact that evaluations of Clinton's job as president not only were undamaged by the scandal but actually reinforced, was not due to a particularly brilliant defensive strategy on the part of the president's office. Clinton's defence from the first moment of the scandal (at the end of January 1998) up to his enforced statement before the grand jury in August of the same year consisted of a flat denial of any kind of sexual relationship with the former White House intern. But this strategy did not seem particularly persuasive, as the main witness, Monica Lewinsky herself, did not support it. She not only did not help the presidential strategy but very soon started to semi-publicly negotiate a deal with special prosecutor Starr to obtain immunity in exchange for her testimony. Clinton's sole hope – the one that maintained and even reinforced his credibility as president – was the favourable political context in which the scandal erupted. The mixture of economic prosperity, peace and ideological moderation which Clinton could present as the results of his performance as president was, in Zaller's view, what led most citizens to remain unimpressed by the huge media attention devoted to the affair.[14]

Analysing the 1996 Spanish general election, Caínzos and Jiménez (2000) suggested a similar explanation to account for the unexpectedly good electoral results obtained by the Socialists: many of those who voted for this party apparently discounted the negative effect of the wave of scandals in the first half of the 1990s in exchange for the defence of certain policy positions (such as, for example, the system of publicly financed pensions), which they valued.

We do not want to suggest, however, that it is always possible to exchange the defence of certain policies for toleration of corrupt behaviour. It is likely that the extent to which implicit trading is possible depends on the types and levels of corruption that may be involved. When a scandal reveals practices within what Heidenheimer (1970) called the black zone (that is, the zone describing those acts on which there is a broad societal consensus regarding them as undesirable) the likelihood that voters will tolerate the practices in question will be lower. In such situations it is almost certainly harder to solve the problem of cognitive dissonance that we encounter when we try to reconcile our rejection of certain abusive behaviour with our desire to satisfy a particular policy preference. In cases like these, it is harder to find adequate frameworks allowing us to eliminate such dissonance.

But the implicit trading theory has implications not only for our evaluation of scandals. It is also very important when the voter calculates the costs and benefits of the possible victory of a rival candidate, as we shall see in a moment. Two other conditions of our model will be considered first: responsibility and saliency.

Responsibility

As we have stated, the electoral effect of a scandal also depends on voters' abilities to attribute direct or indirect responsibility for it to one or more of the parties or candidates competing in the election in question. The literature offers a number of examples of the importance of this condition and of the factors that affect it. Some have to do with the accounts that politicians give of their involvement in the scandal. But, first, we shall pay attention to certain factors concerning the institutional characteristics of the political system.

Differences in the way parties are organised in different countries (with differences in the degree to which they are internally democratic) as well as such differences in the characteristics of electoral systems as district size and the structure of the ballot: all these make for important differences in the degree to which voters can hold particular agents responsible for scandals.

Due to the fact that scandals are very often mere external shocks having short lives and transitory effects, it seems reasonable to expect that their electoral impact will depend upon how close or distant they are from the most decisive moment of the electoral process. This decisive moment is not the same in all political systems. If in Spain the key moment is usually the election itself, in the US the moment at which candidacies are decided is more important. If, for example, a scandal affecting an incumbent emerges when there is still time to register new, alternative candidacies, it is quite likely that the incumbent will suffer a greater loss of votes than if the scandal erupts closer to election day when there is no time to improvise more solid rival candidates. The incumbent's weakness will in the first case attract stronger challengers with better chances of obtaining financial and other resources (Alford *et al.*, 1994). With regard the Lewinsky case, Jacobson (1999) has pointed out that had the Democrats fielded stronger and more experienced candidates in a number of districts in Republican hands, they would have achieved better results in the 1998 election. What was hard for Democratic tacticians to foresee at the moment at which candidacies had to be registered (and most of them had to be registered during the first weeks of the scandal) was that this affair could benefit them in the long term.

From a more abstract point of view and using game theory analysis, Roger Myerson (1993) found that electoral systems vary in terms of their effectiveness in reducing government corruption. Both of the basic assumptions in Myerson's game are worth commenting upon. First, he chose a complex model to describe a repeated game. This adds some realism to his model, for, as he himself points out, it is easy to think that in a situation with two competitive non-cooperative parties, the corruption of one of them would bring the competitor into government and would thus eliminate the incentives to get involved in corruption. However, in a repeated game, the higher the barriers of the electoral system to the entry of new competitors who might campaign against corruption, the greater the incentive on the leaders of both parties to be collusively involved in corruption. The second assumption Myerson makes recalls the implicit trading theory. In his words (1993: 119):

> difficulty in removing corrupt officials can arise because, under some electoral systems, voters who desire some specific government policy may find that, to maximize the probability of achieving their desired policy, they must give support to corrupt candidates who are committed to this policy . . . Even if there exist non-corrupt candidates who are committed to the same policy, some electoral systems can make it disadvantageous for individual voters to transfer support away from corrupt candidates, when others' expected votes are taken into account.

Thus, for Myerson, voters take into account two different goals when they make their electoral calculus: to eliminate or reduce corruption, but also to get their preferred policy approved by the government. What he was interested in underlining was that all other things being equal, some electoral systems make it possible to reconcile these goals better than others.

In his account of the electoral impact of scandals in Japan, Reed (1999) also refers to the role of the electoral system. The Japanese electoral system, based on multi-member districts, allows for competition among candidates of the same party. This, according to Reed, allows Japanese voters to punish corrupt LDP candidates without punishing the party as a whole.

The second group of factors affecting the responsibility condition are located in the accounts or explicative strategies used by the politicians against whom charges are levelled in order to defend themselves. As Hanna Pitkin (1967) pointed out several years ago, the accountability of representatives to the represented is the essential core of the concept of political representation. The accountability of representatives means above all that they are obliged to render an account of their performance to those they represent. A moment when this rendering of accounts is especially necessary is when the representative is affected by a scandal. The scandal calls into question the fiduciary basis upon which the authority position of the representative rests and can demolish it. For this reason, the representative has to offer a convincing account of the case in question if he wants to retain citizens' trust. Although the final success of this enterprise will depend, as we are seeing, on a range of factors, several laboratory research results have suggested that different types of accounts have different degrees of efficacy. Chanley *et al.* (1994) and Gonzales *et al.* (1995), using real and invented examples of scandals respectively, undertook analyses similar to the one McGraw (1991) applied to a different situation. Their results were very similar: although the party identification variable had a large impact on the level of credibility the political agent in question reached, the type of account was also important. In particular, both analyses found that 'refusals' (the denial of deeds or of the agent's own involvement in them, as well as denial of the right of other actors to criticise or to blame others) were particularly inefficient in reducing the damage caused by charges.

Saliency

For a corruption scandal to have an effect on electoral choice the voter must place corruption highly in his hierarchy of public concerns. In the 1996 Spanish election, the scandals that monopolised public debate during the first half of the 1990s led most political pundits to expect voters to punish the PSOE more harshly than they did. As various studies (for example, Andréu Abela, 1998; CECS, 1995) have shown, political corruption had become prominent in the media. However, Jiménez and Caínzos (2003) have shown that, despite continuous media attention, both the extent and the intensity of public concern about corruption did not remain at the same level during these years (the period just prior to the 1996 election being one when concern was at its lowest) and that corruption was always below a number of other concerns, such as unemployment, terrorism or narcotics.[15] Thus, it seems that the high visibility of the problem and its intense politicisation in the first half of the 1990s did not translate itself into a substantial modification of the priorities defining citizens' agendas. Had political pundits had a more soundly based idea of this agenda, their expectations would probably have been more accurate.

In an account of the June 1989 Greek general election, Dimitras (1989) found a similar difference between the almost monopolistic role of scandals in the agendas of the parties and the media, and the much more complex set of problems concerning citizens. Since the actual results achieved by PASOK were, like those of PSOE in Spain, also at variance with most pundits' expectations, we would again speculate on the extent to which such expectations were based on mistaken ideas about citizens' concerns.

Alternative

It is obvious that, since voting is a choice among different possible alternatives, the calculus made by the voter has to take into account the expectation of a victory of his or her least preferred option. Jacobson and Dimock (1994) and Jacobson and Kernell (1983) had already developed this idea with regard to the Watergate and the House overdraft scandals respectively. According to them, the electoral fortunes of a politician weakened by a scandal depend to a great extent on the appearance of a solid (experienced and well-financed) challenger who can capitalise on that weakness. If this does not happen, it is less likely, at least in the US context, that a scandal will have a real impact on the electoral outcome.

In an analysis of how scandals affected the Conservatives in the 1997 British election, Farrell *et al.* (1998) argued that the persistent charges of sleaze during the 1990s were a significant factor in the defeat of Major's government. However, the authors added that the main impact of the scandals was to contribute to a national desire for change rather than to lead to the direct punishment of individual incumbents. There was however a small number of districts where such electoral punishment was inflicted and the authors remark in particular on what happened in the Tatton constituency. There the Labour party and the Liberal Democrats chose not to nominate candidates to oppose the sitting Conservative who had been subject to allegations of impropriety, but rather chose to back an independent ex-BBC war journalist who won the seat with an almost 25 per cent swing against the incumbent. Thus, an especially attractive voting alternative makes it easier for voters to punish an incumbent affected by a scandal.

The same idea that the nature of the opposition parties affect the extent to which voters discount the negative information conveyed by a scandal appears in the study by McCann and Domínguez (1998) on the 1988 and 1994 presidential elections in Mexico. According to their data, concerns about electoral fraud and political corruption had a small direct effect on the probability of voting for the opposition. McCann and Domínguez (1998: 495) found that

'Mexicans accord relatively low salience to electoral fraud and corruption in their assessment of the country's principal problems; consequently, for the most part they vote on the basis of considerations other than their perceptions of electoral fraud and corruption' – such as policy-making expertise and efficacy. For this reason they thought that, if the opposition parties wanted to profit from widespread perceptions of the dishonesty of the PRI, they should emphasise not so much their own honesty but their capacities to govern efficaciously. In an article which reviews an earlier work by Dominguez and McCann (1996) among others, Joseph Klessner (1998) extends Domínguez and McCann's argument to suggest that both the state and local elections in 1994, 1995 and 1996, and the 1997 congressional elections (won by the opposition parties in the middle of a profound economic crisis and the corruption scandals affecting the Salinas family) are amenable to the same kind of explanation. When Mexican voters concluded that the PRI no longer guaranteed efficacious decision making, they largely abandoned it.

Steven Reed's account of the electoral punishment inflicted on the Japanese Liberal Democratic Party from 1967 to 1990, to which we have already referred, also relates to our fifth condition. As Reed explains:

> before 1955 conservative voters had conservative alternatives to the party implicated in a scandal. After 1955 voters still had conservative alternatives to individual scandal-tainted candidates, but not to the scandal-tainted LDP; they continued to punish the former but were unable to punish the latter. In 1993, when they were again offered the option of voting for conservative parties other than the LDP, they responded to a degree not seen since the 1950s. (Reed, 1999: 146)

Caínzos and Jiménez's (2000) analysis of the 1996 Spanish general election provides a further example of this kind of voter reaction. Concern about a People's Party victory was of more importance in decisions about whether or not to vote for the Socialists than was concern for corruption.

Voters' evaluation of the alternatives also depends on how much they think is at stake at the election in question. Thus, the type of election, especially whether it is a first- or second-order election, is a very important factor in the likelihood that voters will punish an incumbent affected by scandals. A number of works on Japan (for example, Bouissou, 1994; Richardson, 1997) make it clear that Japanese voters have had a greater propensity to punish the LDP for scandals in elections to the Senate (the less important and powerful chamber) than in those to the key lower chamber. And the same phenomenon seems to have been present in Spain, where the Socialist party was able to mobilise a greater number of voters in the general elections of 1993 and 1996 than in either the 1994 European or the 1995 local and regional elections. It seems that second-order elections allow for a greater degree of 'expressive tactical voting'[16] in order to send warning signals to the party in government, while this does not necessarily mean that the voter will not support that party in the general election.

Conclusion

Our aim in this chapter has been to argue that it is not possible to talk about a direct or automatic electoral effect of scandals because the consequences they can have are mediated by a large number of different factors. Rather, for a scandal to influence the individual voter's electoral choice, several conditions must be met. These conditions are contingent on a broad set of external and internal factors. In brief, such factors have to do with three different aspects: first, the characteristics of the scandal itself – the kind and seriousness of the breach that produces it, the identity of the agent(s) involved and of the accusers, the nature of media coverage of the event. The second set of factors relates to the context in which the scandal emerges: the economic situation or the tensions among political elites. The final set of factors has to do with the prior attitudes of voters. These will react to a scandal according to their moral principles, but also according to their partisan identities, their preferred policies, their support for or dislike of the agent involved along with their assessment of the likelihood of his electoral defeat or their evaluation of the political and economic situation.

Notes

1 We are grateful for the comments on an earlier version of this chapter made by participants in the conference, 'Political Scandals, Past and Present', University of Salford, 21–23 June 2001. We should also like to thank Eric Uslaner, Steven Reed and Mariano Torcal who have also read and commented on earlier versions of this chapter. The research upon which it is based would have not been possible without the financial support of the Spanish Ministry of Science and Technology and of the Regional Government of Galicia through, respectively, grants BSO 2000-0747-C02-01 and PGIDT01-PXI21301PR.

2 Following Price and Zaller (1992) and Zaller (1987 and 1991), Laura Stoker (1993: 197) has argued that the actual occurrence of such changes of attitude depends basically on two conditions: 'the degree of exposure to change-inducing information' and 'one's degree of resistance to the information conveyed'. Our aim is to insert these conditions into a more complex framework.

3 In fact, the Lewinsky affair seems to offer an excellent counterexample (see Miller, 1999: 728). Writing on the House Bank overdraft scandal, Shea (1999) found that the extent of local media coverage of an incumbent's misbehavior was not directly related to the extent of the electoral punishment suffered by that representative. He also found, however, that the tone of news stories did affect the extent to which the representative was subject to such punishment. Thus, the frequency of 'negative stories concerning an incumbent's role in the affair played a lead role in the possibility of defeat' (Shea, 1999: 56).

4 The authors think that this is probably due to the fact that it is easier to initiate indictment proceedings in minor cases. However, in research on Japan that is still in progress, Steven Reed has found that those scandals involving formal procedures of investigation cost more votes than other scandals (personal communication).

5 Although it is possible to suggest on the contrary that a very negative economic situation may lead to assessments of a candidate's competence that are more positive than assessments of his integrity. For instance, Gerchunoff and Torre's (1996) analysis of Menem's re-election in the 1994 Argentine presidential elections suggests that the unfavourable economic situation at the time led to fear of a return to the period of high economic instability of 1989–90. This led many people to renew their support for the Peronist candidate in spite of his alleged irregularities.

6 Other research showing the importance of the type of wrongdoing includes that of Funk (1996), Gonzales *et al.* (1995) and Jackson and Smith (1996). On the impact of the severity of the wrongdoing, see Peters and Welch (1978, 1980) and Jackson and Smith (1996).

7 Although McCurley and Mondak (1995: 864) found that 'incumbents' levels of integrity [had a] direct influence on both feeling thermometer scores and the vote choice', while 'competence exerts an indirect effect on the vote by influencing the behaviour of prospective challengers'.

8 Fackler and Lin follow very closely the now discredited idea of the 'community-society' continuum, which Samuel Hays (1967) used to describe major changes in American political life.

9 The exceptions refer either to differences between insiders (the political class) and outsiders (citizens in general) (Jackson and Smith, 1996; similar results in McAllister, 2000) or to marginal disparities in how various social groups regard different types of wrongdoing (in particular, lower status-groups evaluate nepotism more harshly then higher status groups) (Johnston, 1986).

10 In fact, Stoker used data from two different National Election Studies (namely, the 1986 study and the 1987 Pilot Study), which, however, could, when combined, serve as a panel study.

11 In our research on Spain, we have found a clear example of this reaction. Corruption scandals had a strong negative impact on PSOE's image, but this did not translate itself into an electoral rout for the party (Caínzos and Jiménez, 2000; Jiménez and Caínzos, 2003).

12 Although see Richardson (1997, especially p. 34) for some examples of this kind of exchange in Japan. Nevertheless, Richardson adds that this kind of 'traditional' exchange was more frequent in the past than it is now.

13 We can therefore see that the nature of the exchange relationship between citizens and politicians affects not only voters' evaluations of given candidates but their evaluation of the alternative candidates as well. We shall develop this point in a moment.

14 And Zaller's viewpoint has been confirmed by Newman's (2002) analysis of the components of Clinton's presidential approval ratings. Jacobson (1999) explains in a similar way why this scandal had no effect on the 1998 election.

15 In fact, during the whole of the first half of the 1990s, Spaniards' concern about political corruption remained at the same level as their concern about environmental problems – not a very high priority for Spanish public opinion.

16 On expressive tactical voting and its incidence in second-order elections see Franklin *et al.* (1994), Heath *et al.* (1997) and Van der Eijk and Franklin (1996).

References

Ahuja, S., S. L. Beavers, C. Berreau, A. Dodson, P. Hourigan, S. Showalter, J. Walz and J. R. Hibbing (1994), 'Modern Congressional Election Theory Meets the 1992 House Elections', *Political Research Quarterly*, 47: 4, 909–21.

Alford, J., H. Teeters, D. S. Ward and R. K. Wilson (1994), 'Overdraft: The Political Cost of Congressional Malfeasance', *The Journal Of Politics*, 56: 3, 788–801.

Anderson, C. J. and J. Ishii (1997), 'The Political Economy of Election Outcomes in Japan', *British Journal of Political Science*, 27: 4, 619–30.

Andréu Abela, J. (1998), *Los españoles: opinión sobre sí mismos, España y el mundo. Análisis longitudinal. Escala de Cantril*, Granada, Universidad de Granada.

Banducci, S. A. and J. A. Karp (1994), 'Electoral Consequences of Scandal and Reapportionment in the 1992 House Elections', *American Politics Quarterly*, 22: 1, 3–26.

Barreiro, B. and I. Sánchez-Cuenca (2000), 'Las consecuencias electorales de la corrupción', *Historia y Política*, 4, 69–92.

Bouissou, J.-M. (1994), 'Les elections legislatives au Japon (18 juillet 1993). La chute du parti libéral-démocrate et la recomposition du système politique', *Revue Française de Science Politique*, 44: 3, 379–423.

Caínzos, M. and F. Jiménez (2000), 'El impacto de los escándalos de corrupción sobre el voto en las elecciones generales de 1996', *Historia y Política*, 4, 93–132.

CECS [Centro de Estudios del Cambio Social] (1995), *España 1994*, Madrid, Fundación Encuentro.

Chanley, V. J., L. Sullivan, M. H. Gonzales and M. B. Kovera (1994), 'Lust and Avarice in Politics: Damage Control by Four Politicians Accused of Wrongdoing (or, Politics as Usual)', *American Politics Quarterly*, 22: 3, 297–333.

Clarke, H. D., M. C. Stewart and P. F. Whiteley (1998), 'New Models for New Labour: The Political Economy of Labour Party Support, January 1992–April 1997', *American Political Science Review*, 92: 3, 559–75.

Conway, M. M. and M. L. Wyckoff (1980), 'Voter Choice in the 1974 Congressional Election', *American Politics Quarterly*, 8: 1, 3–13.

Criado, H. (2003), 'Competir para ganar. La lógica estratégica de la movilización electoral del PP y el PSOE en 1996 y 2000', PhD dissertation, Instituto Juan March and Universidad Autónoma de Madrid.

Dimitras, P. E. (1989), 'Greece', *Electoral Studies*, 8: 3, 270–80.

Dimock, M. and G. Jacobson (1995), 'Checks and Choices: The House Bank Scandal's Impact on Voters in 1992', *The Journal of Politics*, 57: 4, 1143–59.

Dobratz, B. A. and S. Whitfield (1992), 'Does Scandal Influence Voters' Party Preference? The Case of Greece during the Papandreou Era', *European Sociological Review*, 8: 2, 167–80.

Domínguez, J. I. and J. A. McCann (1996), *Democratizing Mexico: Public Opinion and Electoral Choices*, Baltimore, Johns Hopkins University Press.

Fackler, T. and T. Lin (1995), 'Political Corruption and Presidential Elections, 1929–1992', *The Journal Of Politics*, 57: 4, 971–93.

Farrell, D. M., I. McAllister and D. T. Studlar (1998), 'Sex, Money and Politics: Sleaze and Conservative Incumbency in the 1997 British Election', in D. Denver (ed.), *British Elections and Parties Review 1998*, London, Frank Cass.

Fiorina, M., S. Abram and J. Pope (2003), 'The 2000 US Presidential Election: Can Retrospective Voting Be Saved?', *British Journal of Political Science*, 33, 163–87.

Fraile, M. (2001), 'Does the Economy Enter the Ballot-Box? A Study of the Spanish Voters' Decisions', PhD dissertation, Madrid, Instituto Juan, March.

Franklin, M., R. Niemi and G. Whitten (1994), 'The Two Faces of Tactical Voting', *British Journal of Political Science*, 24: 4, 549–59.

Funk, C. L. (1996), 'The Impact of Scandal on Candidate Evaluations: An Experimental Test of the Role of Candidate Traits', *Political Behaviour*, 18: 4, 1–24.

Gerchunoff, P. and J. C. Torre (1996), 'La política de liberalización económica en la administración de Menem', *Desarrollo económico*, 36: 143, 733–68.

Glass, D. P. (1985), 'Evaluating Presidential Candidates: Who Focuses on their Personal Attributes?', *Public Opinion Quarterly*, 49, 517–34.

Gonzales, M. H., M. B. Kovera, J. L. Sullivan and V. Chanley (1995), 'Private Reactions to Public Transgressions: Predictors of Evaluative Responses to Allegations of Political Misconduct', *Personality and Social Psychology Bulletin*, 21: 2, 136–48.

Groseclose, T. and K. Krehbiel (1994), 'Golden Parachutes, Rubber Checks, and Strategic Retirements from the 102nd House', *American Journal of Political Science*, 38: 1, 75–99.

Hays, S. P. (1967), 'Political Parties and the Community-Society Continuum', in W. N. Chambers and W. D. Burnham (eds), *The American Party Systems: Stages of Development*, New York, Oxford University Press.

Heath, A., I. McLean and B. Taylor (1997), 'How Much Is at Stake? Electoral Behaviour in Second-Order Elections', Working Paper no. 59, Centre for Research into Elections and Social Trends, Glasgow.

Heidenheimer, A. J. (1970), 'Introduction', in A. J. Heidenheimer (ed.), *Political Corruption: Readings in Comparative Analysis*, New Brunswick, NJ, Transaction.

Jackson, M. and R. Smith (1996), 'Inside Moves and Outside Views: An Australian Case Study of Elite and Public Perceptions of Political Corruption', *Governance*, 9: 1, 23–42.

Jacobson, G. (1999), 'Impeachment Politics in the 1998 Congressional Elections', *Political Science Quarterly*, 114: 1, 31–51.

Jacobson, G. and M. Dimock (1994), 'Checking Out: The Effects of Bank Overdrafts on the 1992 House Elections', *American Journal of Political Science*, 38: 3, 601–24.

Jacobson, G. and S. Kernell (1983), *Strategy and Choice in Congressional Elections*, New Haven, Yale University Press.

Jacobson, G., S. Kernell, E. M. Uslaner and S. S. Conway (1986), 'Interpreting the 1974 Congressional Election', *American Political Science Review*, 80: 2, 591–95.

Jiménez, F. and M. Caínzos (2003), 'Political Corruption in Spain: Perceptions and Problems', in M. J. Bull and J. L. Newell (eds), *Corruption in Contemporary Politics*, London, Macmillan-Palgrave.

Johnston, M. (1986), 'Right and Wrong in American Politics: Popular Conceptions of Corruption', *Polity*, 18: 3, 367–91.

Kiewiet, D. R. and L. Zeng (1993), 'An Analysis of Congressional Career Decisions, 1947–1986', *American Political Science Review*, 87: 4, 928–41.

Klessner, J. L. (1998), 'An Electoral Route to Democracy? Mexico's Transition in Comparative Perspective', *Comparative Politics*, 30: 4, 477–97.

Krosnick, J. A. and D. R. Kinder (1990), 'Altering the Foundations of Support for the President Through Priming', *American Political Science Review*, 84: 2, 497–512.

Ladd, E. C. (1998), 'Nixon and Watergate Revisited', *The Public Perspective*, April–May.

Lafay, J.-D. and M. Servais (2000), 'The Influence of Political Scandals on Popularity and Votes', in M. S. Lewis-Beck (ed.), *How France Votes*, New York, Chatham House.

Lupia, A. and M. D. McCubbins (1998), *The Democratic Dilemma. Can Citizens Learn What They Need to Know?*, Cambridge, Cambridge University Press.

McAllister, I. (2000), 'Keeping Them Honest: Public and Elite Perceptions of Ethical Conduct Among Australian Legislators', *Political Studies*, 48, 22–37.

McCann, J. A. and J. I. Domínguez (1998), 'Mexicans React to Electoral Fraud and Political Corruption: An Assessment of Public Opinion and Voting Behaviour', *Electoral Studies*, 17: 4, 483–503.

McCurley, C. and J. J. Mondak (1995), 'Inspected by # 1184063113: The Influence of Incumbents' Competence and Integrity in US House Elections', *American Journal of Political Science*, 39: 4, 864–85.

McGraw, K. (1991), 'Managing Blame: An Experimental Test of the Effects of Political Accounts', *American Political Science Review*, 85: 4, 1133–57.

McLeod, J. M., J. D. Brown and L. B. Becker (1977), 'Watergate and the 1974 Congressional Elections', *Public Opinion Quarterly*, 41, 181–95.

Miller, A. H. (1999), 'Sex, Politics and Public Opinion: What Political Science Really Learned from the Clinton-Lewinsky Scandal', *PS: Political Science and Politics*, 32: 4, 721–9.

Miller, A. H., M. P. Wattenberg and O. Malanchuk (1986), 'Schematic Assessments of Presidential Candidates', *American Political Science Review*, 80, 521–40.

Myerson, R. B. (1993), 'Effectiveness of Electoral Systems for Reducing Government Corruption: A Game-Theoretic Analysis', *Games and Economic Behaviour*, 5, 118–32.

Newman, B. (2002), 'Bill Clinton's Approval Ratings: The More Things Change, The More They Stay The Same', *Political Research Quarterly*, 55: 4, 781–804.

Pérez Díaz, V. (1996), *España puesta a prueba*, Madrid, Alianza.

Peters, J. G. and S. Welch (1978), 'Political Corruption in America: A Search for Definitions and a Theory', *American Political Science Review*, 72, 974–84.

Peters, J. G. and S. Welch (1980), 'The Effects of Charges of Corruption on Voting Behaviour in Congressional Elections', *American Political Science Review*, 74: 3, 697–708.

Pierce, P. A. (1994), 'Political Sophistication and the Use of Candidate Traits in Candidate Evaluation', *Political Psychology*, 14, 21–35.

Pitkin, H. F. (1967), *The Concept of Representation*, Berkeley, CA, The University of California Press.

Popkin, S. (1991), *The Reasoning Voter: Communication and Persuasion in Presidential Campaigns*, Chicago, The University of Chicago Press.

Popkin, S. (1993), 'Information Shortcuts and the Reasoning Voter', in B. Grofman (ed.), *Information, Participation and Choice*, Ann Arbor, University of Michigan Press.

Price, V. and J. Zaller (1992), 'Who Gets the News? Predicting News Reception and Assessing Its Impact', Revised version of the paper presented to the 1990 annual meeting of the American Political Science Association, San Francisco, California.

Reed, S. R. (1999), 'Punishing Corruption: The Response of the Japanese Electorate to Scandals', in O. Feldman (ed.), *Political Psychology in Japan*, Commack, NY, Nova Science Publishers.

Renshon, S. (2002), 'The Polls: The Public's Response to the Clinton Scandals, Part 2: Diverse Explanations, Clearer Consequences', *Presidential Studies Quarterly*, 32, 412–27.

Richardson, B. (1997), *Japanese Democracy: Power, Coordination and Performance*, New Haven, Yale University Press.

Rundquist, B. S., G. S. Strom and J. G. Peters (1977), 'Corrupt Politicians and Their Electoral Support: Some Experimental Observations', *American Political Science Review*, 71, 954–63.

Schwartz, N. and H. Bless (1992), 'Scandals and the Public's Trust in Politicians: Assimilation and Contrast Effects', *Personality and Social Psychology Bulletin*, 18: 5, 574–9.

Shah, D. V., M. D. Watts, D. Domke and D. P. Fan (2002), 'News Framing and Cueing of Issue Regimes: Explaining Clinton's Public Approval in Spite of Scandal', *Public Opinion Quarterly*, 66, 339–70.

Shea, D. M. (1999), 'All Scandal Politics is Local: Ethical Lapses, the Media and Congressional Elections', *Harvard International Journal of Press and Politics*, 4: 2, 45–62.

Sonner, M. W. and C. Wilcox (1999), 'Forgiving and Forgetting: Public Support for Bill Clinton during the Lewinsky Scandal', *PS: Political Science and Politics*, 32: 3, 554–7.

Stewart, C. (1994), 'Let's Go Fly a Kite: Correlates of Involvement in the House Bank Scandal', *Legislative Studies Quarterly*, 19: 4, 521–35.

Stoker, L. (1993), 'Judging Presidential Character: The Demise of Gary Hart', *Political Behaviour*, 15: 2, 193–223.

Uslaner, E. M. and M. M. Conway (1985), 'The Responsible Congressional Electorate: Watergate, the Economy and Vote Choice in 1974', *American Political Science Review*, 79, 788–803.

Van der Eijk, C. and M. Franklin (1996), *Choosing Europe? The European Electorate and National Politics in the Face of Union*, Ann Arbor, The University of Michigan Press.

Welch, S. and J. R. Hibbing (1997), 'The Effects of Charges of Corruption on Voting Behaviour in Congressional Elections, 1982–1990', *The Journal of Politics*, 59: 1, 226–39.

Wilson, J. Q. and E. C. Banfield (1964), 'Public-regardingness as a Value Premise in Voting Behaviour', *American Political Science Review*, 58, 876–87.

Wilson, J. Q. and E. C. Banfield (1971), 'Political Ethos Revisited', *American Political Science Review*, 65, 1048–62.

Zaller, J. (1987), 'Diffusion of Political Attitudes', *Journal of Personality and Social Psychology*, 53: 5, 821–33.

Zaller, J. (1991), 'Information, Values and Opinion', *American Political Science Review*, 85: 4, 1215–38.

Zaller, J. (1998), 'Monica Lewinsky's Contribution to Political Science', *PS: Political Science and Politics*, 31: 2, 182–9.

14

How scandals affect the values and policies of decision makers

Jeroen Maesschalck

Introduction

Scandals, particularly when they involve some failure in the administrative or political system (rather than merely individuals transgressing boundaries), are often followed by policy makers rushing to television studios, loudly proclaiming that they will do everything possible to prevent the scandalous events recurring. Such pronouncements usually include vague promises of new legislation, or of organisational or other types of policy change. Often, however, these promises remain unfulfilled. This chapter focuses on one particular case where a scandal *was* followed by significant policy change – the Dutroux scandal in Belgium – and in doing so tries to draw some general conclusions about how and why scandals produce such changes.

In what follows, I aim to analyse the relationship between scandal and policy making in a way that is both sensitive to the context in which the specific case was located, and is theoretically informed. Thus, two fundamental approaches inform this analysis. First, by adopting a narrative approach, I conceive of 'scandal' and 'policy change' as consecutive 'events' (Abbott, 1992) that can be linked by a theoretically informed narrative. Narratives 'are composed of sequences of events and the temporal ordering of the events in the sequence is a central aspect of the analysis . . . The central claim narrativists make about temporality is that the order in which causal factors occur will affect outcomes' (Kiser, 1996: 254). Linked to this is their notion of 'the path-dependent nature of social processes' (Kiser, 1996: 255): the idea that past events impact upon later historical periods. Applied to policy making this means previous decisions form the context and background for subsequent policy decisions: they both limit and facilitate them.

Second, the narrative will be 'codified' in theoretical language. This has two advantages. First, it ensures the systematic and explicit application of selection criteria in the process of data gathering. Selectivity in data gathering is unavoidable since sequences of events consist of unlimited numbers of facts amongst which the researcher must choose. Systematic codification of the narrative in the language of a theoretical framework makes this selectivity explicit. Second, theoretical codification enables us to draw conclusions that have relevance beyond the specific case study. This can be done by means of 'analytic generalisation' (Yin, 1994): the generalisation of empirical findings to theory. Moreover, placing the empirical facts within a theoretical framework makes it possible to apply the framework to other cases and thus, through the logic of 'replication' (Yin, 1994), to refine the theory and increase its range of applicability.

The obvious place to look for a theoretical framework is, of course, in the scandals literature itself. Yet, this literature has traditionally been descriptive, with elaborate factual accounts but without much systematic 'codification'. Until recently, theoretically informed contributions were very limited, both in quantity and theoretical ambition. This changed during the 1990s, following the spectacular proliferation of scandals across the Western world. Not only was there a significant increase in the number of publications about the topic but social and political scientists were also induced to ask more ambitious questions about the causes and the effects of scandal. Most theoretically informed contributions focused on causes (e.g. Della Porta and Mény, 1997; Pujas and Rhodes, 1999) and a few also focused on effects (e.g. Thompson, 2000). However, none (as far as we are aware) provided an encompassing and systematic framework enabling one to understand the effects of scandal on policy making. Hence, in order to understand this issue we are forced to turn to other sources of theory. Specifically, this will be 'grid–group theory', first developed by the anthropologist Mary Douglas and later applied to a wide range of social and related sciences, including political science (e.g. Thompson, Grendstad and Selle, 1999) and public administration (e.g. Hood, 1998).

At a more general level of abstraction, my aim in this chapter is to answer the question: what effects do scandals have upon the perceptions, values and policies of politicians, and what governs their impact? This question will be answered in two stages. First, I will present a theoretical framework that suggests two mechanisms through which scandals can bring about policy change. Then I will apply this framework to a particular narrative of policy change that was strongly affected by scandals and eventually produced the most comprehensive police reform in Belgian history. Finally, I will draw some general conclusions about the value of the theoretical framework in accounting for the particular case and about its more general use for research on scandals and their relationship to policy making.

Theoretical framework

At a very general level, there are two ways in which scandals can affect policy making. First, they can affect the political power balance, thereby fostering policy change. Scandals provide new opportunities for institutional and individual actors to defend their interests and contest the legitimacy of powerful policy elites. Thompson (2000), for example, describes and theorises the impact scandals have on the symbolic power of decision makers. Second, scandals will not only affect policy makers' opportunities to give effect to their beliefs, but sometimes they will also affect policy makers' beliefs themselves: their 'way of looking at the world' or, as noted below, their 'belief systems'. Here, the belief systems of policy makers constitute the crucial intervening variable through which scandals affect policies. Until now, interest in this variable has been very limited.[1] Thus I aim to help fill a gap in the literature by focusing particularly on this variable. My underpinning theoretical framework, 'grid–group theory', claims to be one of the few social science theories seriously tackling the question of belief formation, rather than taking it for granted (Thompson *et al.*, 1990: 55–68).

Grid–group theory's basic hypothesis is that, in any social setting, there is always a mutually supportive relationship between, on the one hand, the way social relations are structured, and, on the other, dominant values and beliefs (or 'cultural bias') (Thompson *et al.*, 1990). Grid–group theorists call this 'the compatibility condition': 'Relations and biases are reciprocal, interacting and mutually reinforcing: adherence to a certain pattern of social relationships generates a distinctive way of looking at the world; adherence to a certain worldview legitimises a corresponding type of social relations' (Thompson *et al.*, 1990: 1).

Only certain combinations of values and social relations – that is, certain 'ways of life' – are 'viable'. These combinations can be caught in two dimensions: 'group' and 'grid'. Thompson *et al.* (1990: 5) explain them as follows:

> Group refers to the extent to which an individual is incorporated into bounded units. The greater the incorporation, the more individual choice is subject to group determination. Grid denotes the degree to which an individual's life is circumscribed by externally imposed prescriptions. The more binding and extensive the scope of the prescriptions, the less of life that is open to individual negotiation.

Thus each dimension refers to one of two very basic questions: 'Who am I?' (group) and 'What shall I do?' (grid). Put together, they form four ways of life that can be presented graphically in a 2×2 matrix. Applying the typology to public management, Hood (1998: 9) formulates them as 'four styles of public management organisation' also applicable to police organisation (see Table 14.1).

From this description we can derive two mechanisms (Elster, 1998) that can explain how the beliefs and preferences of actors and groups in the policy-making process are formed. The first follows naturally from the previous description of the theory. If there is a mutually supportive relationship between cultural biases and the structure of social relations, and if these tend to go together in a limited number of ways of life, then we can expect people to derive their preferences from their respective ways of life. When confronted with new facts or changes in circumstances, people will react in ways predictable from the worldview that goes with their way of life. Scandal, a particularly shocking confrontation with new facts, is then also interpreted from the worldview. 'In responding to changes in circumstances, adherents of a culture are more

Table 14.1 Four styles of public-management organisation: grid–group theory applied

Grid		Group	
	Low	*High*	
High	*Fatalism* Low co-operation, rule-bound approaches to organisation	*Hierarchy* Socially cohesive, rule-bound approaches to organization	
Low	*Individualism* Atomised approaches to organisation stressing negotiation and bargaining	*Egalitarianism* High participation structures in which every decision is 'up for grabs'	

Source: Hood (1998: 9).

likely to adjust their institutions so as better to support their way of life than they are to transfer their allegiance to a rival culture' (Lockhart, 1997: 95). Hence, the usual strategy for dealing with scandal will be a process of 'pattern-maintaining' change (Lockhart, 1997: 95). Hood (1998: 24–7) has discussed this strategy, focusing on 'public management disasters' as a particular kind of scandal. He has devised a grid–group typology of responses to 'public management disasters' focussing on the questions: who is blamed, and what is the preferred remedy? People with a hierarchical perspective usually blame poor compliance with the rules and lack of professional expertise. To avoid similar disasters in the future, they seek a more secure managerial grip and greater expertise. The egalitarian bias usually leads people to blame the whole system for the failure, particularly focusing on managerial abuses of power, while preferring participation and empowerment as the remedy. The typically individualist response is to blame 'over-collectivisation and lack of price signals' (Hood, 1998: 26) for the failure, and to propose market mechanisms and increased competition as solutions. Finally, a fatalist bias leads people to focus on 'the fickle finger of fate' (Hood, 1998: 26) to make sense of disasters. Such people are very pessimistic about the likely success of strategies to avoid disaster and at most believe in *ad hoc* responses after the event. These four types of reaction show that this pattern-maintaining mechanism works in a dynamic way: even when they keep their basic bias, people do not simply stick to their old recipes. Confronted with new situations and facts, they develop and adapt their ideas. Each way of life 'constantly has to generate within itself the behavior and the convictions that will hold it together' (Thompson *et al.*, 1990: 66).

However, as Lockhart (1997) suggests, shifts to rival worldviews are also possible. Eventually, the pattern-maintaining reaction might not suffice anymore. 'The cumulative impact of successive anomalies or surprises' (Thompson *et al.*, 1990) can lead people to doubt the fit between their worldview and the actual world. This, in turn, can lead them to change their worldview, thereby changing how they deal with the world: this is comprehensive policy change.

These 'pattern-maintaining' and 'comprehensive policy change' strategies can be conceived as two mechanisms through which scandal influences policy making. As 'mechanisms' in Elster's (1998) sense, they 'allow us to explain but not to predict' (Elster, 1998: 45). When scandal results in modest incremental changes, this can be explained by referring to the first mechanism (pattern maintaining). When scandal produces a comprehensive policy shift to another worldview, this can be explained by referring to the second mechanism: the accumulation of surprises so great that change to another worldview becomes inevitable.

A 'policy venue' (Baumgartner and Jones, 1993) consists of the policy makers: those institutions, groups or individuals that have authority to make decisions concerning a particular issue and can limit access to the policy process. A 'belief system' is defined as 'the policy-goals plus causal and other perceptions' (Sabatier and Jenkins-Smith, 1993: 5) that are shared by the members of a policy venue. Such a belief system consists of secondary elements and core assumptions (Sabatier and Jenkins-Smith, 1993), with the former being highly stable over time and the latter more flexible (and hence more susceptible to change). We therefore expect that, when individuals in a policy venue are confronted with surprise, they first change the secondary elements of their belief system, only very exceptionally changing their core assumptions. Combining this with the two mechanisms described above, we can suggest four possible types of policy reaction to a scandal (see Box 14.1). The first is complete immobilism: no decision is made. The second reaction is pattern-maintaining change: policy venue members take decisions consistent with the cultural bias of their belief system, both on core assumptions and secondary aspects. If that is not satisfying they might turn to a third possible reaction: comprehensive change in the secondary aspects of the belief system, combined with a pattern-maintaining strategy for core elements. Mars (1982, cited by Hood, 1998: 20) provided a useful metaphor for this situation when he proposed using grid–group theory at different levels of detail: 'it is always possible ... to slip a more powerful ... lens into any quadrant by ...

Box 14.1 Cumulative policy reactions to a scandal

---

1 Inertia.
2 Pattern-maintaining (*mechanism 1*) both on secondary aspects and core assumptions.
3 Comprehensive change (*mechanism 2*) on secondary aspects, but pattern-maintaining (*mechanism 1*) on the core assumptions.
4 Comprehensive change (*mechanism 2*) on both secondary aspects and core assumptions.

dividing it into a further 2×2 matrix'. When examining a belief system with a rough lens, we can only see the overall bias of the core assumptions. A more powerful lens, however, allows us to see that the secondary aspects might have different cultural biases, for example resulting from second mechanism-type change in those secondary aspects.[2] The fourth reaction to scandal is comprehensive change in both secondary aspects and core assumptions, that is, a collapse of the belief system.

The case study

On 9 August 1996, a fourteen-year-old girl was kidnapped in Bertrix, Belgium. Following police investigations, Marc Dutroux, his wife and a collaborator were arrested. Two days later, the police found the girl, together with another girl who had been kidnapped more than two months previously, alive in a cage in one of Dutroux's houses. In subsequent weeks, the remains of four other girls, who had been kidnapped in previous years, were found on his premises. These events shocked the country to an almost unprecedented degree – especially after it emerged that Dutroux had previous convictions for sex offences and that the police, though suspecting him in this case also, had failed to find the girls during previous investigations. Shortly after these discoveries, Parliament established a Committee of Inquiry to investigate what had gone wrong in the previous investigations and what could be done to prevent these failures in the future. After some months of very intensive work, amply covered in the media, the Committee presented a lengthy report containing recommendations for revolutionary police reforms. Although there was remarkable consensus about the report's contents when it was published in April 1997, the consensus turned out to be very weak, and the plenary debate in Parliament revealed sharp divergences of view over how the recommendations were to be interpreted. The debate continued in subsequent months, and the reforms eventually implemented would probably have been rather modest had it not been for one of the most spectacular events in recent Belgian history: Marc Dutroux's escape from prison on 23 April 1998. Although he was caught within hours, the whole of the political establishment knew quick and decisive action was necessary in order 'to restore trust in the institutions'. The leaders of the four governing parties and four opposition parties, supported by their police and judicial experts, started the 'eight party' or so-called 'Octopus' negotiations chaired by Prime Minister, Jean-Luc Dehaene. The earlier divergences of view were reconciled remarkably quickly and general agreement was reached within a few weeks (on 24 May). At the end of 1998, the Belgian parliament passed laws to implement the agreement, thereby producing the most important changes to the structure of the Belgian police ever implemented. After some two centuries of debate about the alleged competition between Belgium's multiple police forces, the Dutroux scandal led to the decision to merge the forces into a single, 'integrated police force, structured at two levels' – local and national.[3]

Presented thus, the narrative seems a typical example of a scandal that produced important and far-reaching policy change. But is it? Did the scandal indeed have a causal effect on the policy shift and, if so, how? A theoretically codified narrative can provide an answer to these questions. Central to such an approach is the above-mentioned path-dependency assumption. This means that one must not only study the Dutroux scandal and its effects, but also the preceding period. The narrative starts in the mid 1980s. At that time, the most significant features of criminal justice policy were very much as they had been in preceding decades – while the late 1980s marked the start of change culminating in the 'Octopus agreement' of May 1998 that enacted the spectacular police reform this study seeks to explain.

The narrative will show that, as a policy domain, policing in Belgium is informed by a single dominant belief system with several firmly held and commonly shared core assumptions. Given the theoretical framework described above, there are three levels of analysis at which the policy reaction to the Dutroux scandal can be studied: the overall belief system itself, the groups sharing the belief system's core assumptions (while differing on secondary aspects) and the individuals belonging to these groups. Purely for reasons of space, empirical application of the theory below will be confined to the former two levels, leaving aside the individual level.

The first episode: building up to the Pentecost Plan
During the first half of the 1980s the activities and outlooks of policy makers in the area of policing could best be described as 'stable'. At the political level, there were three ministers responsible for policing matters[4] together with the advisors they appointed to their ministerial cabinets. At the administrative level, there were the senior officers belonging to the three large police forces, with the *Gendarmerie* (the national police force) as the strongest party. The 'local police' were not really a police force but rather a patchwork of municipal forces without any national command. The Judicial Police was much smaller than the *Gendarmerie* and closely bound and largely subordinate to the judiciary. Although scattered over different institutions and different levels, this restricted group of political and administrative decision makers could be seen as the members of a policy venue, particularly since levels of interest and expertise in policing matters, both in Parliament and in the wider society, were limited. The belief systems of those belonging to the venue could be summarised as ones exemplifying a 'law and order' image consistent with the traditional 'military policing' approach that had dominated Belgian policing since the nineteenth century (Easton, 2000: 25–7). In grid–group terms, both the structure of the policy venue and the bias behind the belief system were strongly hierarchical.

This consistency, or the 'mutually supportive relationship between structure and values', explains why the reaction to a number of violent events in the mid-1980s was pattern-maintaining. A series of bombings by the Communist terrorist organisation, the *Cellules Communistes Combattantes*, and a number of very violent supermarket robberies by the so-called 'Gang of Nivelles', deeply shocked the country, without, however, destabilising the belief system. Indeed, the events reinforced the hierarchical character of both the venue and the belief system. As for the former, the government kept powers firmly within the venue in a way consistent with its more general policy of ruling by decree, which allowed it to promulgate laws without prior parliamentary approval.[5] As for the belief system, the violent events were perceived as caused by too much individualism ('anarchy'), egalitarianism ('terrorism is committed by Communist sectarian groups') and fatalism ('the police do not react firmly to crime'). Hence, for those in the policy venue, the solution could only be hierarchical. This bias is obvious from the stream of measures that were taken in reaction to the violence, such as the centralisation of anti-terrorism policy, the deployment of paramilitary troops in the streets, and the plea by the Minister of Justice for reintroduction of the death penalty. Overall, then, reaction to the events was one of pattern-maintaining change. Real change would require not only further 'surprises' but, more importantly, surprises of a rather different kind.

While the aforementioned hierarchical decisions were being taken in the mid–1980s, certain slow but significant changes were taking place outside the policy venue. These would lead to comprehensive change in the belief systems of those within the venue, and eventually to the Pentecost Plan of June 1990. First, a growing body of research and seminars outside the policy venue was gradually preparing for a move from the previous policy alternatives, which were a continuous stream of unsystematic hierarchical anti-terrorism measures, to more comprehensive policy proposals for police reform. Second, in Parliament and the media, the perception of the central policy problem in policing was shifting. Thus, the hierarchical focus on terrorism and banditry gradually began to give way to more egalitarian and individualist concerns about the lack of democratic control over the police forces, where such concerns were strengthened by several scandals. The fact that the inquiry into the Gang of Nivelle's killings was not advancing, for example, undermined the general public's hierarchical trust in the policy venue's capacity and integrity. Overall, several 'surprises' in grid–group terms changed the cultural bias of the broader policy community, thereby increasing pressure on those in the policy venue to change their belief systems.

However, it took the elections of December 1987 and subsequent government negotiations to produce the crucial change in the policy venue and belief system that would eventually produce the changes embodied in the Pentecost Plan. The Socialists returned to power after more than six years in opposition, bringing with them several proposals that were a clear departure from the policies typical of the prevailing hierarchical bias. The proposals included 'demilitarising' the *Gendarmerie* and strengthening parliamentary control of the police and intelligence services (Van Outrive *et al.*, 1992: 310–11).

These and other changes were agreed to in the Pentecost Plan of 5 June 1990. The changes proposed in the plan and implemented in subsequent years can clearly be described as pattern maintaining with regard to the core elements of the belief system. The fundamental structure of the Belgian police remained hierarchical and a significant number of new instruments had a basic hierarchical bias.[6] However, there were significant shifts away from hierarchy with regard to some secondary aspects of the belief system. The establishment of a body for deliberation among the different actors involved in local criminal justice policy, for example, had an egalitarian bias, being intended to increase co-operation and mutual trust. The most telling example, however, was the Plan's proposed reform ('de-militarisation') of the *Gendarmerie*. This reorganisation programme was dominated by the force's 'community-policing' rhetoric. 'Community policing' has become the preferred label for a wide range of reforms in countries worldwide.[7] Generally speaking, two groups of reform measures fall under the community-policing label, each having a particular grid–group bias. First, as suggested by the term itself, community policing embodies an egalitarian rhetoric that depicts police officers as working in and for the local community: they are there to serve and are directly accountable to citizens. An example was the appointment of police officers as 'sector workers', sent out on to the streets to improve relations with the public (De Kimpe and Ponsaers, 2001: 8). Visits by the head of the *Gendarmerie* to local brigades (Easton, 2000: 125) and other measures to increase bottom–up communication indicate a similar egalitarian emphasis, but with regard to internal management. The second group of community-policing measures can be described as 'managerialist'. These are largely analogous to the New Public Management reforms in public administration. The latter have been identified in grid–group terms as largely hierarchical, but with strong individualist elements (Hood, 1998) and the same can be said for community policing's managerialist strand. The *Gendarmerie* launched, in implementation of the Pentecost Plan, a programme of managerialist reform. This included such individualistic measures as a mandate system for high-ranking police officers, but maintained a basic hierarchical bias.

The comprehensive policy change sanctioned in the Pentecost Plan was produced by the 'surprise effect' of the scandals described above, affecting the cultural bias both of the general public and of the belief system of those in the policy venue. The Socialists' opportunity to take power, for example, was (partly) caused by changing preferences among the electorate. Further empirical analysis could test the hypothesis that this change occurred following an accumulation of surprises among voters. For the belief system of those in the policy venue as well, the hypothesis is that accumulated surprises about the drawbacks of the hierarchical approach led members of the venue to turn to individualist and egalitarian approaches. This increased the opportunities available to the advocates of these approaches (such as the Socialists and the more community-policing-oriented officers in the *Gendarmerie*) to acquire the power they needed to enable them to implement their ideas. Thus a change in the overall belief system produced a change in opportunities for some. A more ambitious empirical analysis would aim actually to test these hypotheses about preference changes, thereby revealing how, at the individual

level, preferences and opportunities interact and reinforce each other to produce policy change.

*The second episode: the Dutroux scandal and the Parliamentary Committee of
Inquiry's report*
The chosen strategy of implementing proposals that were basically hierarchical, while having egalitarian and individualist components, was reinforced
in subsequent years. In particular, increasing numbers of measures designed
to stimulate co-operation between police forces at the local level made a considerable contribution to the police forces' later integration. As mentioned,
the arrest of Marc Dutroux, his wife and a collaborator on 13 August 1996
initiated a series of events that together gave rise to one of post-war Belgium's
most serious scandals. The first and most widespread public reaction was
one of 'system blame', a typically egalitarian reaction. The general public experienced a deep crisis of trust in everything that represented 'the system':
politicians, administrators, the police, the judiciary and even the intellectual
elite. Public outrage reached its peak following allegations of official attempts
at a cover-up arising out of a judgment of the Court of Cassation (the highest
Belgian appeal court) on 14 October.[8] The protests following the judgment
culminated in the 'White March' on Sunday 20 October 1996: Belgium's largest
post-war demonstration, bringing together 250,000–300,000 protesters on
the streets of Brussels. The strongly egalitarian bias behind these events was
exemplified by the White March's spontaneous and unorganised character,
together with the 'White Committees' that soon sprang up all over the country.
The government's response (after an initial period of silence) was 'symmetric'
(Hood and Jackson, 1991) with these demands and hence also had a (partly)
egalitarian bias, as indicated by two examples. First, in the weeks following
the outbreak of the scandal, the government repeatedly announced that it
would pass legislation leading to 'more respect' for and better care of, crime
victims along with more powers for their lawyers during judicial proceedings.
Second, the government promised to implement measures to stimulate a
'New Political Culture', including measures to increase citizen involvement in
policy making.

In the event, however, the Prime Minister referred further debate to a
newly created venue, the 'Dutroux' Parliamentary Committee of Inquiry,
established under the presidency of Marc Verwilghen, an opposition MP. By
explicitly referring police and justice reform for discussion in this separate forum
the Prime Minister not only made the issue more manageable, but also
allowed for a restoration of the policy image of this issue, somewhat detached
from the egalitarian 'crisis-of-trust' issue. Thus, the Committee's bias at the
start of its hearings was similar to the bias of the dominant belief system in
the police domain, having some egalitarian and individualist features with regard
to secondary aspects, but hierarchical as far as its core was concerned.

From the beginning, the Dutroux Committee acquired a strong position
in the policing policy venue. Levels of interest in its hearings were high and

continuous, stimulated as they were by live television coverage. The hearings brought to public attention the problems that policy makers had already recognised before, but now, through some symbolic examples – such the telling images of a *Gendarmerie* officer and a magistrate giving completely contradictory accounts of the same events – gave them a higher profile. In their April 1997 report (Kamer der Volksvertegenwoordigers, 1997), the Committee's members indicated they perceived three main inter-linked problems, in this way revealing their basically hierarchical bias. First, they concluded there was too much competition between the three main police forces and within different sections of the same force, referring to the situation as a 'police war'. They saw this as the main cause of the inefficiencies of the Dutroux inquiries and of the insufficient levels of information exchange between forces more generally. Second, in some police forces, the Committee perceived a general crisis in moral standards, mainly explained by the fatalistic attitudes of the supervisors. The Committee notably complained that, although extensive procedures for disciplinary sanctions were provided by statute, they were very rarely used, even when thought necessary. Third, the Committee found a lack of professionalism and expertise in police inquiries. The police tended to investigate in an overly 're-active way', rather than 'pro-actively' searching for evidence, thus being excessively fatalist in their approach.

The Committee's recommendations were consistent with this definition of the problem and with the strategy adopted since the Pentecost Plan. That is, they were pattern maintaining on the core issues, but egalitarian and individualist as regards the secondary aspects. First, the proposal for an integrated police force, with a unified command (at least at national level) was clearly hierarchical in essence. On the other hand, the idea that the force be structured at two levels, keeping important powers in the hands of local mayors, added a somewhat egalitarian element. Second, the recommendation to restore discipline and sanction those who failed to do their jobs properly clearly had a hierarchical bias, but the recommendation to make disciplinary procedures simpler again somewhat relaxed this bias. Third, the Committee recommended that senior police officers be trained in 'modern management techniques', an approach to public sector management that has been identified as predominantly hierarchical in conception, though with individualist elements (Hood, 1998). Finally, it was recommended that all police officers learn to investigate in a 'pro-active' way and be trained in modern investigatory techniques. This recommendation revealed a typically hierarchical trust in expertise. Meanwhile, the proposed new investigatory techniques fitted in with the broader 'community policing' rhetoric that had both individualist and egalitarian elements (see above).

The third episode: Dutroux's escape and the Octopus Agreement
The weeks and months following the unanimous approval of the Committee's report saw the re-emergence of controversies on secondary aspects of the belief system. A central role here was played by those MPs who were also

mayors. These had a strong interest in police reform, since integration of municipal police forces within single police zones, and with local *Gendarmerie* brigades, would reduce mayors' powers *vis-à-vis* the police. Due to their cultural biases, Flemish and Wallonian 'mayor-MPs' were deeply divided over this issue. Wallonian mayors have traditionally seen themselves – as opposed to the police commissioners and senior municipal officials – as the heads of their municipal police forces (Ackaert, 1998: 61–6), and their voters, administrators and police officers expect them to act in accordance with this assumption. Flemish mayors, on the other hand, emphasise their role as policy makers (Ackaert, 1998: 61–6), leaving the daily management of police forces to the police commissioners, an attitude also expected of them by those in their immediate environments. In short, a police reform that incorporates small municipal forces into larger and more professional units is more foreign to Wallonian than it is to Flemish practice and bias. As such, the contrasting backgrounds of Wallonian and Flemish mayors help account for their different positions in the parliamentary debate (De Kimpe and Ponsaers, 2001).

Within hours of the news of Marc Dutroux's escape (23 April 1998), the Ministers of the Interior and of Justice both resigned, and they stuck to these decisions even when it emerged that Dutroux had been caught a few hours after his escape. Prime Minister Dehaene invited the opposition parties to co-operate in reforming the police and justice system. After fierce criticisms and calls for the government to resign, four opposition parties agreed to participate. The historic 'eight party' or 'Octopus' negotiations started on 11 May, chaired by Prime Minister Dehaene.[9] Pressure on the negotiators was strong. The media in particular were again demanding action to 'restore trust in the institutions'. The Octopus agreement, proposing an integrated police force both on national and local levels, was presented to the press on 24 May, just over a month after Dutroux's escape. The agreement included a proposed reform of the police that was consistent with the position taken in the Dutroux Committee report. More generally, in terms of the grid–group framework, the proposals of the Dutroux Committee (April 1997) and the Octopus Agreement (May 1998) were not significantly different from those contained in the 1990 Pentecost Plan, important though they were. Thus, while they embodied comprehensive changes of an egalitarian and individualistic kind on secondary aspects, they contained a core that remained clearly hierarchical. In other words, in spite of the enormous number of scandalous events, there was no collapse of the belief system.

Conclusion

From the early nineteenth century there had been concerns about the co-existence of several police forces (Van Outrive *et al.*, 1992), but it took the Dutroux scandal at the very end of the twentieth century to draw a conclusion which, with the benefit of hindsight, seems to be self-evident: that there was a need to integrate the different police forces and thereby terminate the competition between them. As this comprehensive policy change was enacted after the Dutroux scandal, the assumption is easily made that the two were causally linked. The foregoing analysis has suggested, however, that to understand the effects of scandal, one should concentrate not so much on the scandal itself, but rather on its context and the 'path' preceding it. Using the grid–group framework, we observed that it was not simply the seriousness of the Dutroux scandal that caused the policy change, but rather its role in an already lengthy process of accumulation of surprises about the gap between the dominant worldview and the actual world. It was important to look back at the past and at the path travelled to that point, since people perceive and approach scandals through the 'lens' or bias of their worldviews. Such worldviews are developed during long processes of mutual reinforcement of structure and culture, influencing the biases of the individuals who work and live in the contexts established thereby. These worldviews define the biases guiding their 'carriers'' reactions to scandal. While such reactions are usually of a 'pattern-maintaining' variety they can also exemplify a second type, namely comprehensive policy change.

The theoretical framework we have adopted has turned out to be very useful in explaining how, at the end of the 1980s, the hierarchical belief system with its pattern-maintaining attitude was, because of accumulating surprises, replaced by a belief system that was still hierarchical in its core, but also egalitarian and individualistic concerning its secondary aspects (the Pentecost Plan). An important conclusion was that the Dutroux Committee report of 1997 and the Octopus agreement of 1998, although widely seen as producing far-reaching changes, were in grid–group terms, little different in terms of their biases than those of the Pentecost Plan. How should this conclusion be judged? On the one hand, it is true that the most important departure from earlier periods occurred with the Pentecost Plan of 1990. On the other hand, the significance of this conclusion should not be exaggerated. For it is based on an analysis not permitting much detail because of the length of the period covered (more than a decade) and because the emphasis has been on presentation of the framework rather than on case specifics. More detailed analysis of the Committee's report and of the Octopus agreement would show that, albeit to a lesser extent than is usually assumed, they differ from the Pentecost Plan in at least two ways. First, the individualist and egalitarian elements in 1997 and 1998 were much stronger and more developed than in 1990. Hence, although the overall biases did not change, their relative importance did. Second, although the Dutroux scandal's effects on the overall belief system may have been rather modest, this does not imply that there were no important effects on particular groups or individuals within the belief system. As Thompson *et al.* (1990: 77–8) argue, there is a potential difference between a macro-change, and the micro-changes by which it came about. Similarly, micro-changes might cancel each other out, wrongly suggesting that at the macro level there is no change at all. Hence, research empirically more ambitious than the present should take up the challenge of opening the 'black box' of the belief system and investigate these micro-effects of the scandal, ultimately even at the individual level.

The grid–group framework proved useful in two particular respects: as a device for organising the data and as an explanatory framework. First, it structured the narrative and acted as a powerful data reduction tool. It allowed us to summarise all the complex policy options and changes of the last two decades of the twentieth century, and it can act as a basis for future comparisons, across both countries and policy domains. Second, it delivered on its promise to explain preference formation. It conceives of a scandal as a shared feeling of surprise, which people can cope with in one of two ways. The usual reaction is pattern-maintaining – involving incremental changes without fundamental changes to overall 'world-views' or 'belief systems'. However, an accumulation of surprises can lead people to doubt the appropriateness of their shared worldview thus inducing them to shift to another way of life in a second type of change: comprehensive policy change. As such, the grid–group framework explained how a scandal, through its role in an accumulation of surprises, could work to change the preferences of the carriers of a belief system and hence the decisions they make. Thus, cultural theory appears to be a valuable candidate to fill the gap in the literature about the effects of scandals on policy making. Of course, future empirical research is necessary to support this claim and answer the many remaining questions. Can the same mechanisms of policy reaction to surprise, also be found in other cases? Can the framework also explain the vast number of cases where scandal is not followed by comprehensive policy change? Additionally, it would be useful to combine the grid–group account with other frameworks that focus on 'opportunities' rather than 'beliefs' as the intervening variable between scandals and policy change.

Notes

This chapter is adapted from Maesschalck (2002).

1 Several authors (for example, Bovens and 't Hart, 1996) have emphasised the important role values and beliefs play in identifying an event as a scandal, but few, if any, have analysed the effects of scandal on the belief systems of decision makers.
2 It would then be particularly interesting to try to discern different groups of people sharing a similar 'secondary bias' within the overall bias of the belief system.
3 This narrative and all the other descriptive elements of the case study below are based mainly on De Kimpe and Ponsaers (2001), De Mulder and Morren (1998), Deweerdt (1997, 1998, 1999) and Van Outrive *et al.* (1992).
4 The Minister of Justice, the Minister of Defence and the Minister of the Interior.
5 This clearly hierarchical instrument was very popular during the 1980s, particularly in social and economic policy making, and was justified on the grounds that the pressing economic crisis required quick and decisive action. It seemed only natural that similar arguments would be deployed when crises of internal security arose as well.
6 An example was the attempt to eliminate competition between police forces by introducing a law containing a detailed description of their respective duties and powers.

7 A somewhat similar role is played by the 'New Public Management' label in civil service systems (e.g. Barzelay, 2001; Bouckaert and Pollitt, 2000; Hood, 1991).
8 This removed investigating magistrate Connerotte from the case, supposedly to 'guarantee impartiality', because he had been at a party with the parents of the kidnapped and murdered children where he had been given a pen. The judgement strengthened suspicions of a cover-up, particularly since Connerotte had launched, a few days previously, a general request for information from 'all persons who [had] ever been the victims of paedophilia'. This had strengthened rumours that he was tracking down other paedophilia networks involving high-level officials.
9 The four government parties were the Flemish and Francophone Christian Democrats and Socialists, and the four opposition parties were the Flemish and Francophone Liberal parties and the Flemish and Francophone nationalist parties. The extreme-right parties and the Flemish and Francophone Green parties did not participate.

References

Abbott, A. (1992), 'From Causes to Events: Notes on Narrative Positivism', *Sociological Methods and Research*, 20: 4, 428–55.
Ackaert, J. (1998), 'Belgische Burgemeesters in Noord en Zuid', *Kultuurleven*, 65: 5, 60–7.
Barzelay, M. (2001), *The New Public Management. Improving Research and Policy Dialogue*, Los Angeles, University of California Press.
Baumgartner, F. R. and B. D. Jones (1993), *Agendas and Instability in American Politics*, Chicago, University of Chicago Press.
Bouckaert, G. and C. Pollitt (2000), *Public Management Reform: A Comparative Analysis*, Oxford, Oxford University Press.
Bovens, M. and P. 't Hart (1996), *Understanding Policy Fiascoes*, London, Transaction.
De Kimpe, S. and P. Ponsaers (2001), *Consensusmania. Een Onderzoek Naar De Achtergronden Van De Politiehervorming*, Leuven, Acco.
De Mulder, M. and M. Morren (1998), *De Zaak-Dutroux Van a Tot Z*, Antwerpen, Icarus.
Della Porta, D. and Y. Mény (eds) (1997), *Democracy and Corruption in Europe*, London, Pinter.
Deweerdt, M. (1997), 'Overzicht Van Het Belgisch Politiek Gebeuren 1996', *Res Publica*, 39: 4, 468–521.
Deweerdt, M. (1998), 'Overzicht Van Het Belgisch Politiek Gebeuren 1997', *Res Publica*, 40: 3–4, 311–75.
Deweerdt, M. (1999), 'Overzicht Van Het Belgisch Politiek Gebeuren 1998', *Res Publica*, 41: 2–3, 162–238.
Easton, M. (2000), *De Demilitarisering Van De Belgische Rijkswacht Tussen 1940 En 1998. Een Positionering Op Het Continuüm Van Een Militaire Tot Een Civiele Politieorganisatie. Proefschrift*, Brussel, Vrije Universiteit Brussel.
Elster, J. (1998), 'A Plea for Mechanisms', in P. Hedström and R. Swedberg (eds), *Social Mechanisms: An Analytical Approach to Social Theory*, Cambridge, Cambridge University Press.
Hood, C. (1991), 'A Public Management for All Seasons?', *Public Administration*, 69: 1, 3–19.
Hood, C. (1998), *The Art of the State. Culture, Rhetoric, and Public Management*, Oxford, Clarendon Press.

Hood, C. and M. Jackson (1991), *Administrative Argument*, Aldershot, Dartmouth.

Kiser, E. (1996), 'The Revival of Narrative in Historical Sociology: What Rational Choice Theory Can Contribute', *Politics and Society*, 24, 249–71.

Kamer der Volksvertegenwoordigers [Belgian Chamber of Representatives] (1997), *Parlementair Onderzoek Naar De Wijze Waarop Het Onderzoek Door Politie En Gerecht Werd Gevoerd in De Zaak 'Dutroux-Nihoul En Consorten'. Verslag Namens De Onderzoekscommissie*, Brussels.

Lockhart, C. (1997), 'Political Culture and Political Change', in R. Ellis and M. Thompson (eds), *Culture Matters*, Boulder, CO, Westview Press.

Maesschalck, J. (2002), 'When Do Scandals Have an Impact on Policy Making? A Case Study of the Police Reform Following the Dutroux Scandal in Belgium', *International Public Management Journal*, 5: 2, 169–93.

Mars, G. (1982), *Cheats at Work: An Anthropology of Workplace Crime*, Aldershot, Ashgate.

Pujas, V. and M. Rhodes (1999), 'A Clash of Cultures? Corruption and the Ethics of Administration in Western Europe', *Parliamentary Affairs*, 52: 4, 688–702.

Sabatier, P. A. and H. C. Jenkins-Smith (1993), *Policy Change and Learning: An Advocacy Coalition Approach*, Boulder, CO, Westview Press.

Thompson, J. B. (2000), *Political Scandal: Power and Visibility in the Media Age*, Cambridge, Polity Press.

Thompson, M., R. Ellis and A. Wildavsky (1990), *Cultural Theory*, Boulder, CO, Westview Press.

Thompson, M., G. Grendstad and P. Selle (eds) (1999), *Cultural Theory As Political Science*, London, Routledge.

Van Outrive, L., Y. Cartuyvels and P. Ponsaers (1992), *Sire, Ik Ben Ongerust. Geschiedenis Van De Belgische Politie 1794–1991*, Leuven, Kritak.

Yin, R. K. (1994), *Case Study Research: Design and Methods*, 2nd edition, Thousand Oaks, Sage Publications.

Index

Page references to notes are followed by n